"Psychology Of Evil"

PROFILES OF SERIAL KILLERS

Florence McLean
"As told to Søre Flott"

"Psychology Of Evil"

PROFILES OF SERIAL KILLERS

"Psychology of Evil: Profiles of Serial Killers"

ISBN: 978-87-27-014715

Authors: Florence McLean as told to Søren Flott

Publishing editor Elise H. Nørholm

Graphic Design: Demuth Grafisk

Cover: Simon Lilholt/Imperiet.dk med image from Shutterstock & Drawing from Florence McLean

Author Photo: Mew.dk

Printer: Livonia Print

lindhardtogringhof.dk BOG.DK – Your online book magazine

Lindhardt and Ringhof is part of Egmont. Egmont is Denmark's largest media group and a foundation that annually donates almost 100 million Danish kroner (approximately 14.5 million USD) to children and young people facing difficulties.

ACKNOWLEGMENTS

I would like to express my gratitude to John E. Douglas who help me in 2000 regarding my thesis and understanding the method of Criminal Profiling for the Master of Science in Psychology and to my mentor Bent Isager-Nielsen Merits: Knight of the Dannebrog. Education: Military and police, studies with the FBI in the USA, Scotland Yard in England and RCMP in Canada, Police Superior Leader Training (POL). (19.04.2023)., for his help and support all the way from 2018.

CONTENTS

FOREWORD

In the early 1980s, I was visiting my sister, who lived in Muswell Hill in North London with her boyfriend. There was a somber atmosphere of nervousness and unrest in the area. I often stayed up late into the night talking with my sister's boyfriend about the murders that had occurred there and the fear that had spread. The murders were committed by an as-yet unknown perpetrator who had been dubbed The Muswell Hill Murderer. After each killing, he followed a specific ritual: he bathed the body and dressed it. He kept the deceased for an extended period until they could no longer be handled due to decomposition and stench. Then he dismembered the body and burned it or flushed smaller parts down the toilet. When Dennis Nilsen (The Muswell Hill Murderer) was arrested in 1983, he was suspected of up to 15 murders and received a life sentence. He died behind bars in 2018.

At that time, I never would have imagined that I would come to communicate with, and in some cases get quite close to, people like Dennis Nilsen. Today, it is an important part of my method for trying to understand the mind of the serial killer. I have been working with serial killers since 1997, and this initially resulted in an empirical thesis, *Serial Killers, Understanding and Prevention*, which I began preparing in 2000 and completed in 2004. In that connection, I conducted a questionnaire survey where 34 serial killers from the USA, Australia, and the UK recounted their childhoods and upbringings, and how they themselves related to their cases. The overall goal of my thesis was to investigate whether one could, by using theories behind criminal profiling, formulate a method that could be used to find potential serial killers before they commit their first murder. I sought answers to what serial killers are like and why they end up becoming serial killers. For example, I asked about violence and abuse in the family, bullying at school, loneliness, mental health problems, and brain injuries, all in the quest for an answer.

In 2012, I wrote a research report titled *Prevention: A Case Description of the Arthur Shawcross Case*, and in 2021, I published the book *Serial Killer – The Human Behind the Monster*, which is about how serial killers are made. However, the book was a long time coming. My report supervisor was the first to push me: "Now write that book; you have unique material!" But I was busy with my job. I had realized that the research path wasn't for me. I chose instead to work with children and young people in Struer, Skanderbeg, and finally Aarhus Municipality, which has greatly enriched my professional life. But the thought of writing a book was still there, and in 2021, I finally succeeded.

It was completely overwhelming to hold the finished book in my hand, and I never in my wildest dreams imagined that there would be another. Since its publication, I've completed two professional courses in criminal profiling, and in 2023, I finished my Masters of Science in criminal profiling. This has given me deeper insight not only into how serial killers are formed but also how psychological understanding can provide law enforcement with a vital tool in the hunt for some of the worst criminals out there. This is knowledge I want to share with readers who do not necessarily have a professional background, because I often encounter many myths when I give lectures. There can be a big difference between profilers in movies and TV series and how serial killers work in reality.

The book is primarily based on my analyses of cases from the USA, Europe, Australia, and a few other locations. These cases have been reconstructed using, among other sources, video recordings of entire trials, crime scene photographs, police reports, books, and films. They appear detailed and occasionally include dialogue. It's important to emphasize that this is not fiction; the events, thoughts, details, and dialogue all stem from the sources.

It's also crucial to highlight that my analyses are, by their very nature, retrospective, meaning the cases are closed. However, I've done my best to only use information that investigators had access to when they were in the midst of solving the cases. Only later in the process do I incorporate my knowledge of the serial killers' backstories to create a connection between their upbringing and their crimes.

After finishing this book, you won't be able to go out and create profiles of serial killers and serial rapists. However, you will gain insight into the method and an understanding of what it can and cannot do. At the same time, you'll hopefully also get a sense of the connection between the offenders' upbringing and their later actions, not that these are excuses, but they are possible explanations, which also leads to something very close to my heart: prevention. True crime can be exciting to read about, but it can be more than that. By seeing the connection between the person and the serial killer, perhaps we can gain greater insight, and understanding is crucial if we are to have a chance at preventing violent crime, of which serial murder is, of course, the absolute worst kind.

I'm working toward that understanding, among other things, by still corresponding with convicted serial killers, both from my thesis and new contacts I've made. Among the letters is a stack from Douglas Clark, whom you'll encounter in this book. I won't reveal his story here, but I can mention that, on his own initiative, he wrote a foreword for my book in 2004.

I've chosen not to use it in its entirety, but I think these lines fit well here:

> Florence McLean's research into serial murder and serial offenders is of great importance because she has inquired into all the possible factors that can lead to such crimes and which might help prevent some of them. I believe I've gained an in-depth understanding of serial killers and their lives, from their childhoods through school age to adolescence and the time before their first murder. I know them in their criminality. I have insight into how they perceive themselves, as well as their own explanations for why they ended up the way they are. Some of that, I'll share with you in this book.

It is important to note that when I talk about serial killers, I define them as a subcategory of multiple murderers.

The super category is multiple murderers, which includes all persons who kill more than one person, including mass murderers, spree killers, contract killers, serial partner killers, family murderers, healthcare serial killers, gang murders, and serial killers.

So, I define serial killers (a subcategory of multiple murderers) as individuals who kill two or more people in different events and situations with a cooling-off period. The motive for the killings is killing itself, not money, jealousy, revenge, lust, hatred, fanaticism, or anything else, but serial killers are people who kill to gain power and control, and they kill because of some psychological need they are acting on.

There may well be several motives at once, but the overall motive is power, control, and some psychological need they are acting on.

CHAPTER 1: A CRUCIAL PROFILE: THE BACKPACKER KILLER

On September 19, 1992, a minibus carrying eight runners from The Scrub Runners Orienteering Club turned off Hume Highway approximately 100 kilometers southwest of Sydney, Australia. A few kilometers later, they reached the entrance to Belanglo State Forest.

"Welcome," a green sign with white letters read. "Take care."

The forest, owned by the state of New South Wales, was one of the oldest pine plantations in the country, bordering typical Australian bush where hikers and runners often encountered some of Australia's iconic animals that inhabited the rugged terrain.

The orienteers passed one of the local rangers' cabins and continued into the wilderness. They parked and divided into teams of two, which soon disappeared among the trees. Two of the runners hurried up a slope toward an area ominously named Executioner's Drop. Late in the afternoon, they reached a small gorge where eucalyptus trees stretched toward the sky. They stopped at a boulder where a sweet-nauseating stench caught in their throats. They moved closer. On the west side of the rock, they spotted a mound of branches and twigs, about two meters long and half a meter high. In the middle of the pile, something resembling brownish fur was visible, and the two runners had no doubt. "It must be a wombat," one of them said.

Still, they moved closer. A whitish bone protruded from the pile, and the heel of a shoe. The runners looked at each other and stared at the pile until they realized it wasn't the fur they had seen at first. It was hair attached to a human skull. The two bolted and didn't stop until they reached the ranger's cabin, from where the alarm was raised. When the police arrived, the runners led them to the gorge and the boulder. As dusk fell, officers cordoned off the area and set up floodlights, allowing them to examine the pile of branches and twigs more closely. Beneath it lay the body of a young woman. She was lying face down on the forest floor and had been gagged with strips of fabric. Close to her lay a homemade garrote, which might have been the murder weapon.

At daybreak, the police began to meticulously search the gorge. Just 30 meters from the young woman, they found a similar pile of branches and the body of yet another young woman. A sweatshirt full of holes was wrapped around her head. Near the deceased, police found a number of Winchester brand shell casings and six cigarette butts of an unknown brand. 40 meters away, officers stumbled upon a ring of bricks. In the center were the remains of a bonfire.

The bodies had been in the gorge for so long that it was impossible to identify them before forensic examinations. Two days later, police were able to inform the press of the victims' identities. They were 22-year-old Joanne Walters and 21-year-old Caroline Clarke. The former was Welsh. After graduating from high school with good grades, she decided to travel to Australia to alternate between working and traveling around the vast country. The latter was from England. She wanted to make a difference for her fellow human beings and had therefore applied to the police force, who, however, thought she was too young. Since her brother had already traveled down under, she followed to gain some life experience.

The two young women teamed up, and in Sydney's Kings Cross district, notorious for prostitution, drug abuse, and cheap hostels, they agreed to go to Western Australia, where backpackers could easily find jobs as fruit pickers. First, however, they wanted to see the state of Victoria. Like so many others, they went to the Liverpool district, where the southbound Hume Highway began—from here it is possible to hitchhike toward Melbourne.

After this, Joanne Walters and Caroline Clarke disappeared without a trace until their bodies were found in Belanglo State Forest about six months later. At the press conference, journalists wanted to know if the police expected to find more bodies in the area, as the two young women were not the only backpackers who had disappeared in Australia. Then, as now, the country was an extremely popular destination for young travelers. The beaches, coral reefs, wildlife, rainforests, and nightlife lured over 200,000 tourists aged 20 to 25 there every single year in the 1990s. For travelers on a tight budget, hitchhiking was an obvious choice, especially on the Hume Highway, which connected the country's two largest cities. Around 300 of them disappeared annually. Most reappeared shortly after, having simply changed their travel plans without calling home to their parents in the USA or Europe. Some were never found—including several who, like Joanne Walters and Caroline Clarke, had decided to hitchhike on the Hume Highway.

"However, there is no indication that we are dealing with a mass grave out there, although we certainly aren't ruling anything out," said the police spokesperson.

When I hear about the case from Belanglo State Forest, several things immediately stand out to me. Firstly, there's the discovery site itself. It's not easily accessible. You either have to hike or you need a four-wheel drive vehicle. This tells me that the perpetrator possessed local knowledge; otherwise, they likely would have dumped the bodies closer to the road. It also suggests that the killer might have wanted to spend a significant amount of time with the victim. Those who spend a long time with their victims are acting out something psychological. It can also be a way to prolong the experience, and it can give them the opportunity to experiment with the victims. All of this requires them to feel reasonably certain they won't be discovered.

Secondly, there were cigarette butts. Of course, we can't know if they were killer's or one of the victims', but it's hard to imagine one of the deceased smoking six cigarettes while the assault was underway. So, if we assume it was the killer who smoked them, it also indicates he took his time. The same applies to the remains of the bonfire, if he was the one who made it. In that case, we're dealing with a person who has a fantasy that extends beyond the killings, which can be over quite quickly. This is also a person who managed to plan what they wanted to do, as they were able to keep the two women in check from the moment they overpowered them until they left their bodies deep within the forest.

Forensic examiners determined that Joanne Walters had been killed with 14 stab wounds, far more than necessary if one simply wants to kill another person. Something similar happened to Caroline Clarke, only she had been shot 10 times in the head. In both cases, we can talk about overkill, which often points toward a perpetrator who harbors a violent rage. However, it's important to examine stab and gunshot wounds more closely. For instance, if there are many defensive wounds because the victim fought back fiercely, it's not necessarily overkill. In such a case, it might even say something about the killer's physique if a female victim manages to counterattack. Therefore, it's crucial that the autopsy report describes which stabs or shots were fatal and which were defensive lesions.

Had I been present then, I would have told the police to look for a younger, locally knowledgeable man with access to a four-wheel drive vehicle and firearms, and that this individual undoubtedly had experiences in his past that had made him extremely enraged at his surroundings. That profile could fit many people, I readily admit. And that's often how it is with profiling. As much as one might wish, a profiler cannot pinpoint a specific perpetrator, although I almost got that impression when my interest in the subject was first sparked. It began in 1997 when I was studying psychology at Aarhus University and one evening happened to stumble upon an American documentary series on television. In it, police officers, forensic pathologists, and psychologists talked about some of the world's most notorious criminal cases. They showed images from crime scenes and detailed how the crimes took place. Along the way, you followed the detective work itself, where profilers, based on the crime scene and the way the murders were committed, could say a great deal about the person who had done it.

You often see something similar in films like *The Silence of the Lambs* and series such as *Criminal Minds*. Here, profilers are portrayed almost as psychics who sense what happened at crime scenes and can then describe the culprit in such detail that the police can find and arrest them. That's not how it happens in reality, and I hope this book can help debunk some of the many myths associated with the method.

My path to profiling went via my thesis in psychology. Inspired by the American documentary series, I began to wonder if the profiling method could be used even before a series of murders was committed. As a psychologist, I was especially interested in the perpetrators and their past, and it was a topic I got the opportunity to delve into when I had to write my final assignment at university. Through the FBI, I got in touch with John E. Douglas, the now-retired FBI agent who, in his time, together with his team, developed the American federal police's method by interviewing a wide range of different serial killers for hours. He became a kind of mentor for my project. He helped with contact information for a large number of serial killers, so I eventually had contact with 34 of the world's most disturbing criminals. At the time, though, I wasn't interested in the murders themselves.

I wanted to know about their upbringing and the time leading up to the first murder instead. Based on my knowledge from child psychology, I created a questionnaire designed to clarify whether there had been any common warning signs along the way. To put it very briefly, there were. I've written about this in the book *Serial Killer – The Human Behind the Monster*. When I later in my career came to work with children and young people who had experienced massive neglect in the form of violence, sexual abuse, humiliation, and isolation, I found that their backgrounds strikingly resembled those of the serial killers from my thesis. This is not to say that everyone who has experienced such suffering in their upbringing becomes a serial killer; far from it. Some recover, while many react inwardly, which can manifest as self-harm, depression, anxiety, or eating disorders. Still, others react outwardly and become violent, and ultimately, it can indeed end in murder. The central point here is that adults can destroy and damage children, and that this can have severe consequences later in life, which can manifest in various ways. This connection, childhood and the most horrific crimes, has interested me for many years.

I was utterly exhausted by serial killers when I finished my thesis, and when, later in my career, I returned to one of them for a research report, I thought it would be the last time I opened the door to humanity's darkest side. But I was wrong, and in 2019, I enrolled in my first course in Criminal Profiling and Crime Scene Analysis with the American criminologist, Ph.D., and forensic psychologist Brent Turvey. He has, among other things, worked as a consultant for the police on numerous murder cases and testified as an expert in countless trials. It might sound crazy at first glance, considering I've never wanted to look at crime scene photos. But there was no way around it now. As a profiler, you must study them down to the smallest detail: How many stab wounds are there? Are they deep or superficial? Where on the body are they? Could the murderer look the victim in the eyes during the act, or did they turn the deceased onto their stomach?

When I started my Master of Science, I asked one of my lecturers how he handled it, and he specifically recommended focusing on the detail, not on the person who had been murdered. That way, I see the gunshot wound, but not the person. I see the semen stains in connection with a rape, but not the victim. This way, the analysis becomes technical and clinical, and I can better keep a clear head. It's not easy, and when I occasionally took a break during an assignment, I often saw the whole person again. I had to remind myself that the deceased was no longer suffering, and I also thought about how the work a profiler does can help solve cases and thereby bring just a little relief to the bereaved.

The teaching was conducted online, and the assignments mainly involved analyzing cases that had already been concluded. As students, we were given access to photographs, video recordings, autopsy reports, witness statements, and interrogation transcripts. Based on these many different pieces of information, we had to try to reconstruct what had happened at the crime scene and propose what type of perpetrator was responsible.

I remember one example involving a younger man found in his bedroom. He was undressed and had a rope around his neck. The police initially concluded it was a fatal sex game, where one brings oneself close to asphyxiation which is said to give a more intense orgasm. However, something didn't add up. Firstly, there was nothing in the man's computer search history or in conversations with his friends and acquaintances that suggested he was into that type of sex. Secondly, the man had two small dogs, which those closest to him described as his children. When the officers arrived at the house, the dogs were running around on a busy street, which completely contradicted the victim's character as a "dog dad." If you consider your pets like children, you wouldn't let them out into traffic while having sex, especially when there was an enclosed backyard they could have been in. Therefore, I thought it could be a murder rather than an accident, which I primarily based on the victim's behavior.

These are the kinds of small details that reveal something about both the victim's and the perpetrator's behavior, which a profiler keeps a keen eye on, especially if they stand out from what you'd expect to see. Imagine, for example, a crime scene where a woman has been shot and killed, where all drawers and cabinets have been rummaged through, and where everything from books to pillows is scattered everywhere. Immediately, most people would probably guess it was a home invasion that ended in murder, but what should you think when you know that most burglars know exactly which drawers and cabinets to search? And if many valuables are still in the house, including the victim's partner's expensive watch? And does it matter if you can see that the woman's clothing was arranged after her death in a way that her body can't be seen, a behavior you don't typically associate with home invaders? In such a case, alarm bells would ring for a profiler, because something doesn't add up. Something suggests that you're dealing with an entirely different motive in that situation. I would quickly start investigating the couple's background to see if the family might have problems that could have triggered a spousal killing.

I didn't give it much thought before I enrolled in Brent Turvey's program. That's often how I am. If something interests me, I just start investigating it. For me, one of the most exciting things about life is that you can make a choice and then have no idea where it will lead or what will happen tomorrow. I've been asked quite a few times if I'm going to start working as a profiler. I probably won't—I'm a psychologist and have been since 2004. I'm just fundamentally interested in serial killers, their backgrounds, and the methods underlying profiling. It was somewhat the same when I was admitted to psychology study back then. I had a somewhat different profile from my fellow students, because when I decided what I wanted, I had no qualifying education and had a long list of different unskilled jobs behind me. One of my fellow students once asked me if I was afraid that I wouldn't succeed in completing the education, but I hadn't considered that at all. When I set my mind to something, and especially if others doubt me, I keep going until I succeed.

The following year, I enrolled in another course, this time a diploma program at Heritage University in the American state of Washington. The course was called Criminal Profiling and had a number of different lecturers with experience from both the police and the healthcare system. It was quite similar to

Brent Turvey's course, but more in-depth, perhaps because it was at a university level. While the FBI's method is very practical and based on investigators' experiences, here I encountered a more theoretical approach to the method. I was especially pleased that the instructors placed great emphasis on psychology to understand the perpetrators. This was certainly true in the case of the two murdered hitchhikers in Belanglo State Forest in Australia, because even though the police interviewed more than 500 people and a reward of $100,000 was offered, investigators were at a dead end for a long time.

On October 5, 1993, a little over a year after the bodies of Joanne Walters and Caroline Clarke had been found, a local man drove into Belanglo State Forest, as he often did, to collect firewood. He drove along a fire trail and parked deep in the bush, where, as always, he kept an extra eye out for anything the police might have overlooked when they searched the forest around the gorge. After a hundred meters, he stopped. On the ground in front of him lay a thigh bone. He had no doubt it was human. A little further ahead, he could see more bones and a skull. He turned around, ran back to his car, and drove out of the forest to alert the police. Inside the trees, the police found more bones and teeth under branches and twigs, along with a necklace with a crucifix and a bracelet. Among the bones lay a pair of pantyhose with several knots, which could have been used to bind or gag the victim, and some strips of electrical tape.

About 20 meters to the west, officers discovered yet another body under a pile of branches and twigs. Judging by the shoes, it was the body of a man. Approximately 400 meters away, they found a tree trunk that someone had apparently used for target practice. The projectiles were of the same brand and caliber as those used when Caroline Clarke was shot. And just like at the first crime scene, someone had also built a bonfire here, although it was difficult to determine if it had been lit in connection with the crime.

"A casual passerby would hardly venture that far into the forest," one of the lead investigators concluded.

The body parts were sent to forensic examiners, and while the investigations were ongoing, both the police and the press speculated on the identity of the two victims. Many thought of two young German backpackers who had disappeared shortly after Christmas the previous year, after planning to hitchhike along the Hume Highway from Sydney to Melbourne. That theory fell apart when forensic examiners reported that the bones had been in the forest for up to five years. They turned out to belong to 19-year-old Australians Deborah Everist and James Gibson, who had been missing since December 30, 1989. The couple, both keenly interested in the environment, had attended a demonstration and, on their way home, wanted to take the opportunity to camp and hike in various natural areas. James Gibson told his parents over the phone that, like so many others, they would hitchhike from Sydney, which his mother advised against. He said, however, that she shouldn't worry: "There are two of us, so it's safe enough."

Deborah Everist didn't dare tell her parents about the plan; she was sure they would veto it.

Forensic examiners could further report that Deborah Everist had a fractured skull and a broken jaw. Her skull bore marks from a large knife or sword. Her spine showed damage from a different type of knife. James Gibson had also been stabbed; a total of 17 marks were found on his bones. Similar to the two British backpackers, neither of the two Australian victims showed marks that could indicate they had tried to defend themselves before they were killed.

Two other clues would prove important in the case. Shortly after Deborah Everist and James Gibson disappeared, the latter's camera and backpack were found at two different locations about 100 kilometers north of Belanglo State Forest. Inside the backpack, investigators found pine needles, which puzzled them because there were no pine trees in the area where the bag turned up, but there could now be an explanation for that.

Fear spread throughout the local community. Police warned against entering the forest and pleaded with backpackers not to hitchhike. People stayed home and began locking their doors. Alarm companies had boom times, while officers and volunteers continued to meticulously search the forest where the bodies of the four backpackers had been found. On November 1, 1993, they gathered for a final search in a part of the forest called Miner's Despair. They moved slowly through the bush in a long line until one of them raised an arm and shouted, echoing through the trees, "FIND!"

Investigators were met with a sight they had grown accustomed to: human bones, jewelry, and some coins. 50 meters away lay a T-shirt that had been cut open with a knife. Beside it was a piece of wire shaped like a loop. Police ordered the search to continue and expand, now focusing on the northern part of Belanglo State Forest in an area between three fire trails. After three days, an officer spotted a brown woman's sandal. Nearby lay the familiar pile of branches and twigs, and within it, the body of a woman. Just 20 meters from there, yet another body appeared. Here, too, lay a pair of shoes, some jewelry, a watch, and a plane ticket, in addition to a bra, a pair of leggings, and a pair of pink jeans that had been ripped with a knife. Police also found some black electrical tape and a length of blue and yellow rope with a loop at each end.

Forensic examiners identified all three victims: 21-year-old Simone Schmidl, a German backpacker who had disappeared on her way from Sydney to Melbourne on January 20, 1991, and the couple Gabor Neugebauer (21) and Anja Habschied (20), who had disappeared shortly after Christmas in 1991 when they left Sydney. Simone Schmidl had caught travel fever, and when she met an Australian in Alaska, she decided to go to Australia for her next trip. She often hitchhiked, and even when friends in Sydney advised against it and offered to pay for a bus ticket when she wanted to go south to Melbourne, she declined the offer. The couple had not planned to go to Australia, but when the weather in Indonesia didn't cooperate, they traveled further south and ended up at a Christmas party in Sydney, after which no one saw them again.

Simone Schmidl had been stabbed multiple times with a knife. The same was true for Anja Habschied, but in her case, the killer had also used a larger weapon, a machete or an axe. Her skull was never found. Gabor Neugebauer had been shot six times in the back of the head with a .22 caliber rifle. There was strong evidence he had also been strangled. At any rate, a garrote was also found, tied in the same way as the one lying next to Joanne Walters' body.

The Australian police now had seven bodies of young backpackers of both sexes, who had been killed in various ways. One of the country's leading criminologists told the press that they were dealing with a highly unusual case. "Serial killers generally don't target victims of both sexes, nor do they usually kill multiple people at the same time," he stated.

One particular detail puzzled investigators. Forensic examiners had found four of the projectiles in Gabor Neugebauer's skull, but not the last two, which had passed through his head and exited the other side. Despite using sieves and metal detectors, police also didn't find them near where the body was discovered. The killer must, therefore, have shot the young German somewhere else. Investigators might have found the place just 150 meters away. They called it "The Shooting Range." 47 shell casings of the same type already found near several of the bodies were scattered around. They had been fired from a rifle of the same kind the killer had used against several of the backpackers. 46 shell casings from another type of rifle were also found. Experts concluded that the rifles had been used at the same time, and that the shooter or shooters had fired from different angles towards the center of The Shooting Range. A pair of empty ammunition boxes didn't help investigators much. They merely revealed that the cartridges could be purchased in many stores around New South Wales. It was time to call in experts on killer behavior and psychology.

It's easy, of course, to be smart about a historical case, but I'm surprised that the police initially didn't expect to find more bodies in Belanglo State Forest. There are several reasons for this. Firstly, there's the way the young people were killed. If, for instance, it was a robbery gone wrong, you wouldn't have seen the kind of "overkill" that also appears in the five other cases; a single shot would have been enough. There would be no reason to use other methods like strangulation and stabbing, and it certainly wouldn't make sense to also decapitate a victim. In my opinion, even the first victims already bore signs of being killed because the perpetrator genuinely wanted to kill them. And that is precisely the motive when it comes to serial killers. For them, the motive lies in the killing itself. Even though, after the discovery of Joanne Walters and Caroline Clarke, one couldn't definitively say there was a serial killer at large, one could at least have a strong suspicion that the perpetrator would kill again, if they hadn't already.

Another thing I notice is that the killer apparently spent longer and longer time with the victims. Something suggests he enjoyed drawing out the time, and that tells me the power he held over the victims was central to him. You also get the sense that he evolved. It's as if he needed more and more, until he eventually finally cut off Anja Habschied's head. He was also clearly capable of overpowering two people at once, even if they were young men. There could be several explanations for this. Belanglo State Forest is a popular destination for outdoor enthusiasts, and since bonfires were found near the bodies, he might have offered to guide the young people on a camping trip. The fires could, of course, also have been lit after the victims were overpowered or after the killings, because the perpetrator undoubtedly had a good handle on firearms and could have threatened the young women into tying up their boyfriends. If that was the case, the killer had spent time building fires as part of the act, which again could be about prolonging the pleasure he derived from it, regardless of whether the backpackers were alive or not at the time.

As mentioned, police, forensic scientists, and psychiatrists were astonished by the vastly different methods of killing. This led many to believe that there were multiple perpetrators. As noted, one criminologist pointed out that serial killers don't target both men and women, and they don't kill multiple people at once. It was also said that serial killers don't usually kill in different ways. This is often how it's portrayed in films or TV series, but in reality, it's not accurate. When the American serial killer David Berkowitz terrorized New York in 1976 and 1977, he shot couples sitting in their cars in several instances, and he also used a knife in his first two attacks. Edmund Kemper became notorious in the early 1970s as The Co-Ed Killer because he targeted young female students. He started by shooting his grandparents at age 15 in 1964 during an outburst of rage, but when he evolved into a serial killer years later, he used a knife, firearms, and strangled his victims, much like The Backpacker Killer, as the unknown Australian perpetrator was called in the media.

The fact that all the victims were backpackers also says a lot about the killer. Young people tend to take greater risks than adults, for example, by hitchhiking. One must also remember that the times were different. "Stranger-danger" was not a widespread phenomenon, and many initially trusted that they could rely on other people, even if they didn't know them.

Hitchhikers are and were low-risk victims for serial killers because they are easy to pick up, they willingly get into strangers' cars, and they aren't missed immediately. These are all advantages for a serial killer. In this specific case, it's also worth noting that the victims all hitchhiked and disappeared from approximately the same area in the southern part of Sydney, where the Hume Highway begins. This means the killer must have knowledge of this particular road and the fact that many backpackers used it when hitchhiking. Perhaps he was a truck driver? He could also have been a road worker or a forest worker. Of course, one cannot know for certain, but such suggestions might help the police focus their investigation, especially if at some point they had several possible suspects.

Three years earlier, in 1989, a woman was driving her Toyota on one of the roads bordering Belanglo State Forest. Further up the road, she suddenly saw two men. A short distance from them, a four-wheel drive vehicle sat with its doors open. It looked as though the two men were fighting, and she stepped on the brake. At that very moment, one of the men managed to break free, sprinting towards the female motorist.

"HELP!" he screamed.

The woman drove closer, and the young man jumped into the road in front of her. She stepped on the brake again, and before she could react, the young man yanked open the passenger-side door and threw himself in.

"Get out!" she screamed.

"He's got a gun!" the guy shouted with an unmistakable British accent.

A second later, the woman made a U-turn and floored the accelerator. She just managed to glimpse the other man in her rearview mirror. He had a large, dark mustache that reached all the way down to his chin. And it was as if he were smiling at her.

She drove the young man to the nearest police station, where he gave a statement. His name was Paul Onions, and he had arrived in Australia shortly before Christmas in 1989. His plan was to work and travel around. From Sydney, he had gone to the Hume Highway to find a lift to Melbourne. A man calling himself Bill stopped, and Paul Onions got in. At first, "Bill" seemed nice and chatty. He said his parents were from Yugoslavia and that he worked as a road worker. When he mentioned he had just gotten divorced, the mood shifted, and soon after, "Bill" expressed some very racist views that made the young Brit uncomfortable. At one point, the road worker made a move to pull over, saying he wanted to find some tapes in the trunk so they could listen to music. This puzzled Paul Onions, because there were already several cassette tapes inside the car. When "Bill" got out and opened the trunk, the Brit stepped onto the shoulder. At that point, "Bill" pulled out a revolver and said it was a robbery. Paul Onions' gaze dropped to the trunk, where he spotted a bag with ropes—then the young man ran in a zigzag pattern away from "Bill," who shot at him. Several cars passed them, but no one stopped for the desperate backpacker. It was at that moment that Paul Onions spotted the woman in the Toyota.

The police noted Paul Onions' testimony, including that the assailant drove a silver Nissan Patrol without license plates. They also wrote that the man had a thick, dark mustache. But otherwise, the case stalled there. Paul Onions traveled back to Sydney, where he warned all the backpackers who would listen to his story. Later, he returned home to the UK, where years later he read about The Backpacker Killer in newspapers and contacted the Australian police. The young Brit would prove to be one of the most crucial witnesses in the case, for he had met The Backpacker Killer and escaped alive.

At that time, several perpetrator profiles were developed. The Australian police, among others, approached their American colleagues at the FBI, under which the B.S.U., Behavioral Science Unit, belonged. (The unit is now called the B.A.U., Behavioral Analysis Unit). According to the B.S.U., the perpetrator was a white, muscular male aged 25 to 45. He was a loner who struggled with close relationships. On the surface, he might appear friendly and wouldn't immediately arouse suspicion. He most likely came from a large, working-class family. He had experienced problems in school, and the profilers predicted that he had started his 30s. He likely started his criminal career in his teenage years. He enjoyed outdoor life and knew the forest inside out, and he had a strong fascination with weapons, probably because owning them gave him a sense of dominance. In the time leading up to the murders, he was angry and depressed, but afterward, he would seem relaxed and content. Something suggested that holidays or vacations triggered stress in him, as many of the killings happened around these kinds of events that often bring families together.

However, it wasn't possible to determine if this stress was due to financial, work-related, or family problems.

As previously stated, a profiler cannot definitively identify a specific perpetrator. The profile formulated by the B.S.U., while initially appearing broad, contained nuances that distinguished it. In parallel, the police had, of course, undertaken extensive investigative efforts. This included questioning a vast number of individuals, contacting various roadwork contractors, and endeavoring to trace the owners of the rifle type used. The local police also possessed a detailed understanding of the residents in the smaller towns surrounding Belanglo State Forest. It is precisely at this juncture that the profile, in some cases, can prove its utility as one of the essential tools available to law enforcement. When officers received the description of a man from a large family, with a history of criminal convictions and a keen interest in firearms, their course of action became clear: they needed to focus on the Milat family.

The Australians' consultation with the B.S.U. was entirely intentional, as the FBI had originally developed and systematized these profiling methodologies, which developed the foundation for the methods profilers use today. Early in his career, John E. Douglas served as a sharpshooter on a federal police tactical team and subsequently trained as a hostage negotiator. In 1977, he was transferred to the Behavioral Science Unit to teach negotiation techniques and forensic psychology, which led him to police stations across most of the United States. During his travels, he began interviewing a wide range of notorious serial killers and other dangerous criminals, including Edmund Kemper, Ted Bundy, and John Wayne Gacy, also known as The Clown Killer because he performed as a clown at children's birthday parties when he wasn't torturing and murdering young men and burying them in his yard and under his house.

As mentioned, the profiling method is based on the premise that a perpetrator's personality and behavior can be deciphered from a crime scene. There's always a reason why a serial offender acts the way they do. For most of us, this might seem immediately incomprehensible, but for the profiler, it's about narrating the story that makes sense in the criminal's mind. The method has evolved over the years, with many more tools added to the toolkit. What most people think of when discussing profiling, and what they recognize from films and TV series, is usually criminal profiling. If you ask the FBI, this is equivalent to what is known as crime scene analysis, where a profiler attempts to interpret the personality behind the observed behavior. It's during this phase that it can, for example, be crucial whether the fires in Belanglo State Forest were lit before or after the murders, or if The Backpacker Killer committed his crimes around holidays or vacations.

However, criminal profiling is only one part of the FBI's entire approach to profiling. Among the other tools is, for example, victimology, which focuses on the victims and what they can reveal about their killer. In the Australian case, it was significant that the victims were young backpackers who had all hitchhiked on the same road. Profilers also utilize link analysis, where they attempt to connect one crime with others to determine if it's a serial offense or an isolated case. It's been observed in several cases that investigators only realized they were hunting a serial killer late in an investigation. It's this toolkit that we'll delve into in this book to better understand how profilers work, and how their methods might also be used to prevent not just crimes, but also a range of social problems that can arise when children grow up with emotional scars.

These are the people, both children and adults, I've sat across from during my 20-year career as a psychologist. When I give lectures on serial killers, the audience often assumes I'm a profiler. While I do have the formal qualifications to call myself one, I am first and foremost a psychologist. It is very much my experiences in that role that I draw upon when I delve into profiling. And that's also why I believe it was absolutely correct for the Australian police to investigate the Milat family more closely when the B.S.U. delivered the profile of The Backpacker Killer.

The profile, among other things, predicted that the killer came from a large family. Stjepan Milat, the son of Croatian immigrants, married Margaret Elizabeth Piddleston in 1936 when she was 16. Together, they had 14 children, 10 boys and 4 girls. Stjepan Milat was the undisputed head of the family, and even by the standards of the time, he was a tough man and father. Violence was a part of daily life, affecting both the mother and children severely. This pattern of violence was inherited by the boys, who quickly learned to use their fists in their attempts to establish a place in the family hierarchy. Several of the children exhibited signs of behavioral disorders early in life, but the family created a protective barrier around themselves to keep the police and social services at bay, partly by moving between different properties around the state. There's also evidence to suggest sexual abuse occurred among the many siblings.

Boys who grow up in such conditions, with a very strong father and a weak mother who fails to stand up for herself, can, in some cases, develop intense hatred towards their mother. I've witnessed this myself as a psychologist when treating children and adults. Seeing one's mother being abused is so traumatic and difficult to process that the anger can turn against her, especially if the boys, as in this case, have also been subjected to physical, psychological, or sexual abuse, because she "tolerated" the assaults. In the children's eyes, the mother betrays them by staying with the abuser and allowing them to experience the violence. In some instances, she even uses the children as an excuse to remain with the father. This creates a great deal of confusion and internal conflict that can be very difficult to manage, potentially developing into outright hatred. In the Milat family, the sons experienced their mother as largely reduced to a "baby-making machine," which could easily have influenced how at least some of them viewed women in general.

There were plenty of brothers to choose from, but suspicion eventually focused on 39-year-old Ivan Milat. He had a history of burglaries and thefts and had spent time behind bars on numerous occasions. He had worked as both a truck driver and a road worker and spent a significant portion of his free time on weapons and outdoor pursuits. He had purchased a Nissan Patrol in his brother Bill's name. In 1980, he met and married a 16-year-old girl, subjecting her to physical, psychological, and sexual abuse and control until their divorce in 1992. This divorce further intensified his volatile temperament. After the separation, he moved with a new girlfriend into a house near the Hume Highway on the outskirts of Sydney.

As police delved into Ivan Milat's past, they uncovered an old case where two female hitchhikers accused him of rape. However, he was acquitted when it emerged that the two women were lesbians, a fact the defense lawyer exploited to the jury in the then-homophobic society. Police received assistance from Paul Onions, who traveled to Australia and, from a selection of 30 photos of potential perpetrators, identified Ivan Milat as the man who had assaulted him four years prior.

Furthermore, a part of the investigation revealed that Ivan Milat had been in the vicinity of the areas from which the backpackers had disappeared.

In this instance, it's clear that the profile developed remarkably well with the rest of the investigation, making it understandable that the police subsequently prepared for an arrest.

*

Ivan Milat and his girlfriend were asleep when the phone rang at 6:36 AM on May 22, 1994. Drowsily, he answered, and an unfamiliar voice introduced himself as a police officer. The officer informed him that the house was surrounded by armed personnel and instructed him to exit the front door with his hands raised.

"Okey-Dokey, I just need to put some pants on," Ivan Milat replied, his voice sounding both bewildered and strangely cheerful.

Five minutes later, the phone rang again. This time, his girlfriend answered and handed the receiver to Ivan Milat. He told the officer, who wanted to know why he hadn't come out, that he'd figured it out: it was a practical joke by his colleagues.

"No, mate, I'm from the police, and this isn't a joke," came the response.

"If you are, why the hell didn't you just knock on the door?"

The police officer insisted he was simply following procedure, and Ivan Milat chuckled on the other end: "Okay, I'll play along."

Minutes passed, and outside, police could hear a car door opening and closing inside the garage. At 6:48 AM, the officer called again. This time, the girlfriend explained that Ivan Milat was looking for his keys. "He always misplaces them," she added.

Then the door opened, and Ivan Milat emerged with his hands above his head, as instructed. He was ordered to lie on the lawn, whereupon two officers arrested him and placed him in handcuffs. The search then began. Among a multitude of items, police found many interesting things: a postcard addressed to "Bill" and a driver's license with the same name featuring a photo of Ivan Milat. There were also coins and banknotes from various countries, including Great Britain and Indonesia. Ammunition of the same type used by the killer in the forest. Police also found parts of a weapon matching the murder weapon, a map of Belanglo State Forest, black electrical tape, and a camera of the same model Caroline Clarke had brought to Australia, a model only available in the UK. Simone Schmidl's sleeping bag, Deborah Everist's sleeping bag, and various camping gear were recovered. Furthermore, inside a cavity in a wall, a magazine and parts of a .22 caliber Ruger rifle were discovered.

Searches at the homes of other Milat family members also yielded results, in the form of camping equipment, sleeping bags, backpacks, and tents belonging to the various victims. A brother and sister-in-law presented a photo album with pictures from a family Easter celebration, claiming these provided Ivan Milat with an alibi. They had simply forgotten that the correct date was printed on the back of the photographs.

While there was a wealth of circumstantial evidence, the prosecution lacked tangible proof, such as fingerprints or eyewitnesses to the abductions or murders, when the case went to trial on March 26, 1996. A DNA analysis was conducted, but a chemical error rendered the results unusable. This, however, did not impact the outcome. The defense attempted to shift the blame to Ivan Milat's brothers, but this claim was quickly dismissed by the accused himself when he took the stand. When the prosecutor inquired about some gloves police had found during the search, Ivan Milat began, "I never used…" then quickly tried to rephrase himself. The jury found Ivan Milat guilty. He was sentenced to life in prison without the possibility of parole and died at 74 years old in 2019.

Ivan Milat was one of the serial killers I wrote about while working on my thesis. He declined to participate, maintaining his innocence right up until his death. This isn't uncommon; some serial killers will admit and talk about the murders, while others refuse to confess, regardless of the evidence against them. Personally, I have no doubt that Ivan Milat was guilty. As mentioned, the case was based solely on circumstantial evidence, and one might reasonably wonder if he would have been convicted on just a few pieces of it. However, the sheer volume of evidence was so extensive that I fully understand the verdict, especially when considering Paul Onions' testimony.

The Backpacker Killer had a number of supporters in Australia who believed in his innocence. They often pointed to the different methods used in the killings and the cigarette butts police found in the forest near the bodies as proof of Ivan Milat's innocence. I've already mentioned that serial killers often kill in similar ways, but it's by no means unheard of for them to experiment or simply have a fantasy about trying different methods.

Regarding the cigarettes, there's a valid point. Ivan Milat didn't smoke. One possibility is that one or more smokers, completely unrelated to the murders, discarded the butts in the forest. Of course, it's also possible that Ivan Milat did smoke during the killings. And then there's a third consideration, which was already discussed at the time: perhaps there was more than one killer. The profilers, because others besides the B.S.U. were involved in the case, were divided on this. If there had been two perpetrators, I would initially look within the immediate family. Many have pointed to the fierce competition among the brothers, but I'd look closer at one of the sisters who smoked the exact brand found on the forest floor. She lived in the same house as Ivan Milat and his girlfriend, and there were rumors of an incestuous relationship between the two. Whether I'm right, we'll likely never know.

Looking at the crime scenes, I certainly don't find a definitive answer, as the behavior could point in either direction. The family has largely remained silent, except when Ivan Milat's siblings attempted to create false alibis for him. However, according to author Clive Small, he confessed to his mother shortly before her death in 2001. The sister Ivan Milat lived with was aware of what happened.

CHAPTER 2: BIND, TORTURE, KILL: WHAT THE CRIME SCENE TELLS

On the afternoon of January 15, 1974, 15-year-old Charlie Otero walked home from school. His house was on the corner of North Edgemoor Street and East Murdock Avenue in Wichita, Kansas. He lived there with his parents and four younger siblings. The Otero family had lived in the white wooden house for about three months, so much still felt new, but they were used to it.

Joseph and Julie Otero both came from Puerto Rico but grew up in New York City. Joseph Otero, whose father was in the military, had lived in several different countries. He was in the Navy himself and was regularly stationed around the country, and Julie Otero and their five children, ranging from 9 to 15 years old, always joined him. They always managed to settle in well. Julie Otero was deeply religious and involved herself in the local Catholic church, where she did volunteer social work. It wasn't unusual for the family to host guests for Christmas who had fallen on hard times. One of her more unusual interests was judo, in which she held a brown belt.

As usual, Charlie Otero went in through the back door. Behind the house, their dog, Lucky, greeted him, which puzzled him. The dog was normally always inside unless someone was walking him. Charlie Otero opened the kitchen door and stepped inside. On the stove, he noticed his mother's purse. It was overturned, and its contents were scattered everywhere, which was unlike Julie Otero, who highly valued order.

"Is anyone home?!" Charlie Otero called out.

"Charlie, hurry! Mom and Dad are playing a stupid practical joke!"

His younger brother and sister had arrived home shortly before him and were now in their parents' bedroom. Julie Otero lay on the bed, while Joseph Otero lay on the floor. The children's mother was bound, and they struggled to recognize her. Charlie Otero was briefly paralyzed as he watched his siblings try to cut a rope to loosen a plastic bag around his father's head. Charlie felt as if his heart was being ripped from his chest, but he still managed, along with his brother and sister, to run to a neighbor, who called the police.

The officers also entered through the kitchen. Dishes were on the dining table, and it looked like the family had been in the middle of making lunch. They continued to the bedroom. There, they found that Joseph Otero's ankles were tied together with a piece of white cord, and his hands were bound behind his back. A plastic bag was over his head. Julie Otero was also hog-tied, and they could see she had been strangled.

The police officers moved on to the house's other rooms. In the floor of one of them, they found nine-year-old Joseph Jr. His ankles and hands were bound with a cord from the blinds. He had a pillowcase over his head, in addition to two plastic bags and a T-shirt.

An officer turned on his flashlight and descended the stairs to the basement. There, he encountered the body of 11-year-old Josephine. She was hanging from a thin but strong cord attached to a water pipe on the ceiling. She was wearing socks and a sweatshirt, but her underwear had been pulled down, and her bra had been cut into pieces with a knife. Cords from blinds were tied around her ankles and knees, and her hands were bound behind her back. On her legs, there was a dried substance, which turned out to be semen. The officers noted that the knots the killer had used looked professional. There was no doubt the person knew how to make them hold tight.

Outside the house, police quickly discovered that the telephone line had been cut and the family's car, an Oldsmobile Vista Cruiser, was missing. The surviving children reported that their father had driven them to school in it that morning but had driven back home because he had been injured in a car accident and was still on sick leave. Witnesses said they had seen the car driven away that morning. The driver was described as a dark-skinned man. Besides the car, Joseph Otero's watch was gone, as was a radio that Joseph Jr. had had in his room. Otherwise, nothing else seemed to be missing from the home.

Later that day, a priest and a police officer informed Charlie Otero and his brother and sister that Joseph Jr. and Josephine had also died. Since that day, Charlie Otero thanked God that it wasn't him or his two siblings who had found the youngest members of the family dead.

Police in Wichita had never seen anything like it. The city was relatively peaceful, a place many families moved to, either because the father was in the Air Force, which had a base in the area, or because of work at the aircraft manufacturing plants. This had earned the city the nickname "Air Capital of the World."

Autopsies revealed that the parents and the two children had been strangled. No foreign fingerprints or footprints were found in the house, despite what appeared to be a highly chaotic crime scene. Relatively quickly, the investigation shifted toward a gang-related crime, perhaps a drug dispute, or a violent revenge where the killer or killers targeted the family to settle a score with the father. There was nothing at the crime scene itself to suggest this, but given the family's Latin American background, police apparently considered it a plausible theory.

It's very clear to me that the investigators failed to decode the story the perpetrator was telling them, and thus drew hasty conclusions. Imagine standing at the crime scene and considering the differences among the four victims. They were all bound, and they were all strangled in different ways. Why didn't the police find Josephine Otero in her room like the others? And why was she the only one displayed in such a manner, by being hanged? For me, there's no doubt that, to the killer, the youngest daughter was the most significant (target victim) of the four victims. Unless she was already in the basement, which is unlikely given the family was about to eat lunch, the perpetrator himself had to ensure she got down there. He spent time tying her up and hoisting her to the ceiling, and it was there that he ejaculated, even though there was no sign that he had direct sexually assaulted the girl. This tells me she was the central figure in his fantasy.

Analyzing a crime scene and the perpetrator's behavior is probably the aspect of a profiler's job that outsiders are most familiar with. In movies and on TV, profilers are often depicted walking around crime scenes, almost psychically sensing what happened and who the perpetrator is. That's not how it works in reality. At the FBI, there isn't even a job title called "profiler." The agents who work with profiling are called behavioral analysts. They spend most of their time behind a desk, looking at photos and video recordings and poring over reports, interrogations, databases, and statistics. They're usually only brought into a case once it has gone cold, and their work typically concludes with a written report sent to the head of the investigation. When you see behavioral analysts in a show like *Criminal Minds* flying out to crime scenes, collecting evidence, questioning witnesses, and finally arresting "the unsub," the unknown subject, as it's called in the jargon, it's pure fiction. The FBI would never send their profilers into a firefight, as that's simply not what behavioral analysts are trained for.

When a profiler delves into even the smallest details of a murder case, it's about telling a story from beginning to end. They try to figure out what the perpetrator did first and what they concluded with, knowing that everything along the way can be significant, even if it might point in different directions. This was the case in the Otero family home. On one hand, the house showed signs of chaos. Things were overturned, and it was evident the victims had struggled to break free and might even have been tied multiple times, as if the perpetrator hadn't done it before. Conversely, the knots were of a type that suggested the killer had experience with binding. And although the scene bore the marks of chaos, it was clear that planning lay behind the murders, as one doesn't simply walk in off the street and assault an entire family without having thought through the process. Especially not in a residential neighborhood at a time when many women were at home, meaning there could be many witnesses in the area. The disconnected telephone points in the same direction. The perpetrator knew where the line was and how to cut it. The killings themselves also tell me that this was a killer for whom the murders themselves were significant. If it had been a gang dispute, the family would likely have been executed with a single shot or two to the head. Instead, a long time was spent binding, torturing, and killing the victims, something that's entirely unnecessary if the sole purpose is simply to kill them. Furthermore, if it had been about revenge on the father, the perpetrator would have killed him last so he could witness his family die. There was no sign of that. There's also something mysterious about the way Joseph Otero's body was found on a pillow, as if the killer wanted to consider the injury he had sustained in the car accident.Was this an empathetic person, or was it about calming the victim and avoiding panic at the crime scene? Did the perpetrator know that by faking empathy, he had a greater chance of maintaining control? Similarly, the T-shirt over Joseph Jr.'s head is interesting. The killer had no problem looking at Josephine in the basement, but the boy's face was covered. Why? Was the perpetrator affected by what he was doing? Perhaps there was something in his personality that made him identify with the boy, or it could be a sign of remorse because he "had to" kill the youngest family member as well. In this case, my hypothesis would be that the perpetrator saw something of himself in the boy and therefore felt empathy for him. I would remember this identification and use it in a profile or my recommendations for a future interrogation if the police managed to apprehend the killer.

If I had been at the scene, I would also have examined the murder method. In all cases, the victims were strangled, which isn't as easy as it looks in movies. In the real world, it takes several minutes to strangle a victim, whether with hands, a rope, or a bag. It takes time, and it's very personal because the perpetrator literally holds the victim's life in their hands. It turned out that the bags the family members had over their heads did not come from the home. So, the killer brought them, which again speaks to the planning and the fantasy he wanted to live out. He could have shot them or cut their throats, but he chose to strangle them, indicating it was crucial for the act to unfold in that specific manner, even though it was far more difficult and required much more effort.

Of course, it's easy to be wise after the event, but when I look at what happened to the Otero family, much suggests that this was a killer for whom the murders were the motive in themselves. It was highly probable that this was a sexual sadist who derived great pleasure from the suffering he inflicted on the four victims, especially Josephine Otero. I'm also certain that today, there would be fear that the perpetrator would strike again, because the urge behind this type of killing is very strong. I would also find it hard to imagine that this was the perpetrator's first murder, given that it was so extensive. On the other hand, the crime scene showed that the killer was close to losing control several times. It's impossible to know if things would have turned out differently had police known they were hunting a serial killer at that point, but the signs were there if you knew what to look for.

In the police's defense, the horrific events in Wichita began in 1974, a time when criminal profiling as a method didn't yet exist. John E. Douglas and his colleagues were just starting to interview serial killers in American prisons, and there was still a long way to go before coming up with a model that future profilers could work from. This doesn't mean behavioral analysis was an unknown phenomenon until then, but it was more tied to the experiences skilled investigators had gained if they'd encountered similar cases earlier in their careers. However, by no means did everyone even consider behavior. For many, both professionals and amateurs, psychology was irrelevant, as murder was simply about evil, and that was that.

Nevertheless, examples of profiling can be found quite far back in time. One of the first profiles was developed in London in 1888, when Jack the Ripper terrorized Whitechapel in the East End, cutting the throats of a number of women, especially prostitutes. In several cases, he mutilated the bodies and removed organs. At that time, newspapers could sell far more copies than usual, and readers had ample opportunity to revel in the bloody details while police fruitlessly tried to solve the case. Forensic pathologist Thomas Bond was tasked with evaluating the perpetrator's anatomical knowledge and skills. Bond examined the most disfigured body and thoroughly reviewed the other autopsy reports. In his notes, he wrote that he believed the murders were sexually motivated and that the perpetrator must have been driven by misogyny and rage. He also attempted to reconstruct the murder and analyze the perpetrator's behavior, after which he wrote:

"The murderer must have been a man of physical strength and great coolness and daring. There is no evidence he had an accomplice. He must in my opinion be a man subject to periodic attacks of homicidal and erotic mania ... The murderer in external appearance is quite likely to be a quiet inoffensively looking man probably middle-aged and neatly and respectably dressed. Assuming the murderer be such a person as I have just described, he would be solitary and eccentric in his habits, also he is likely to be a man without regular occupation, but with some small income or pension."

Twenty-three years later, in 1911, psychiatrist Nelson Wilson played a role in solving a gruesome case in the US when seven-year-old Joey Joseph disappeared from a street in Lackawanna, New York. Police launched a massive investigation, but it was as if the boy had vanished into thin air, until officers and the victim's parents began receiving postcards from the perpetrator, detailing the murder and expressing remorse. There was no doubt the killer enjoyed what he was doing. Nelson Wilson read the postcards and developed a description of the type of killer he must be. However, this wasn't enough to catch the culprit, so investigators decided to publicize the postcards, which led them to John Frank Hickey, as several readers recognized his handwriting.

It turned out that Nelson Wilson's profile was quite accurate. Hickey had been abused by his father when he was young; he was an alcoholic, and when drunk, he was often overwhelmed by rage combined with a sexual attraction to children. He confessed to the murder of Joey Joseph and a 10-year-old newspaper boy, as well as a colleague he had worked with in a store. There were about 10 years between each murder, and to this day, he remains the prime suspect in 12 other unsolved cases. Hickey, dubbed The Postcard Killer by newspapers, was one of the first known American serial killers to achieve the kind of notoriety that became part of US popular culture in the 1970s and 1980s.

During World War II, British psychologists and psychiatrists developed a number of profiles on Hitler to predict his actions under various circumstances. One profile concluded that the German leader would commit suicide if it became clear the war was lost, which is precisely what happened.

While profiling was initially used sporadically, the work became far more targeted from the 1970s onward, after John E. Douglas and his colleagues began their interviews and started systematizing their knowledge of serial killers. Even then, and for some time after, there was a tendency to believe it was possible to identify criminals simply by their appearance. In old films, it's often glaringly obvious who the killer is based solely on their looks, but FBI agents established once and for all that one must focus on behavior when dealing with an unknown perpetrator.

One of my instructors, Mark Safarik, a former FBI agent, recounted that behavioral analysts at the beginning were mocked. Colleagues thought they were crazy and described their work as hocus pocus, but there's no doubt they performed crucial work that has made it easier to solve not only serial murders but also other serial crimes.

"Stop right there!"

Nineteen-year-old Kevin Bright and his 21-year-old sister, Kathryn Bright, were walking together. It was April 4, 1974, and the siblings had just entered Kathryn Bright's home on East 13th Street in Wichita. From the hallway, they made eye contact with a white man in the bedroom who pointed a firearm at them.

"I'm not here to harm you," the man said, explaining that he was an escaped convict and needed money and a car to drive to New York.

He forced Kevin Bright to tie his sister with a white rope, the kind often used for clotheslines, after which she sat on the bed. Then the "convict" forced him down the hall and into another room, where he was tied to the bedposts. The young man noticed that the unknown assailant was wearing a large, heavy parka and gloves, and that he was sweating profusely. From the room, Kevin Bright could hear him rummaging around the house, as if searching for something. A moment later, the radio was turned on and the volume cranked up before the "convict" returned to Kevin Bright's room. The stranger had a pair of pantyhose with several knots tied in them. He placed the pantyhose around Kevin Bright's neck and began to tighten with all of his strength. However, the young man had managed to free himself from the ropes, and when he suddenly sprang up, the other man pulled a firearm from his waistband. Twice the weapon clicked, without a projectile being fired, but the third time it succeeded. A bang echoed through the house, and Kevin Bright fell to the floor with a bleeding wound to his head.

The perpetrator disappeared from the room. Meanwhile, Kevin Bright regained consciousness. Despite the gunshot wound to his head, he was still alive. Apparently, the man had heard him, because he returned and tried again to strangle him with the pantyhose. The young man fought for his life once more, and again the "convict" pulled a weapon and fired while the two struggled. This time, Kevin Bright was hit in the mouth and collapsed onto the floor in a pool of blood. The perpetrator left the room, believing the young man was dead. He was not. From the floor, Kevin Bright could hear commotion and screams from his sister's bedroom. He managed to get back on his feet, and still with the pantyhose around his neck, he staggered out into the hallway and to the kitchen door, from where he managed to escape to some neighbors and raise the alarm.

As police cars arrived at the house with sirens blaring, the perpetrator was gone. Officers found Kathryn Bright in the bedroom, bleeding heavily from countless stab wounds. Her hands and ankles were bound with pantyhose, and she had a blue scarf and a piece of white cord or rope around her neck.

"I can't breathe," she moaned as police officers waited for the ambulance.

After Kathryn Bright was taken to the hospital, officers searched the house. The radio was still blaring at full volume, and nearby, the young woman's bag had been ransacked, its contents strewn everywhere. A telephone cord had been pulled from the wall, and a drawer full of pantyhose stood open. In several rooms, they found various bloody articles of clothing tied together, and a bullet hole appeared in the bathroom door. No one doubted how the killer had entered, as the pane in the back door was shattered, and glass shards lay on the floor inside.

Later that day, Kathryn Bright died on the operating table due to the multiple stab wounds, but her brother survived and was able to provide police with a description of the killer: approximately 25 years old, about 180 centimeters tall, robust build, weighing over 80 kilograms, with dark hair and a mustache. Despite the numerous physical clues, police were largely at a dead end in the case. The same was true for the Otero murders.

Investigators ended up wasting considerable time when three mentally disturbed men, with a history of sexual offenses, hinted they knew something about the crime. Suspicion focused on one of them, and newspapers wrote extensively about the possible perpetrator, especially the journalists at the local paper, the *Wichita Eagle*.

On October 22, 1974, Don Granger's phone rang in the newsroom. On the other end was a man with a coarse voice. He spoke with a local dialect and instructed Granger to go to the library and look at a book titled *Applied Engineering Mechanics*. "In it, you'll find a letter detailing the Otero murders," said the man, who insisted that the three sexual offenders had nothing to do with the case.

Granger couldn't ignore the mysterious call, so he immediately contacted the police, who found the book on one of the library shelves. The man was right. Inside the book's pages lay a typewritten letter riddled with spelling errors. In addition to an accurate description of the crime scene, he described himself as a monster who would continue to kill to satisfy his fantasies, and he hinted that he was already in the process of finding his next victim.

"Since sex offenders do not change their mode of killing or by nature are unable to, I will not change mine. The keywords for me will be bind them, torture them, kill them. BTK (Bind,

Torture, Kill). You will see he is at it again," he wrote as a parting shot.

If there's one thing that sets BTK apart from other serial killers, it's his communication with the media and the police. It's not unusual for serial killers to be fascinated by the police and their work, even trying to befriend investigators. For an extended period, I corresponded with Arthur John Shawcross, who murdered two children and 12 women in New York State in the late 1980s. He bonded with several of the officers on the case and even offered them coffee and doughnuts. For some serial killers, it's about the fascination with uniforms and authority, which they themselves wish to attain, while for others, it's a way to gain insight into the case. This was not the case for BTK. According to him, it was a matter of "professional pride." He naturally knew he couldn't fully conceal himself, but he couldn't stand the thought of others taking "credit" for his murders. This also reveals a great deal about his personality. You'd have to be an incredibly proud and meticulous individual to complain to the media about not receiving recognition as a murderer. It also tells me we're dealing with someone who genuinely feels like a "Superman," unable to imagine that anyone else could be intelligent enough to figure him out. He even chose his own nickname, something neither seen before nor since. I have no doubt that this game with the media and police gave him a power rush. He felt omnipotent and was convinced he'd never be caught, and that feeling helped prolong the pleasure derived from the murders.

As mentioned, at least the early crime scenes suggest a person who plans his crimes but then discovers how difficult it is to execute in reality. It would undoubtedly have been much easier for him to attack prostitutes, like Arthur John Shawcross and many other serial killers. These are victims who are easy to get into a car and who won't likely be missed immediately. But BTK preferred to break into middle-class homes, where the risk of detection was significantly higher, all things considered. This speaks partly to the power he wanted to demonstrate to the world, but also indicates that considerable planning must have preceded these acts and that they must have taken time. This fact may have been a contributing factor to his eagerness to taunt the police with his communications, because if it gave him the power rush I mentioned earlier, it might have allowed him to postpone the point when the urge to kill became so strong that he had to strike again.

Another aspect I would have focused on is the sexual component of the murders. Police found semen on Josephine Otero and in Kathryn Bright's bedroom, yet there were no signs of sexual assault. There's no doubt their killer was sadistic and sexually aroused by his actions, but penetration wasn't necessary for him. All indications pointed to the acts of binding, torturing, and taunting the victims as central, rather than the sexual act, at least, it wasn't a prerequisite. This makes it abundantly clear that the killer had a paraphilia.

Paraphilia is a condition where an individual's sexual arousal and satisfaction depend on fantasizing about or engaging in sexual behavior that is atypical and extreme. There's inherently nothing wrong with this if it occurs consensually among adults and no one is harmed. However, when sex-acts causes harm to others, it is categorized as a disorder, and therefore a paraphilia. For instance, a couple can engage in role-play where one "attacks" the other, but it's unequivocally a crime if one party hasn't consented to the act. Many well-functioning individuals are interested in different sex games. For example, they might enjoy sex in leather or be aroused by receiving pain, so a diagnosis is only made if the sex games negatively impact their quality of life, their ability to function in social contexts, and/or if their behavior harms others.

While many paraphilias seem foreign or extreme, they are easier to understand if viewed as behaviors that, in less extreme versions, are quite common. For example, for some people, it can be arousing to have a partner "talk dirty," but if talking dirty is the only way sexual arousal or satisfaction can occur, and make the person talk dirty to people who don't agree with it, then it would be considered a paraphilia.

Aside from sexual masochism, paraphilias predominantly affect men like BTK, but we don't know why. There are only various hypotheses regarding the causes of paraphilia development. Some psychologists believe that paraphiliacs repeat or revert to a sexual habit that originated early in life. Behavioral researchers suggest that paraphilias arise through a process where non-sexual objects can become sexually arousing if repeatedly associated with pleasurable sexual activity. Specific sexual acts, such as voyeurism or exhibitionism, that provide particularly intense erotic pleasure can lead a person to prefer these behaviors.

In some cases, there appears to be a predisposing factor where difficulties in forming personal relationships lead to atypical sexuality. These difficulties, in turn, can stem from childhood problems, as seen in numerous serial killers. For instance, behavioral research suggests that a child who is a victim or observer of inappropriate sexual behavior may learn to mimic this behavior as they get older. It's also possible that the causes are physical and relate to the interplay between hormones, behavior, and the central nervous system, particularly concerning aggression. Some studies indicate that certain abnormalities in the brain's frontal and temporal lobes correlate with pedophilic urges. A hypothesis about foot fetishism stems from the fact that the brain area processing sensory information from the feet is presumably adjacent to the area processing sensory information from the genitals.

There isn't yet a definitive answer to how paraphilia arises, and I am quite sure the answer lies in a combination of different theories. For us, the key takeaway is that paraphilia often appears in serial killers and can give us a clue as to who they are and why they exhibit the behavior they do.

A typical, though also bizarre, example is Jerry Brudos, who was born in South Dakota, USA, in 1939. His mother, who had already given birth to a boy, desperately wanted a girl. As a result of her disappointment at yet another male child, she subjected her son to physical and psychological abuse. Starting at the age five years, Jerry Brudos developed a fetish for stiletto heels after finding some women's shoes at a dump, and he later recounted trying to steal his elementary school teacher's shoes. As a child, he stole women's underwear from neighbors, and although he received psychiatric treatment, the paraphilia escalated when, as a teenager, he began stalking and assaulting women in the neighborhood.

After a conviction, he was hospitalized, where it was confirmed that his sexual fantasies stemmed from an intense hatred of his mother and women in general. During his hospitalization, Jerry Brudos completed high school, and upon discharge, he got married and had two children. On the surface, their lives seemed normal, but he had developed a habit of having his wife clean naked, wearing only stilettos. He invented a female alter ego and wore women's clothing.

In 1968, the paraphilia escalated further when he committed his first murder. It was a young female door-to-door salesperson whom he lured into the basement while his family was upstairs. He struck her with a plank, strangled her, and dressed her in various stolen clothes. Finally, he cut off her left foot and placed it in a freezer, after which he regularly put a shoe on it. He disposed of the body in a nearby river.

As a murderer, he also evolved. Assault, strangulation, and foot amputation were always part of the murders. In two cases, he also cut off the victims' breasts. Then, he began taking photos of the dead and wearing high heels and masturbating when the women were deceased. When police asked female students at a nearby university if they had noticed anything suspicious, one of them told of a peculiar little man who had repeatedly called her to invite her on a date. The strange man turned out to be Jerry Brudos. He was sentenced to life in prison and died behind bars in 2006. In the case of The Shoe Fetish Slayer, as he was called, it's quite easy to see a connection between early childhood and later behavior. The link isn't always that clear, but looking at sexual behavior is a very important part of behavioral analysis because it can help narrow down the killer.

Similarly, BTK's behavior could be an important clue, because in a situation with a number of different suspects, one could investigate their sexual habits. Of course, it's not inherently problematic if a person is aroused by bondage, but if, for example, it turned out that a suspect was a member of a sex club where he exhibited similar desires, he would certainly be worth a closer look. Several studies show that the practice of sadistic sexual behavior can be driven by a desire for power and dominance beyond mere sexual pleasure. This was certainly the case with the crimes in Wichita, and BTK wasn't finished. In 1977, he struck again.

On March 17, police responded to an address on South Hydraulic Street, where two deeply shaken boys had alerted neighbors. In one of the houses bedrooms, officers found the naked body of the boys' mother, Shirley Vian Relford. She was bound with ropes and electrical tape and had a cord wrapped around her neck and a plastic bag over her head. The blinds were open, so the body was visible from the street. The two boys, aged six and eight, told police that a stranger armed with a pistol had forced them and their younger sister into the bathroom, after which he harmed their mother. When it became quiet, the older boy smashed a window, and he and his brother ran for help. The six-year-old had seen the man before. Sometime earlier, he had been going around the neighborhood with a picture of a woman and a child, knocking on doors and asking if anyone had seen them.

Nine months later, on the morning of December 9, an unknown man called the police and stated that the body of Nancy Fox could be found in her home at 843 South Pershing. A patrol car was dispatched, and upon seeing that the telephone line outside had been cut, they had a premonition of what they would find inside. On the bed in the bedroom lay the 25-year-old woman, face down, just like Kathryn Bright and Shirley Vian Relford. Her ankles were bound with a yellow strip of cloth. Another strip held her hands behind her back. She had two pairs of pantyhose wrapped tightly around her neck, and her underwear was pulled down around her legs. By her head lay a blue bathrobe with semen stains.

Shortly after the New Year, BTK communicated again, writing to a local TV station to claim responsibility for the murders of the Otero family and the three women. The letter included a poem about Nancy Fox's death and a description of the "X-factor" that, according to the perpetrator, drove him to kill. After that, there was silence for several years. In 1985, he killed 53-year-old Marine Hedge. She had been strangled with a pair of pantyhose, but uncharacteristically, her body was found in a ditch five days after she failed to show up for work. The following year, Gordon Wegerle came home from work for lunch. In the bedroom, he found his wife, 28-year-old Vicki. Her hands were tied behind her back with a leather cord, which was also used to bind her ankles. Her jeans were unzipped, and her upper body was nude. Around her neck, she had both a pair of knotted pantyhose and a pair of leather shoelaces. Their two-year-old son was unharmed. The family's second car was later found in a nearby parking lot.

Then there was silence again. In 1988, he wrote a letter informing the public that he was not responsible for the murder of a family of three, but that he admired the work the perpetrator had done. On January 19, 1991, a man arrived at a house on North Hillside to repair a friend's car, but 62-year-old Dolores Davis was not home. The man was puzzled. The curtains were drawn, a lamp outside was burning even though it was midday, and the car was in the driveway instead of the garage. The door from the garage to the house stood open, and the telephone line in the kitchen had been pulled from the wall. In the bedroom, linens and sheets were missing, and so was Dolores Davis. Her son informed that she had been nervous because, a few days prior, she had heard someone or something moving around outside the house. It wasn't until February 1st that a boy walking his dog made a shocking discovery when he found the frozen body of Dolores Davis under a bridge. She had been strangled with a pair of knotted tights, and her legs were tied together with another pair just above the knees. Near the body lay a hand-painted porcelain mask. It would prove to be BTK's last murder. After that, the investigation evolved into a cold case.

*

In an attempt to get closer to arresting BTK, several profiles of the unknown perpetrator were developed over the years. They were very similar to each other. According to those profiles, the perpetrator was a White man aged 25 to 35 at the time of the first murder. They agreed that he would not immediately stand out in the local community; on the contrary, he would appear friendly and charming on the surface. However, underneath was a completely different personality, demanding attention and recognition, and someone who enjoyed manipulating other people like a puppeteer. No one believed that the perpetrator was insane, but he showed clear signs of psychopathy. One of the profiles believed that his motive for the sadistic killings was to be found in a violent hatred for women.

One of those who made a profile on BTK was John E. Douglas, whom I have mentioned several times. He believed that the killer spent a long time at the crime scenes taking pictures that he could use to fuel his fantasies without committing new murders immediately. John E. Douglas was also convinced that the killer had a long list of burglaries and voyeurism, though he did not believe that the killer was a rapist. Others agreed with this. Since BTK only masturbated at the crime scenes, several people believed that it was an immature sexuality that could be rooted in childhood experiences or early adolescence. John also pointed out that the killer used a lot of police jargon in his letters. Therefore, he could either be employed in law enforcement or had a great interest in true crime and was most likely an avid reader of magazines and books about crimes. One thing that was common in all the profiles was that BTK was probably a rather miserable person who lived alone and was considered a bit of a loner by the people around him.

Despite the profiles and a huge effort by investigators, BTK sank into obscurity. As the years passed, the memory of one of the most brutal serial killers in American history faded, at least for those not directly involved in the case. Other feared and infamous killers stole the headlines, and investigators in *Wichita* wondered if BTK was dead or seriously ill. Another possibility was that he was in prison for other crimes, or he could have moved to another state.

However, that was not the case. And that is one of the things that separates BTK from serial killers who kill until they are caught and often kill at shorter and shorter intervals. There must be something in this case that allowed the perpetrator to have very long cooling-off periods compared to many other serial killers.

It lasted until the spring of 2004, when a journalist at *The Wichita Eagle* received a letter from someone calling himself Bill Thomas Killman. He wrote that he had killed Vicki Wegerle back in 1988—a crime that police had not previously attributed to BTK. The letter included photos from the crime scene and a copy of Vicki Wegerle's driver's license. At the time, DNA material had been collected from under the victim's fingernails, and technological advancements now made it possible to conduct DNA tests on hundreds of men who had been under police scrutiny over the years. However, there was no match.

In May of the same year, a letter containing a draft of a BTK biography arrived at a TV station. In June, a package taped to a stop sign at an intersection was found to contain graphic descriptions of the Otero murders and a drawing of a sadistic assault. Additionally, there was a list of suggested chapters for a book about the serial killer. For the rest of the year, BTK sent packages and letters or placed them in public locations. In one instance, he included Nancy Fox's driver's license along with a doll that was bound in the same way as her and had a plastic bag over its head. This bizarre behavior continued into the new year. In a letter to the police, BTK asked about a cornflakes box he had placed in the bed of a pickup truck at a Home Depot. It turned out the vehicle's owner had discarded the package, but officers managed to find it. Inside was a hog-tied doll. Surveillance cameras showed a figure placing the package and driving away in a black Jeep Cherokee. Subsequently, the TV station received a flood of postcards, and police found another cardboard box with a doll inside.

For me, it's incredibly interesting to follow BTK's communication with the media and police. He had, as far as we know, been in a cooling-off period of 13 years at that point. That's a very long time, though not unheard of. Contrary to popular belief, many serial killers have long cooling-off periods, which makes them particularly difficult to catch because, unfortunately, it's often the murders themselves that help investigators and profilers solve cases. But I have no doubt that the urge resurfaced, evidenced by the almost manic way he behaved, not only writing letters and sending packages but also leaving clues in various public places. It's clear that drawing attention to himself and his actions excited him again. If I had been part of the investigation then, I would have been afraid that it could be a sign he was preparing to kill again. At the same time, his behavior also shows clear signs of the grandiosity and narcissism that characterized him, because even after 13 years, he clearly couldn't stand being out of the spotlight, and he was simultaneously convinced that he was so clever that no one would be able to expose him.

But then he made a mistake, at last!

In one of his letters, he asked investigators if they could trace him if he sent them a floppy disk. The police responded to him through an advertisement in *The Wichita Eagle*, where they had cominicated through, assuring him they couldn't reveal his identity. BTK fell for it, and on February 16, 2005, he sent a purple 1.44-megabyte Memorex floppy disk to KSAS-TV. The diskette came with a letter, a golden necklace with a medallion from one of the victims, and a copy of the cover of a book about a serial killer. The police's IT specialists immediately began working on the diskette. On it, they found traces of previous documents, including the words "Christ Lutheran Church." They could see that the document had last been modified by a "Dennis." It took only moments to find the church online, and after a few clicks, the police knew that the chairman of the congregation was named Dennis Rader. When officers drove by Dennis Rader's house, they saw a black Jeep Cherokee in the driveway. These were all strong circumstantial indicators, but the police wanted more tangible evidence before taking action.

They managed to persuade a judge to allow investigators to use a sample that Dennis Rader's daughter had provided at a hospital. When they compared her DNA with the DNA from Vicki Wegerle's fingernails, there was no doubt: Dennis Rader was BTK.

On February 25, 2005, Dennis Rader, then a 59-year-old family man, got into his car to drive home for lunch with his wife. He held a position with the city as a compliance officer, an official tasked with ensuring city regulations were followed, that people trimmed their hedges and pruned their trees, that children and young people only played ball where allowed, that dogs weren't running loose, and so on. The job suited him perfectly. He enjoyed the details and the power it gave him to reprimand people or issue fines. He had even received complaints because many felt he was excessively zealous.

He turned on the police radio he had installed in his car. Nothing out of the ordinary was happening, though he noticed that the FBI seemed to be involved in something in the city. For a moment, the serial killer wondered if it was related to him, but he concluded that so many years had passed. And where would he flee anyway if the police were indeed after him?

He turned a corner onto Frontage Road, where he spotted a long line of police cars. "Hmm, this isn't good," he thought.

He later recounted that for a second or two, he hoped it was just a routine traffic stop, but when the cars followed him with flashing blue lights, he knew it was over. He pulled over, and in his rearview mirror, he could see officers getting out with their weapons pointed at his Jeep.

"Get out of the car and lie on the ground!" they shouted.

Dennis Rader complied. As he lay on the ground, he felt his arms being pulled behind his back, followed by the click of handcuffs clamping onto his wrists. He was then pulled to his feet and placed in the back seat of a patrol car.

"Mr. Rader, do you know why we're taking you to the station?" a police officer asked.

"Well, I have an idea," he replied, annoyed that he, a compliance officer, was now the one who had to obey orders.

In an interrogation room at the police station, Dennis Rader considered defending himself against the accusations, but it wasn't long before he recounted in gruesome detail to investigators the 10 murders he had committed between 1974 and 1991, and no one doubted that he enjoyed the attention. The same was true when he stood before the judge at his plea hearing, detailing how he had spent immeasurable amounts of time planning his atrocities. He revealed he had over 50 "projects," as he called the women he stalked while deciding whom to bind, torture, and kill.

That summer, Dennis Rader, BTK, was sentenced to 10 consecutive life terms and transferred to El Dorado Correctional Facility, where he remains at the time of this writing.

Since it was a plea hearing, no witnesses were called. The judge read out the details of the case, and Dennis Rader interrupted him at regular intervals to clarify specific points, as if he were reviewing a recipe or a resume. If the judge, the relatives, or the journalists had expected remorse or an apology, they were sorely disappointed. The prosecutor compared Dennis Rader to an actor receiving an award, and many felt a chill down their spines because he seemed completely unfazed and almost bored.

The psychopathic traits, which we'll explore further in Chapters 8 and 9, were reflected in the profiles created for BTK. However, they were completely wrong regarding Dennis Rader's private life, as he was by no means a pathetic loner. He was married and had been with his wife since 1971. They had a son and a daughter and a close relationship with their church, where he served as the congregation chairman. Additionally, he was active in a scout troop and often took children on camping trips, where he taught them, among other things, how to fish. This merely confirms the fact that you can rarely tell or sense that people are serial killers; often, family, friends, neighbors, and colleagues are deeply surprised when they realize they've been close to a murderer for years. While there are, of course, examples of eccentric serial killers, but it is not a widespread characteristic so that you can spot them in social settings.

Dennis Rader is one of the serial killers I corresponded with, until it was stopped when law enforcement suspected he had killed more people and wanted to link him to them. We communicated for approximately two years, and he informed me that he was in the process of answering the questionnaire I developed for my thesis, but, of course, that was also stopped. The questions primarily focus on his childhood, adolescence, and the period leading up to his first murder. I was typically interested in whether anything in his past could help explain why he became BTK.

Forensic psychologist Tony Ruark helped prepare a mental health assessment after Dennis Rader was arrested and wrote: "If Rader were completely honest, which he isn't, I'm sure we'd find some childhood event that Rader immediately associated with sexual feelings. Somehow, at a very early point, Rader experienced an incident after which he immediately connected sexual pleasure with watching a living creature suffer and die. And after that first incident, Rader likely began spending a lot of time fostering those feelings."

Over the many years he's been behind bars, Dennis Rader has recounted several such incidents. In a TV program, for example, he described to American forensic psychologist Katherine Ramsland an episode where his mother's finger got caught and she screamed in pain. That moment remains very clear to him to this day because he remembers how the experience aroused him. Subsequently, he also became sexually aroused when his mother hit him.

Other details from his upbringing resemble what we see in other serial killers. He was bullied and isolated at school, spending a lot of time alone. We know that from a very early age, he began killing cats and dogs by strangling them, and that as a teenager, he developed fantasies of tying up girls and having sex with them. In this way, he shares traits with several other serial killers. When pressed about his childhood, it turns out he had a complicated relationship with his mother and was physically disciplined. He also describes how, from an early age, he experienced isolation and bullying, often even initiated by his teachers. If there's one thing I've observed as a psychologist, it's how devastating it is for a person to be ostracized. I've encountered numerous children who have told me they would always prefer a beating if only they could avoid being isolated by their parents or other children.

The events of that time may help explain his need for revenge and his anger for not receiving the recognition he felt he deserved. Perhaps it's also no coincidence that he began murdering shortly after losing his job at an aircraft factory. He describes how his world collapsed, and he then crossed over to "the dark side." The termination not only gave him a difficult-to-manage feeling of inferiority, but it also gave him a lot of free time where his fantasies, which had never left him, came close to the surface.

He had, over many years, collected police magazines with descriptions of torture and murder, and created collages with images of women and bondage. Sometimes he went even further, putting on women's underwear, tying himself up, masturbating, and taking pictures of it,. He recounted how he started driving around, stalking women, and following them to supermarkets and appointments around town, fantasizing about how he would bind and kill them, and over time, the plans became more concrete. It seems very likely that for Dennis Rader, the planning and the hunt fueled his fantasies as much as the murder itself, which makes sense when you consider the years that passed between the killings. This didn't mean the fantasies stopped, not at all. Right up until his arrest, he was working on his "projects," and he even had a more concrete plan for a murder in 2004. However, he didn't carry it out. According to him, he had grown too old and could no longer overpower young women. He targeted older women, like his last victims, but that didn't fit his fantasy, so he stopped.

Dennis Rader primarily targeted women, but among his victims were also men and boys. Looking at the women, they ranged from children to young adults and middle-aged adults. This confirms that serial killers don't necessarily kill a specific type of person. This can make it difficult for investigators, as seen in this case, where the fate of the Otero family was initially considered to be part of a gang dispute. Therefore, it's also a crucial part of police and profilers' work to be able to demonstrate connections between crimes, even if they differ significantly in key aspects. We'll examine this more closely in the next case.

CHAPTER 3: ONE OR MORE? THE STORY OF THE EYEBALL KILLER

It was easy for the police to identify the body of a heavily built woman found in a run-down and almost forgotten neighborhood in southern Dallas, Texas, on December 13, 1990. One of the officers recognized her as 33-year-old Mary Pratt, a known and well-liked figure in the prostitution scene around the seedy Star Motel on the outskirts of the Oak Cliff district, which was otherwise mostly a typical middle-class neighborhood. Like many other sex workers, she was addicted to drugs, but she had managed to keep that part of her life hidden from her aging parents, with whom she lived. The cause of death was also straightforward: someone had shot her in the head. When the police arrived, a floral sheet covered the body, but they quickly learned that the caller, a deeply shocked local resident, had placed it over the deceased as a respectful gesture. Mary Pratt was dressed in her usual "uniform:" jeans, tennis shoes, and a small T-shirt.

The two experienced investigators, John Westphalen and Stan McNear, drove together to the medical examiner's office. There was almost no blood or brain tissue near the body, so they knew the murder had occurred elsewhere, which would make the case even more difficult to solve. Crimes in the prostitution environment were already challenging to deal with because so many people constantly crossed paths, and few wished to help the police.

The medical examiner put down her coffee cup and examined Mary Pratt's body, which lay on a gurney. Needle marks were evident on her arms. So was a *Playboy* bunny tattoo and a bullet hole from a .44 caliber firearm in her head. The blue and yellow marks on her face and chest showed that the perpetrator had beaten the deceased before killing her. The medical examiner leaned forward to lift Mary Pratt's right eyelid. Without saying anything, she also lifted the left one.

"My goodness!" she exclaimed. "They're gone!"

Westphalen and McNear moved closer and looked down at Mary Pratt's face. The medical examiner was right. A pair of empty eye sockets met their gaze. Someone had removed both eyeballs without leaving so much as a tear in the eyelids. The medical examiner was speechless. Whoever had performed the operation knew how to do it, and it was not exactly a standard procedure for medical students; only highly trained specialists learned that kind of thing.

Westphalen knew that he and the other police officers were facing something unique. He immediately contacted the FBI to have them conduct a search in the Violent Criminal Apprehension Program (ViCAP). The database was a true nightmare of details about the USA's most sadistic, bizarre, and nightmare-inducing cases: severed body parts, decapitations, removed organs, bite marks, you name it. But stolen eyeballs were still a rarity.

Meanwhile, Regina Smith and her partner, John Matthews, had begun their shift. In a patrol car, they kept an eye on the streets around the Star Motel, where they had by now come to know most of the sex workers by name. Not far from the motel, they spotted 25-year-old Veronica Rodriguez, who, despite her age, was already seasoned and rarely let the police's presence stand in the way of a good business deal. John Matthews pulled over while Regina Smith rolled down the window. The young woman had a nasty wound on her forehead and a gash across her throat.

"What on earth happened to you, my dear?" Regina Smith asked.

"Please don't arrest me, I was almost killed!" Veronica Rodriguez exclaimed.

The sex worker then shared a peculiar story with the officers. The night before, she had been picked up by a client who drove a good distance south before raping her. The man then tried to kill her, but she escaped and sprinted toward a nearby house. Coincidentally, the owner of the house turned out to be a man she knew; not only that, he knew the man behind the attempted murder. The two police officers weren't quite sure what to make of it. Veronica Rodriguez was notorious for her stories, which usually aimed to get the officers to let her off with a warning rather than a trip to the station.

Two days later, they saw her again. She was sitting in the cab of a truck with a thin-haired, middle-aged man. While John Matthews took the young woman over to the patrol car, Regina Smith spoke with the driver. According to his driver's license, his name was Axton Schindler, and he lived at 1035 Eldorado Street. He owed money for a couple of fines, but otherwise, there was nothing on him.

"You mustn't arrest him!" Veronica Rodriguez cried. "He's the one who saved me from the murderer!"

Again, the two officers exchanged knowing glances. Eldorado was in the Oak Cliff neighborhood, just a few minutes' drive from the Star Motel, not far to the south. The driver, practically stumbling over his words, said he had no idea what the sex worker was talking about and that he had just intended to give her a lift. Veronica Rodriguez was arrested for prostitution, and Axton Schindler was taken in because of the money he owed the public. It wasn't until later that the officers realized they had stumbled upon an important lead in the macabre murder case involving the missing eyeballs.

It is rare for profilers to be involved in the investigation of a single murder. As previously mentioned, they typically work with cold cases that involve serial crimes, not least because it can be extremely difficult to say much about a single crime scene.

That said, for my part, alarm bells would already be ringing in my head if I had stood at the spot where Mary Pratt was dumped. She was found with her legs spread very wide, a position she was unlikely to have landed in by chance. If my assumption is correct, this was a case of what is called staging, where the perpetrator places the body in a specific way to fulfill a fantasy or to shock those who might find the deceased. In this case, it could be about displaying and humiliating the victim after death, which could be linked to hatred for prostitutes or women in general. If, for example, a pimp had killed her due to a disagreement, simply shooting her would have been enough. And if a pimp needed to make an example, the body would likely not have been dumped in such a remote location.

Then there are the eyes, which truly make the case unique. They were not only removed; they were surgically extracted in a way that very few people are capable of. Eyes are also a very symbolic part of the body. They are a window to the soul, as they say. The fact that the murderer took the time to remove them so meticulously must have had a special meaning for him. It would have led me to think in terms of a potential serial killer in development, even though at that point there was only a single body.

Police undoubtedly had the same thought, as one of the investigators very early in the process used ViCAP to access the database that agents have built over decades. The Violent Criminal Apprehension Program was founded in 1985 at the instigation of Pierce Brooks, a homicide detective with the Los Angeles Police Department. He had noticed that periodically, there were cases that were very similar to each other, regardless of whether they involved the same or different perpetrators. Several times, he spent time in newspaper archives to find similar cases from the past to see if details from back then could help him in the hunt for a killer.

He was particularly fascinated by the case of The Lonely Hearts Killer from the 1950s. The killer's name was Harvey Glatman, born in 1927. He grew up with his family in Colorado and exhibited antisocial behavior and sadomasochistic tendencies from childhood. As a child, he would tie a string around his penis and pull it for sexual pleasure, and at age 12, he began tying ropes around his own neck and performing autoerotic asphyxiation in the bathroom at home. When his mother discovered it, she took him to the family doctor, who, however, reassured her that the boy would grow out of it.

As a teenager, Harvey started breaking into women's apartments, stealing lingerie among other things, which evolved into outright stalking and later assaults and rapes. In 1945, he was sentenced to 5 to 10 years in prison, where he was diagnosed with psychopathy and schizophrenia with extreme sexual thoughts. Nevertheless, he was paroled after three years. In 1957, he moved to Los Angeles, where he began frequenting various modeling agencies, duping hopeful women into believing he was a photographer with work for them. Once they were in his apartment, he would tie them up, rape them, and photograph the entire ordeal. Eventually, he strangled them and dumped the bodies in the desert outside the city. After the first two murders, he sought new victims among the newspaper's personal ads, "Lonely Hearts," as they were called. In 1958, a police officer spotted Harvey Glatman kidnapping a young woman and arrested him on the spot. During interrogation, he confessed to three murders and led police to a toolbox where he had stored the photos of the crimes. The Lonely Hearts Killer was executed in the gas chamber at San Quentin Prison on September 18, 1959.

Pierce Brooks wondered if details from such cases could be centrally collected so that his colleagues across the country could access them. He therefore contacted the Department of Justice and presented his idea. Shortly after, he was appointed ViCAP's first chief, and cases began pouring in from all over the USA. The database contains both solved and cold cases. Investigators delve deeply into details about methods, crime scenes, victims, weapons, and much more, primarily in cases of serial murderers or serial rapists. In an American context, ViCAP is particularly advantageous when perpetrators commit crimes across police jurisdictions and state lines. It was previously not uncommon for police officers in different parts of the country to be working on the same case without realizing it.

The database can also be an inspiration for investigators, who can compare their cases with already solved ones, much like when Pierce Brooks delved into newspaper archives. Databases like ViCAP are, of course, most helpful the more details one has available. If you search solely for gunshot murders, you will quickly drown in the more than 150,000 cases, in 2024, in the system. However, if a rape also occurred, the victim was disfigured with a knife, and their hair was cut off, you will end up with a much smaller list of similar cases. In some instances, it might involve a perpetrator who has already been convicted, in others, there might be a match with several unsolved cases. Sometimes, investigators can gain insights into other cases involving a perpetrator who behaves similarly to the one they are hunting.

From conversations with Danish police officers, I know that databases are frequently used in Denmark for solving crimes like murder and rape. It's important to note, however, that this involves statistics, and therefore the work is based on probabilities. Reality, of course, doesn't always fit neatly into a spreadsheet. As we saw with the case of The Backpacker Killer, a serial killer can indeed commit murders in vastly different ways. In the case of BTK, several investigators considered the possibility of a serial killer even after the Otero family murders, but dismissed the idea when the FBI reported that the probability was minimal.

Due to privacy concerns, the FBI cannot disclose details about specific cases. However, the bureau has made a scenario, based on real investigations, available to the public. A case involves a young woman in Portland, Oregon, who was kidnapped as she left her local gym. Her body was found several days later on an undeveloped plot several kilometers from the gym, where her car is still parked. Near the car, police found traces of chloroform. Since no one in the woman's immediate circle could have committed the murder and the preceding rape, investigators entered the case details into ViCAP. The system matched the murder with a three-month-old case from Seattle, Washington, Oregon's neighboring state. Here too, a young woman was kidnapped after exercising at her local gym. She was raped, murdered, and dumped in a desolate location a few kilometers away. And there were traces of chloroform near her car. The Portland police, therefore, contacted their colleagues in Seattle.

Concurrently, a ViCAP analyst in Virginia was working on a case from Minnesota that resembled the other two. In this instance, though, the victim had survived and could describe the perpetrator, including a special tattoo on his forearm. The analyst saw that two colleagues were working on similar cases and immediately informed them. The collaboration among the three parties leads to a suspect: a salesman whose travel matched the dates of the crimes. His description matched the third victim's account, including the tattoo, and a search of his residence revealed traces of chloroform in the kitchen sink. DNA tests confirmed he was the murderer; the trap has sprung!

Databases like ViCAP alone cannot solve crimes. As the example illustrates, a lot of investigation occurs before and after searches, for instance, crime scene and behavioral analysis, as we discussed in the previous chapter. However, databases can be valuable tools that, combined with other methods, bring police closer to solving serious crimes. It is crucial, though, to maintain a critical perspective when working with statistics. If you investigate a case and find that 80 percent of perpetrators in similar cases were tradesmen, there's a certain probability that the same could be true in the current case. But you must also remember that 20 percent in similar cases are *not* tradesmen, and that's a significant portion regardless. If you take statistics for granted as a kind of oracle, you risk creating an incorrect profile that can delay the investigation and prevent a solution.

Two months later, investigator Larry Oliver arrived at the road where Mary Pratt had been found. Another body was lying there. Larry Oliver was employed by the Dallas County Sheriff's Department. Since the body was just outside the city limits, the investigation was the county police force's responsibility.

The victim was 27-year-old Susan Peterson. She was a prostitute from the area around the Star Motel. She was almost naked and lay with her legs spread wide. Death was due to gunshot wounds to the head, chest, and abdomen. Larry Oliver hadn't heard about Mary Pratt, so he was just as surprised as his colleagues in the city when the medical examiner revealed that both eyes were missing and had been removed with surgical precision.

"They had a similar case a couple of months ago at the Dallas Police Department," the medical examiner stated.

The next day, Larry Oliver met with John Westphalen in the city, and soon, investigators from both forces were on the case. They deliberately avoided talking about serial killers to prevent public panic and sensational headlines in the press. It could complicate the investigation by scaring the perpetrator away from the Star Motel neighborhood. But everyone knew they were dealing with a disturbed, yet intelligent killer who was willing to take the risk of dumping bodies on quiet residential streets for unsuspecting locals to find the next day.

"A repeater," as John Westphalen put it.

John Matthews and Regina Smith continued to patrol the streets around the Star Motel. Nervousness spread, but only few women stayed away; their drug addiction was too strong for that. The two officers feared what awaited them. Susan Peterson had been one of the toughest on the street, and if the killer had managed to get hold of her, anyone could be next. They were convinced he must be one of her regular clients; otherwise, she would have been on guard and pulled the razor blade she always carried.

John Matthews and Regina Smith encountered Veronica Rodriguez several times. She kept changing her story about the attempted murder. First, the perpetrator was White, then he was Latino. Then she had met a man who knew something about Mary Pratt's death, and then she had never heard of it. The drugs affected her brain, but there was always a core in the story that repeated itself: Axton Schindler. Did he know the murderer? Was he the murderer? Was Veronica Rodriguez so afraid of him that she changed her narrative? The officers regularly discussed the case, but they had passed the information on to the homicide department, so as street officers, there wasn't much more they could have done.

Investigators followed every lead, no matter how unlikely, without results. On March 19, 1991, another body appeared. This time, it was an African American sex worker named Shirley Williams. It was early morning, and she had just left the Avalon Motel. There she cleaned during the day and had clients in the evenings and nights, when she was attacked. This time, the body was on a different street in the middle of the Oak Cliff neighborhood, close to a school, where schoolchildren had a clear view of the deceased, and was placed sitting up against a curb.

"Check her eyes and tell me if they're there," John Westphalen said to the medical examiner on site.

"They're gone," was the reply.

John Westphalen turned to his colleague, Stan McNear: "That makes three."

When reading about The Eyeball Killer, as the perpetrator was obviously called, I particularly noted the autopsy report prepared after the third murder. The autopsy showed an important difference between Shirley Williams and the first two victims. The eyes were indeed gone, but it was sloppy work, and the tip of an X-Acto knife was stuck in one eye socket. When determining if a serial killer is at large, it is crucial to be able to connect the murders to the same perpetrator. This is called linkage analysis, and it is performed by examining the killer's *modus operandi.* The focus is especially on ritual and signature.

Ritual refers to actions by the perpetrator that are not necessary to commit the murder, that is, things that go beyond what is required to cause death. These ritualistic elements must have occurred with at least two of the victims in a series, but they do not necessarily take place every time. The perpetrator might have been interrupted, the victim might have done something unexpected, or the killer might have chosen a victim who, for some reason, did not live up to the fantasy.

Rituals can encompass many things. In BTK's case, bondage was a central part of his fantasy. Many serial killers also feel the need to display their victims, for example, in obscene positions or in a way that shocks those who find the body. There are also perpetrators who insert foreign objects into the deceased, cut the body, or take body parts or belongings as souvenirs. It's crucial for a profiler to distinguish ritual from MO, *modus operandi,* which covers the actions necessary to commit a murder. MO can include stalking to learn the victim's routines, breaking and entering, abduction, and binding. As is evident, there can certainly be an overlap between MO and ritual. Mutilation of the body can be a ritual, but it can also simply be a practical way to obscure the deceased's identity. Similarly, arson can be part of the fantasy, but it can also be a method to dispose of a body.

Signature falls under the ritualistic category, but it is so specific and unique that it can often be considered the perpetrator's calling card. If a signature appears at the crime scenes, it is a very strong indicator of a link between two or more different murders. A good example is Richard Ramirez, who, under the moniker The Night Stalker, terrorized Los Angeles and San Francisco for a year and a half in the mid-1980s. Ramirez was by no means particular and murdered children, adults, and the elderly, men and women alike. He killed in different ways, which would have made it difficult to link the crimes to the same perpetrator, if not for his signature. At a number of crime scenes, he drew a pentagram with, for example, the female victims' lipsticks on the wall, the mirror, or in one instance, on the victim. At one of the subsequent court hearings, he shocked the jury members by extending his pentagram-adorned palm toward them and shouting, "Hail Satan!" He was sentenced to death but died of cancer in 2013 before his execution. Signatures can also be found among serial rapists.

Many years ago in Denmark, we had a case involving a perpetrator known as "The Yachtsman" because he was an elite sailor at a yacht club in the affluent "Whiskey Belt" region. The prosecution lacked conclusive evidence. Investigators found semen at the crime scenes, but in the era before DNA evidence, they could only confirm that The Yachtsman shared the same blood type as the perpetrator. Instead, the prosecutor focused on the man's *modus operandi*. It wasn't particularly unique that the victims resembled each other, or that he threatened them into sex by choking them or using a knife. Nor was it especially distinctive that he ordered the women to take off their clothes and shoes. However, the fact that he took the time to force them to put their shoes back on before the assaults was entirely different and unique, which helped to convict him.

Not all serial offenders have a signature, but when they do, they find it difficult not to leave it, because it is such a vital part of their fantasy and, in many cases, stretches far back in time. As we shall see, this was very much the case with The Eyeball Killer. For now, it's sufficient to establish that he has a very clear signature. It can hardly get more unique, bizarre, and unnecessary for committing a murder. It is, however, worth noting the change that occurred with the third victim. The ritual was performed in a slightly different way, prompting profilers to speculate on the reason.

Like other tools in a profiler's toolbox, linkage analysis rarely stands alone. It's one of many puzzle pieces that can aid in solving a case, but there are instances where linkage analysis has played a central role. This is illustrated by a case from South Africa, where a serial killer was sentenced to life imprisonment in 2006 for more crimes than there was physical evidence or eyewitness testimony for. The convicted man, Themba Sukude, would sneak up on couples having sex in a park in Newcastle, in the eastern part of the country. He would beat the men to death and rape the women. His method was so specific that Themba Sukude was found guilty of four murders, even though in several instances, there was nothing but linkage analysis to convict him.

In the aforementioned cases, the link between the perpetrator and the crimes is very clear. This is not always the case, and it's common for a serial killer not to be convicted of all the murders they are suspected of. Conversely, one can also mistakenly include murders for which the suspect turns out to be innocent. Most frustrating are cases where, long after and perhaps forever, there will be doubt about who was behind the crimes, even when a perpetrator has been convicted.

After the murder of Shirley Williams, the number of sex workers on the streets patrolled by Regina Smith and John Matthews began to thin out. Brenda White, one of the veteran women, however, was still holding out, but said she would probably soon pack up her bags and find a new place.

"The other night, I had to use my pepper spray when a client tried to attack me," she told the officers.

The client had stopped in his dark station wagon. He was robust, had streaks of gray in his dark hair, and wore jeans and cowboy boots. He suggested they drive to a discreet place he knew, but Brenda White refused. She always took her clients to one of the nearby motels, so she told him to drop her off immediately. Then the client flew into a rage. In an outburst, he screamed that he hated prostitutes and that he would kill them all. In that moment, Brenda White grabbed her pepper spray.

"Me and my Black ass are out of here!" she told Regina Smith and John Matthews.

The two officers pondered the story and returned again to Veronica Rodriguez's account. They decided to check out the truck driver, Axton Schindler, on their own. It quickly became clear that the house at 1035 Eldorado was owned by a Fred Albright. A further search revealed that Fred Albright also owned a house on Cotton Valley Street in the neighborhood where the bodies of the first two victims were found. The only snag was that Fred Albright was dead.

"Could this have something to do with a man named Charles Albright?" asked the colleague at the keyboard.

He explained that a few weeks earlier, he had been contacted by an anonymous woman who had been friends with Mary Pratt. Through her, she had met a man whom she briefly dated. His name was Charles Albright, and he had a strange fascination with eyes and X-Acto knives at home. He also shared an address with Axton Schindler. Could he be one of

Schindler's friends who had tried to kill Veronica Rodriguez? A check of his criminal record showed that Charles Albright, born in 1933, had a long rap sheet of thefts, burglaries, fraud, and a sexual assault on a child. His picture showed a middle-aged man who matched the description of the client Brenda White had told them about.

The two patrol officers then contacted their colleagues in the homicide department, and when Veronica Rodriguez identified Charles Albright's picture from a lineup, the trap snapped shut. In the dead of night on March 22, 1991, a task force stormed through the front door of the house at 1035 Eldorado in the heart of the Oak Cliff neighborhood in Dallas. Shortly after, the homeowner was handcuffed, and while his wife, completely oblivious to what was happening, screamed, the police led him away.

Charles Albright was a precocious child, good at almost everything he attempted. He was very young when he learned the names of various constellations, and he played the piano like a dream because he practiced every morning before the school bus arrived. The latter was something his mother had ordered him to do. She and her husband had adopted Charles when he was just three weeks old, and he grew up in Oak Cliff. His mother told her son that his biological mother was a talented 16-year-old law student who had secretly married her boyfriend. The marriage, however, had been annulled at her parents' insistence, which was why he ended up with the Albright family.

No one doubted Mrs. Albright's love for her son, but most agreed that their relationship was peculiar. For example, she kept goats in the backyard because she insisted that goat milk was far superior to cow's milk, and Charles had to drink it, whether he liked it or not, or he would be beaten. Occasionally, she dressed him in girls' clothes and gave him a doll to play with, and she changed his clothes several times a day out of fear of germs. At that time, polio was most parents' worst nightmare. Since the disease came from viruses in feces, she taught Charles the importance of hygiene by taking him to the hospital and showing him patients who couldn't breathe on their own and were therefore in iron lungs.

When Charles was 11 years old, his mother was told that he had been seen several times on roadsides, poking at roadkill animals. Someone also told her that her son was sometimes cruel to animals. This led her to choose a hobby for him: taxidermy. The boy took a taxidermy course and began stuff out birds and smaller animals, but his mother, who was, to put it mildly, frugal, refused to buy the expensive and lifelike eyes that otherwise fascinated Charles. Therefore, guests approaching the display cabinet where the animals stood were met with an eerie sight. The taxidermy was always performed so professionally that one would think it was the work of an expert, but the animals stared back with eyes made from buttons from Mrs. Albright's sewing kit.

Mrs. Albright had many other fixed ideas about upbringing. Once, when her son put her measuring tape in his mouth, he was locked in a dark room. Also, she tied him to the bed and if he didn't want to take a nap. She told him that his father was "greedy" when it came to sex, and often tried to grab her when she was in the bedroom in her underwear. Charles dared not try such things. So when he got older and started dating, she insisted on accompanying him, often sitting at the table next to the couple. She would also call the girl's parents beforehand to assure them that her son would not try anything inappropriate.

On the surface, Charles Albright seemed like a polite, even chivalrous, boy and young man. He quickly became one of the most popular students, engaging in a wide range of extracurricular activities and often taking the lead when it came to practical jokes. He was bored by lessons, and when his grades started slipping, he forged his report card in the school office. Later, this escalated to petty theft and burglaries, which led him into the juvenile justice system. His probation officer from that period later stated:

"He could separate reality sufficiently from his own value system that he could tell you a lie and at the same time actually convince himself that he was telling the truth."

Charles Albright continued his criminal path with some fellow students, collectively responsible for a series of business burglaries. When the case went to court, his mother first tried to pay the store owners for what was stolen. When the judge denied her request to act as defense counsel in the case, she asked if she could go to prison instead of her son. Subsequently, he began studying to become a teacher. The seminary was supposed to be a new start, but his bad habits soon resurfaced. When one of Charles Albright's friends broke up with his girlfriend, Albright decided to play a creepy practical joke. The friend met a new girl and got a picture of her. One evening, he noticed that the photograph looked different. Someone had cut his ex-girlfriend's eyes out of a photo and glued them onto the picture of the new girlfriend. And not only that. His ex-girlfriend's eyes stared down at him from the ceiling and walls of the room, out in the hallway, and in the men's restroom.

As a psychologist, when I read about Charles Albright's upbringing and the young man he developed into, I see a classic story of an overstepping boundaries and extremely controlling mother. This is a child who begins life with the ultimate rejection when his biological mother gives him up for adoption, and instead, he gets a mother who exerts strong control over him, both in terms of school and leisure, and in relation to sexuality. I also see a boy with great potential, but as he aged, he developed a kind of helplessness that prevented him from achieving or being given the opportunity to achieve anything. He failed to form his own inner core, and thus, he struggled to live a healthy, stable life, instead drifting from one thing to another. This often happens when a mother or father tries to take over their child's life; they lose will and initiative. For boys, it also often affects their relationships with women, as the relationship with the mother is the first and therefore most important relationship he has. The same applies to girls, only for them, it's often the father who influences their relationships with other men. For boys, the mother can be perceived as the purest being in the world, against whom they measure all other women, who then pale in comparison and sometimes are therefore reduced to prostitutes.

Apparently, things went well for Charles Albright, who got a good position at a high school in a small town east of Dallas, where he taught science. He quickly became popular among both students and colleagues, none of whom had any idea that he had forged his excellent academic papers after being expelled from the seminary due to theft. When this was discovered, he moved back to his childhood neighborhood with his wife and child, where no one knew about his criminal past. People merely wondered why such an intelligent person seemed uninterested in steady employment. When his wife taught English to high school students, he would embark on an endless stream of projects that never really amounted to anything, except for a period as a bullfighter in Mexico. This was perhaps one of the few things that actually made him feel alive. Bullfighters need guts. They need ice in their stomachs, must stand firm and stare the bull in the eyes, while potentially in mortal danger. Charles Albright seemingly needed that.

Since he had tortured and killed animals as a child, he had no problem with that part of the sport, and it gave him an outlet for a lot of aggression.

People knew that Charles Albright had artistic abilities, and at one point, an acquaintance offered him $250 to paint a portrait of his wife. He worked on it for weeks until the acquaintance grew tired of waiting. He showed up at Charles Albright's house and saw that the large portrait was largely finished, but where the eyes should have been, there were just two round, white holes. Several months passed before Charles Albright was satisfied, but by then, the eyes were so good that it felt as if their gaze followed people as they walked past.

He managed to keep a series of suspended sentences for petty thefts a secret, but in 1985, things looked bleak for Charles Albright again. He had since divorced and joined a local Catholic church, where he sang in the choir and helped with both charity and church duties. "Good Old Charlie," the priest called him. Here, he met a family he became part of, who, after some time, accused him of sexually molesting their minor daughter. Both the family and the now 51-year-old Charles Albright wanted to keep the matter quiet, and he ended up pleading guilty in an empty courtroom. Rumors circulated, but women in the community found it hard to believe the story could be true. Charles Albright was an old-fashioned gentleman and a romantic, who recited poetry and never made advances on women until they permitted him. Many of them were also jealous when he met a pretty, shy widow whom he married.

Neither his new wife nor his friends had any idea that Charles Albright was simultaneously a familiar face in the prostitution scene around the Star Motel. Numerous sex workers knew him as a regular client, and it wasn't unusual for him to help some of the women pay their bills when they were arrested. Witnesses could attest that in his younger days, he had briefly dated a woman who was good friends with Mary Pratt, and that he became one of her regular clients when she started working the streets. He typically visited when his wife was at work. Suddenly, it made sense that he had taken a job as a newspaper deliveryman at night and early morning, which gave him an opportunity to visit the prostitutes without having to explain his whereabouts at home. Most often, it was gentle sex, but a couple of the women recounted that Charles Albright occasionally changed character. Once, in a motel room, he chained two of them to the bed and beat them with a belt. "Scream, bitch! You know you love it!" he yelled.

This altered behavior coincided with the deaths of his parents in 1981 and 1986. As we've already discussed, Charles Albright had an extremely complicated relationship with his mother, who made no secret of her disappointment with the man her son had become. He loved his mother, but hated the influence she had over him. So, when she and his father were finally gone, a lot of the suppressed rage could at long last fully blossom. He was in freefall, and there was no one to restrain him and his dark desires. After his father's death, Charles Albright inherited a sum of money and several houses, one of which was rented out to the truck driver Axton Schindler, an eccentric who soon filled the house with junk and lived without electricity or running water. Charles himself moved into his childhood home at 1035 Eldorado with his new wife.

Shortly after, Charles Albright's friends were puzzled by a strange episode involving their softball team. They knew him as a calm, composed man who never raised his voice but did everything he could to make others like him. After a game, the players spotted a car with some women whom they perceived as prostitutes. One of the men joked that Charles should hurry after them. "I'd kill them if I could!" was the reply. A complete silence fell, and the others stared at him as he spun on his heel and left the field in anger. A couple of days later, the team gathered again, and Charles Albright tried to apologize for his behavior. He explained that the topic was difficult for him because his biological mother was a prostitute. There is nothing to suggest that his mother was a prostitude, but that doesn't mean Charles Albright hadn't convinced himself of it, thereby creating a connection between mothers and prostitutes in his mind, a clash of opposites that might explain why sex workers around the Star Motel experienced him as both caring and decent, and as violent and terrifying.

The bizarre comment is a good example of what's called spillover or a "Freudian slip." This phenomenon is often seen when people try to suppress something they're thinking about and wish to happen. It occurs to all of us in everyday life, but it also happens to serial killers when, for a split second, they reveal their true selves and suddenly become enraged, jumping out like a jack-in-the-box. There are several instances where serial killers have confessed to a murder or stated who they intend to kill, but those who heard it didn't take it seriously. Spillover can play an important role when investigators interrogate a suspect and try to get them to incriminate themselves. You can read more about this in Chapter 9.

Charles Albright's spillover was noted by his friends, but they accepted his apology and explanation about his biological mother, and nothing more came of it. On the contrary, he now had optimal opportunities to realize his fantasies. His job as a newspaper deliveryman gave him an excuse to be out at night, the prostitutes knew him and were generally comfortable with him, and he had access to one of his parents' old, empty properties. There was only one fly in the ointment: Axton Schindler. He had registered his address as Eldorado 1035 because he didn't want the authorities to know where he actually lived. Thus, Charles Albright ended up under police scrutiny anyway.

During the search of the address, investigators found X-Acto knives, an anatomy book, and a stack of true crime books. In a secret cavity behind the fireplace were some pistols and rifles, but they didn't match the weapon the killer had used. The victims' eyeballs also didn't turn up. No witnesses had seen Charles Albright with the victims, and his wife swore that he never left home earlier than usual and always came home on time. It didn't get any better for the prosecutor when Veronica Rodriguez testified that she had never been with Charles Albright, and Axton Schindler denied any knowledge of the story about him saving her during an attempted murder. Everything depended on a single piece of technical evidence: hair found on the bodies, in the accused's pickup truck, and in his vacuum cleaner. Hair isn't as conclusive as fingerprints, but forensic technicians concluded that the hairs on the deceased matched Charles Albright's, while the hairs in the vehicle matched Mary Pratt and Susan Peterson. Finally, the hairs in the vacuum cleaner were with high certainty Shirley Williams's. The defense argued that this was purely circumstantial evidence and that the police should have looked more closely at Axton Schindler, who had even left town during the trial. The problem for him was that while many sex workers knew Charles Albright, no one knew who Axton Schindler was, and no one who had met the latter could in any way imagine that he was capable of removing eyeballs with surgical precision.

The jury was apparently in doubt. On December 19, 1991, it found Charles Albright guilty only of the murder of Shirley Williams. Therefore, many, including myself, have speculated whether there was only one Eyeball Killer. As described, there are significant differences between the first two murders and the last. This could, of course, be because Charles Albright was disturbed in the last instance and had to remove the eyes quickly, but the differences could also be due to there being two murderers. If that's the case, the question arises: Which murders was Charles Albright behind?

Here, there are two possibilities in my view. He killed Mary Pratt and Susan Peterson, and because of his experience with taxidermy of birds and mammals, he was able to remove the victims' eyeballs professionally. In that case, a second perpetrator may have been behind the murder of Shirley Williams without possessing the same surgical skills. Or, it was an unknown perpetrator in the first two cases, and Charles Albright was inspired to murder Shirley Williams. If that's the truth, the first perpetrator must have had a background that enabled him to perform such a complicated operation, and Charles Albright had some experience with taxidermy. In that case, Charles Albright must be classified as a copycat killer, while the real Eyeball Killer was never found. Conversely, it's worth noting that the murders stopped when Charles Albright was arrested.

A final possibility, which I myself lean most toward, is that it could have been a killer couple: Charles Albright and Axton Schindler. This would explain the difference in how the eyes were removed in the first cases versus the last, as well as the fact that Charles Albright could only be definitively linked to one victim. Furthermore, there's Veronica Rodriguez's explanation. She stated that she had seen both men, but that

Axton Schindler was her rescuer. Perhaps she was mistaken? The street officers knew that, due to drugs, she told stories that probably contained some truth but were often jumbled. So perhaps both men were actually involved in the assault.

I have no doubt that Charles Albright committed at least one of the murders. The profile and details from his life simply fit too well for him to be entirely uninvolved. But the ultimate truth was taken by Charles Albright to his grave when he died at the age of 87 in 2020.

CHAPTER 4: GEOGRAPHICAL PROFILING: MANHUNT IN ENGLAND

Darkness had fallen over the large hospital parking lot in the British city of Leeds, about 270 kilometers north of London, on January 3, 1983, a 26-year-old woman found her car key, unlocked her car, and sat in the driver's seat. But before she could turn the key in the ignition, a stranger forced his way in and pushed her to the passenger seat.

"I'll shoot you in the head if you don't do as I say," he hissed.

Shortly after, he drove into the traffic with the terrified woman beside him. On a deserted stretch alongside the Leeds and Liverpool Canal, the longest artificial waterway in England, he stopped and raped his victim. When he was finished, he gagged the woman with a cloth and bound her hands and ankles with electrical cables. He drove right up to the water's edge, where he pressed a plastic bag over her head and pulled her out of the car. For a brief moment, he stood with her on the bank of the canal. Then he gave her a push. She landed with a splash in the water, and the rapist watched as the bag slowly filled with water. But then something unexpected happened. The woman stood up in the canal. By chance, her legs had hit a rock on the bottom, and it was large enough for her to get her head above water by standing on it. She managed to free herself from the cables and swim to the other side, making it to land, while the perpetrator observed her and eventually fled into the darkness.

The woman immediately went to West Yorkshire Police and reported the near-fatal assault. Investigators quickly recognized the details. Less than a month earlier, a 30-year-old woman had reported a rape in Bradford, just 15 kilometers west of Leeds. On a foggy December evening, the woman had gone to a deserted parking lot to retrieve her car when the perpetrator forced his way into the car and pushed her to the passenger seat, then ripped off her clothes and raped her. The *modus operandi* in the two cases was so similar that it could very well be the same man the police were now hunting. Investigators found a number of clues, including hair, on the victims and in the cars, but after knocking on more than 14,000 doors to find witnesses to the assaults, they gave up and discarded the samples. A composite sketch, which the first victim had created by assembling drawings of different facial parts from one of the police's folders, also disappeared and was never found again.

Fifteen months later, in early summer 1984, the perpetrator sat in his car in a parking lot in Leicester, just under 130 kilometers south of Bradford. Several drivers came and went, but he waited patiently for the right opportunity. It came when a 20-year-old woman drove in and parked in one of the bays. She didn't even have time to get out before he forced his way behind the wheel and drove off with her sitting on the floor by the passenger seat. As in the first two cases, he found a deserted stretch where he raped his victim, then cut her several times in the chest, neck, and abdomen with a knife before fleeing.

When I read about the case from England, I see an extremely sadistic serial rapist. I believe it's purely by chance that he didn't kill one or more of his victims. The way he treated the women both before and after the rape testifies to a man who had absolutely no compassion for his victims; he wanted them to suffer even more than they already were. This says something about the true nature of this type of crime.

In my opinion, rape is one of the worst crimes, and that's why I also call it "extreme violence with sex as a weapon." It is not only profoundly degrading, violating, and shameful for the victim; it often affects their loved ones, who may feel they have failed because they couldn't protect their dear one who was victimized. Rape cases are notoriously difficult to prove, partly because it can be very hard for a rapist's family and friends to imagine that among their fathers, brothers, and sons are men who are behind these crimes. This often leads to colleagues, friends, and family members routinely providing false alibis for their friends or relatives because they simply cannot believe that the person could have done something so terrible.

It came as a shock to many that "The Yachtsman," whom I mentioned in the previous chapter, turned out to be behind at least 16 rapes. He was described as a handsome, charming man. He was successful both personally and professionally and had no problems in his relationship with his girlfriend. This merely underscores that rapes are not about sex; they are about power and control. The opportunity to exert ultimate power over another human being, but also to degrade and use the woman and then discard her, is central for a serial rapist. Most often, for example, in the case of "The Yachtsman," they perceive themselves as so unique and powerful that they believe they have the right to take what they want and treat women exactly as they desire to fulfill their own need to feel powerful.

Like serial murderers, serial rapists share a number of common traits. A study conducted by the FBI in the 1980s showed that almost three out of four had experienced physical, psychological, or sexual abuse as children. In most cases, as previously mentioned, one finds a strong anger directed at women, and it is not unusual for this to ultimately be aimed at an extremely dominant mother. In the upbringing of serial rapists, one also often sees examples of rejection. They have experienced being rejected by their closest relation, not necessarily physically, but certainly emotionally. This often occurs in school, where they may have difficulty forming bonds with others. By assaulting women as adults, they act out and thereby strengthen their low self-esteem or seek revenge on all the women who have rejected them throughout their lives.

In general, you find many of the traits of serial killers: chaotic families, bullying, isolation, degradation, trauma, and humiliation. Furthermore, some of them are psychopaths or sociopaths. But here too, it's important to emphasize that one doesn't suddenly start raping women from one day to the next just because they were bullied as a child. A series of events is required, and they will differ from person to person.

Both serial murderers and serial rapists appear on the surface to live relatively normal lives, but the latter often get away with their crimes more easily. There isn't the same focus on serial rapes as on murders, partly because rape is a less extensive crime than murder.

It took a while before the rapist in the parking lots was caught, but not because he didn't strike again. Because he did. In 1985 and 1987, women were raped according to the same sinister plan, where he would wait for a lone woman to get into her car. Then things went quiet, which isn't unusual. Previously, it was said that when a serial killer or serial rapist stops, there are three possible reasons: he is dead, he is sick, or he is in prison. But today, we know that many start committing serial murders or rapes, only to stop again without any obvious reason. Investigators, of course, couldn't have known it then, but in this case, the perpetrator was behind bars for an armed robbery. The sentence was 16 years in prison, but because he behaved exemplarily, he achieved a number of privileges after just a few years, including prison break. Shortly after, he was transferred to an open prison, which made it possible for him to work as an electrician in the very area that had constituted his hunting grounds.

On the afternoon of May 14, 1993, a 23-year-old woman from the countryside drove into Nottingham in her mother's car. She parked on the street level of a centrally located parking garage and briefly studied the contents of her handbag. That's all it took before a stranger ripped open the door and pressed a knife to her throat. He forced her onto the floor in front of the passenger seat, threw a jacket over her head, and drove out of the parking garage and through the city.

"Are you religious?" he asked.

"I'm Catholic," the woman stammered.

"Then you'd better start praying," he added.

A short distance outside the city, the man turned down a gravel road. He pulled over and ripped the woman's clothes off, then raped her. When he was finished, he tied up his naked victim and drove further into the countryside, where he parked in a secluded spot. He got out, opened the fuel tank cap, and tried to set the fuel on fire. For some reason, it failed, and he left the car and the crying woman. What the woman didn't know was that the rapist was out on prison leave.

Two years later, a 22-year-old student in Leeds began packing up at one of the city's libraries after sweating over books all day. She stepped out into the fresh air and stopped at a supermarket to buy groceries for dinner. From there, she strolled to a nearby parking garage to retrieve her car. It was a warm summer day, and since the car had heated up nicely, she sat for a moment behind the wheel, letting the fresh air stream in through the open door. Suddenly, she heard running footsteps approaching. The next second, a man forced his way into the car and pushed her into the passenger seat. He grabbed her by the neck with one arm, held her head tight, and smeared super glue over her eyes, then tied her hands behind her back. Shortly after, he floored her and drove onto the street. Unable to see anything, the woman only sensed they must be leaving the city.

After some time, the vehicle stopped, and the man again seized the 22-year-old. With a knife, he began to cut her clothes to pieces while she fought back as best she could with her eyes closed. It was in vain. The man raped her. Afterward, he again turned the key in the ignition and drove a little further before parking. When the victim heard him leave the car, she rubbed her face against the seat to remove the glue and that enabled her to blink, and she was soon able to make out her surroundings. She was right by the Leeds and Liverpool Canal. The man had long since disappeared. With one foot, she pressed the horn down and kept honking until a motorist pulled over to help her. The motorist was quick-witted enough to immediately write down what the woman told him, as did one of the paramedics who were called. However, the police misplaced the motorist's description, and investigators never asked the paramedic if he had any information that could be used in solving the rape. Even when a colleague from Nottingham called to tell them about the 1993 case, the Leeds police didn't take it seriously and told him to "fuck off." Two important clues did emerge from the investigation of the 22-year-old's car. When she struggled against the rapist, he cut himself and bled in the car, and he had left part of a fingerprint on an envelope in the woman's bag. The blood analysis was ready in January 1996 and turned out to match semen from the crime scene in Leeds. At the same time, investigators began looking at old cases and quickly rediscovered the assaults from the 1980s, which could easily be linked to the recent ones. Finally, the police forces began working together and launched a massive investigation under the name Operation Lynx, which developed into the most extensive manhunt in England since The Yorkshire Ripper terrorized in the second half of the 1970s.

It was an almost insurmountable task that the police in Leicestershire, Nottinghamshire, and West Yorkshire faced. After featuring on the TV program Crimewatch, the 180 investigators had more than 10,000 suspects in an area the size of Zealand, and even though countless men voluntarily submitted to DNA testing, police didn't get any closer to an arrest.

It was at that point in the summer of 1996 that the English police contacted a colleague at the Vancouver Police Department in Canada, Kim Rossmo, who agreed to look at the case.

Kim Rossmo was the first Canadian officer to earn a Ph.D. He was inspired by criminologists, Patricia and Paul Brantingham, at Simon Fraser University, who were specialists in environmental criminology. This is a scientific field based on the idea that geography plays an important role for criminals, and that it matters where the perpetrator and victim first meet, where the assault occurs, where the victim is raped and possibly killed, and where the body is subsequently dumped. Technical examinations of fingerprints, blood, semen, hair, and footprints are still absolutely central, but there may also be important information in the fact that the victim and perpetrator must, in one way or another, cross paths in both time and place. Kim Rossmo's idea was that environmental criminologists' thoughts could be applied to individual crimes, becoming another tool for investigators hunting a perpetrator. This method is called geographical profiling.

In both Canada and Denmark, and many other countries, murders are relatively easy to solve because the vast majority of victims are killed by partners, family members, or acquaintances. Stranger murders, where the victim and perpetrator often either don't know each other or only for a short time or from distance, and this is where serial offenders come into play, because their motive lies in the act itself, not in a personal relationship with the victims, whom they almost never know beforehand.

To create a geographical profile, a certain number of crimes are also necessary in order to have a chance of pinpointing the most probable location of the perpetrator. On the other hand, the method can potentially be used, along with other tools, in a wide range of different types of crimes where the same perpetrator is responsible. The fundamental idea is this: what is most important for arsonists, rapists, and serial murderers? They all want to ensure they are not discovered. And the better they know an area, the safer they feel, and the safer they feel, the greater their opportunities to carry out what their fantasy demands. Setting fire to buildings, raping, or murdering is not something one just does, and for most serial offenders, it's actually very difficult, especially in the beginning. They need to know where they can live out their fantasy without being seen. There must be an escape route, and in the case of murderers, there is also a body to dispose of. This requires local knowledge, and which area do people know best? Where they live or work.

Take, for example, Ivan Milat, who lived near Belanglo State Forest and knew the forest inside out, or Dennis Rader, who spent a long time getting to know the areas where his victims lived, one of whom was almost a neighbor. It's the same with serial rapists, who find even greater security in their own local area. This has been calculated over time, and it has been shown that serial rapists, on average, assault their victims 1.7 kilometers from their own residence, depending of what research result you look at it range from 0 to 10 kilometer from their anchor point. There are many examples of this, in Denmark. In 2013, a 41-year-old family man, , was convicted of 12 offenses, including rape, attempted rape, and robberies, all of which had occurred near a tunnel in a path system in the Copenhagen district of Tingbjerg, where he himself lived. When victims came cycling, he would knock them over and threaten them into oral sex, and in many cases, he also stole their bags. Once he was arrested, it was quite simple for investigators to link him to the various assaults, partly because his method was consistent every time, and partly because they took place in the same tunnels. From our perspective, it seems "stupid" not to vary the method and location, but it says something about how much security and familiar surroundings mean to serial offenders. Fortunately, this is an advantage for those who have to solve crimes.

Just as behavioral analysis cannot pinpoint a specific perpetrator, geographical profiling cannot point out a specific address for the perpetrator's home or workplace. Instead, it operates with probabilities. Generally, it's said that the further a perpetrator is from their home, which could also be their workplace or a place they frequently visit for example family, the lower the probability that they will commit rape or murder. This is known as distance decay, an expression of the relationship between distance from home and the decreasing likelihood of a crime occurring. It's also known that most serial offenders don't comit crimes very close to where they live to minimize the risk of being discovered, and this area is referred to as the buffer zone. Between the buffer zone and the furthest crime scene is the serial offender's comfort zone. As the perpetrator becomes more comfortable, you might observe them committing their crimes closer and closer to their home. Others travel far from their familiar areas and create new familiar areas for themselves, making it harder for the police to find them.

Over time, profilers have developed computer programs that, based on crime scenes, can calculate the perpetrator's most likely whereabouts. A geographical profile thus consists of a map that resembles a topographical atlas, but instead of color codes indicating the area's height above sea level, the colors represent different percentages indicating the probability of a perpetrator's hunt. As mentioned, this is astonishingly often near their own home.

One of the most famous examples of the importance of geographical profiling was the M25 Rapist case from England, where an unknown perpetrator, over a year from November 2001 to November 2002, was responsible for at least 10 rapes of girls and women aged 10 to 52. The perpetrator was particularly sadistic, even for a serial rapist. During several of the attacks, he even called the victims' families and terrorized them with information about the rape. He made no secret of taking souvenirs, so the girls and women could subsequently imagine him fantasizing with their underwear or other clothing items. The assaults took place in an area of 9,000 square kilometers, but an investigator, using a computer program, developed a geographical profile that highlighted an area of 31 square kilometers near the town of Woking, quite close to the M25 ring road that circles London. Since most crimes occurred during daytime on weekdays, it was reasonable to assume that the perpetrator worked in or near Woking.

Two rapes occurred on the same day, and the crime scenes indicated that the perpetrator had driven from a location south of London on his way to work. And then there was the first case, where a 10-year-old girl was kidnapped from a community center in the town of Ashford. This stood out from the subsequent crimes by occurring after dark and thus after normal working hours, leading investigators to adhere to the hypothesis that the perpetrator lived nearby, which also aligns well with serial offenders preferring to stay close to their homes, especially at the beginning of their deeds. On the TV program Crimewatch, the police talked about the rapes and the geographical profile. Among the more than 10,000 who subsequently called with tips was a woman who lived in the village of Appledore, 16 kilometers southwest of Ashford. She had a strange feeling about her neighbor, Antoni Imiela, who worked for a company in Woking. A DNA test showed that the neighbor's intuition was correct, and Antoni Imiela was arrested and brought to trial.

As mentioned, there are many similarities between serial murderers and serial rapists, which becomes very clear when looking at the M25 Rapist's upbringing. He was born in a refugee camp in West Germany in 1954 to a Polish soldier and a German mother. The couple and their five children eventually moved to Newton Aycliffe in northern England. His father had a violent temper, which primarily went beyond his mother, especially in connection with five abortions and the birth of a disabled son. At school, Antoni Imiela was isolated by the other students, who called him "Nazi" because of his German accent. He reacted by becoming tough and violent, and he shocked his classmates by repeatedly dousing cats, dogs, and other animals with lighter fluid and setting them on fire.

When Antoni Imiela was 14, his mother told him and his siblings that she was going to get fish and chips, but she never came back. Shortly after, his violent sexuality emerged when he, along with a couple of peers, sexually assaulted a 14-year-old girl on the school bus. The five siblings were left to their father, whose upbringing was based on physical and psychological violence and, among other things, led to Antoni Imiela being shaved bald as punishment and, another time, nearly losing an eye when his father put out his cigarette on his face. As an adult, a series of thefts, robberies, prison sentences, and changing relationships followed, where he behaved as violent as his father toward his partners. He died at the age of 63 in 2018.

Geography can also play an important role in linkage analysis, which, as we saw in Chapter 3, is a prerequisite for knowing if a crime is part of a series. Let's go to Canada and take a closer look at the Pig Farm Killer, potentially one of the worst serial killers in the country's history, not least because it took the police an uncomfortably long time to even accept that murders were taking place. It all began in the 1990s, when women started disappearing from a rundown former industrial district in Vancouver known for attracting prostitutes and drug users. By 1998, the number of missing women had reached 27, and street workers began raising concerns about what they feared was a widespread murder case.

Upon closer examination of the numbers, there were very few missing women before 1995, after which the number sharply increased. Kim Rossmo concluded that the area was too small and the number of disappearances too high for it to be coincidental. If it had been about medical cases, it would have been an epidemic. An investigator from the police's missing persons unit began interviewing family and friends.

Although she managed to locate two of the women, she subsequently had 37 on the list who had vanished without a trace. Relatives urged the police to offer a reward of 100,000 Canadian dollars, an amount equivalent to what had been offered for information that could lead to the solving of a series of home robberies in one of the wealthier neighborhoods. But this was rejected because Vancouver's mayor did not believe it was the authorities' job to act as a GPS service for prostitutes. There was also skepticism within police leadership.

It was not uncommon for sex workers to disappear for a period and then reappear. Many of them were on drugs and had likely died from overdoses. Others had probably been murdered by their pimps. It was difficult to counter arguments that random deaths would not have clustered together in that way, but would instead have been distributed in other similar neighborhoods. Furthermore, it was also mysterious that not a single body of the women on the list had been found.

A couple of years passed before pressure from the media and the public prompted the police to initiate an investigation specifically targeting the missing women, which led them to a pig farm outside the city owned by brothers Robert and David Pickton. The brothers had previously been under police scrutiny because they had violated planning laws by letting the pigs tend to themselves while they organized large techno parties in one of the farm's buildings, where both prostitutes and bikers participated, up to 2,000 at a time. In 1997, one of the sex workers went to the police and reported that Robert Pickton had tried to kill her with a knife, but even though she had sustained several stab wounds, the case was eventually dropped.

In connection with a case involving illegal firearms, the police searched the farm and found several belongings of the missing women. The brothers were remanded in custody, and investigators placed agents in their cells, where Robert Pickton talked too much and confessed that he had killed 49 female sex workers and drug users. There is evidence to suggest that some of the bodies over the years had been fed to the farm's pigs. The police even suspected Robert Pickton of having mixed human flesh into the ground meat he sold, and the Canadian food authorities therefore ended up issuing a warning against eating products from the farm. The Pig Farm Killer was successfully sentenced to life in prison for six murders, but he remains suspected of at least the 49 he confessed to in his cell. It took investigators a very long time to search the farm and sift through large quantities of soil to find just a few of the women's earthly remains.

In May 1997, Kim Rossmo arrived in England to visit the locations where the serial rapist had attacked young women in their cars. He recognized the difficulty of developing a geographical profile based on only five cases spread across a relatively large area. However, a specific detail in one of the cases piqued his interest: a stolen credit card the perpetrator had used around Leeds. The list of purchases included a Parker pen, a computer game called Scramble, a shirt, alcohol, and cigarettes. These items weren't particularly related, nor were they bought from the same stores. They were, however, commonplace items that most people buy from their usual shops. This, combined with the fact that several of the assaults also took place in Leeds, made it logical for the geographical profile to focus specifically on that city. These numerous details were fed into a computer program for calculation. When the map was ready, two neighborhoods in Leeds glowed red, indicating the highest probability. While the geographical profile couldn't be more precise, it proved to be a significant aid for the police. They then turned their attention to the partial fingerprint found on an envelope in one of the victims' bags. The quality of the print was too poor for computer-based searches through digitized fingerprints of convicted criminals. However, the geographical profile allowed them to narrow down the search to fingerprints of offenders who lived or had lived in the high-probability areas identified.

It took investigators several months to manually examine over 7,000 fingerprints using magnifying glasses. After some time, it became clear that the perpetrator was not in the system if he resided in the first suggested neighborhood. The stack of fingerprints dwindled when focusing on criminals in the second neighborhood. Then, they found a match. The fingerprint, with high probability, belonged to a man named Clive Barwell, a truck driver and married father of three, who lived in Killingbeck in the eastern part of Leeds, precisely within one of the geographical profile's red zones.

The investigators were ecstatic; they finally had their suspect. Their elation momentarily turned to dismay when they discovered that Clive Barwell had been incarcerated when the Nottingham rape (where the perpetrator attempted to set the victim's car on fire) occurred. However, it was then revealed that Clive Barwell had been granted weekend release permission that had not been officially recorded. Furthermore, it was discovered that the serial rapist's mother lived in Mill Garth, the second neighborhood identified by the profile. This evidence was sufficient for the police to demand a DNA test from Clive Barwell. In October 1999, he pleaded guilty in court and was sentenced to life imprisonment. Young female motorists in the area between Leeds, Nottingham, and Leicester could finally breathe a sigh of relief.

Geographical profiling played a role in solving the cases we've examined in this chapter, but it cannot stand alone. Not all serial offenders commit their rapes or murders close to home. In geographical profiling, they are divided into two groups: marauders and commuters. Marauders, like "The Tunnel Man," are active near their homes because that's where they feel most secure; it's estimated that about two-thirds of serial killers are marauders. Commuters, on the other hand, travel away from their immediate surroundings to commit crimes, mostly because they establish a new "comfort zone," perhaps in connection with their workplace. However, some serial offenders become commuters as part of their *modus operandi*, making it harder for the police to detect and apprehend them.

It's also crucial to highlight that geographical profiling can quickly become ineffective in densely populated areas such as Manhattan, New York. In such places, knowing that a murderer lives within a given square kilometer offers little practical help. Furthermore, there can be a tendency to retrospectively confirm the accuracy of a geographical profile after a case is solved, without fully acknowledging all the other investigative work involved. It's important to remember that a geographical profile is based on hypotheses and uncertainties. When told that a perpetrator is 80% likely to reside within a specific area, there's still a 20% chance they don't live there at all. This was clearly demonstrated in the case of the Baton Rouge Serial Killer, Derrick Todd Lee, who murdered at least seven women in Louisiana between 1992 and 2003. A geographical profile was generated during the investigation, leading police to focus on an area where there was a 60% probability the killer lived. It proved to be a waste of time, as Derrick Todd Lee was not located there. The overall profile also erroneously predicted that the serial killer was White, a common misconception in the past that serial killers were exclusively or predominantly White; Lee was Black. For a geographical profile to be effective, it must work in conjunction with other investigative efforts. This is why Kim Rossmo also emphasized other clues in the English case, such as the purchases the rapist had made. Rossmo states that a geographical profile relies on behavioral analysis and all the technical evidence collected at the crime scene.

There are instances of serial killers who are aware that geography can expose them. One of the most cunning among them was Israel Keyes. Born on January 7, 1978, in Utah, he was the second of ten siblings. His family was initially affiliated with The Church of Jesus Christ of Latter-day Saints, but his parents turned away from it to become Christian fundamentalists. They joined a racist church that insisted Aryans were the true descendants of Abraham, Isaac, and Jacob. The family held little regard for the government and homeschooled their children, who grew up in a desolate and primitive cabin without running water or electricity. The parents rejected modern medicine, which led to Israel Keyes losing one eye due to an infection. As a teenager, he rejected his parents' religion. This led his father to disown him, but he reportedly maintained a close relationship with his mother. At that time, he began breaking into neighbors' homes to steal weapons, which he used to shoot various animals. This escalated into outright animal cruelty. How many victims he had on his conscience, we will probably never know, as he committed suicide in his cell before he could be convicted. Prior to that, he had confessed to three murders and some other offenses. He never admitted to more killings, but in prison, he had drawn 11 skulls and a satanic symbol with his blood on a piece of paper. The FBI interpreted the drawing as Israel Keyes having murdered 11 people. The number could easily be higher, however, as he traveled a lot, including abroad.

The travels were part of his *modus operandi*. In 2011, for example, he flew to Chicago, where he rented a car and drove all the way to Vermont, a 1,500-kilometer trip, to kill a married couple. He had selected the victims two years earlier and had already buried a box with equipment, so he had easy access to weapons, ammunition, and chemicals to dissolve the bodies. On the night of June 8, he broke into their home, tied them up, and drove them to an abandoned farm, where he shot the husband before raping and strangling the wife. The bodies were never found, but Israel Keyes partially admitted to the police later what he had done. After the murders, he collected his equipment and buried it outside the town of Parishville in New York State, where it was found after his arrest. On these excursions, he always made sure to turn off his mobile phone and only used cash obtained through burglaries and robberies. Overall, he was extremely cautious and well-organized until he used a victim's credit card, but by then, he also felt he was losing control, he told investigators. In that way, he reminded them a lot of his idol, Ted Bundy, whose methods he had studied thoroughly. But where Ted Bundy murdered in different states because he lived in several different places, Israel Keyes' travels were part of a strategy designed to make it difficult for the police to catch him.

A special group of commuters are serial killers who work in the transportation industry, especially long-haul truck drivers. They have their home with them, one might say, and therefore they can feel safe wherever they are. At rest stops and along the roads, they have the opportunity to find low-risk victims in the form of sex workers, hitchhikers, or migrant workers. This was a trend that the FBI became aware of in 2004 when an analyst discovered a pattern in the way female bodies were dumped along Highway 40, which runs through Oklahoma, Texas, Arkansas, and Mississippi. The analyst and a colleague entered their information into ViCAP, and it turned out that similar patterns existed along several other highways across states in the USA.

That many of the women whose bodies were found along American highways, in the perpetrator's eyes, belonged to low-risk groups, is no coincidence. In fact, victims of serial offenders often tell at least as important story as the perpetrators and their behavior. Studies of crime victims are called victimology. It is an important discipline for profilers, even though it may seem controversial; we will look more closely at this in the next chapter.

CHAPTER 5: LISA MCVEY: WHAT THE VICTIMS CAN TELL

17-year-old Lisa McVey had written a suicide note during her evening shift at a donut shop in Tampa, Florida. Now she was pedaling her bike and riding the usual route home to her grandmother's house. There, she intended to take her grandmother's boyfriend's revolver and shoot herself in the head. Life had not been kind to the teenager. Her mother was a drug addict and alcoholic, and, after a number of years with various foster families, she forced Lisa to move in with her grandmother, who needed help. Here, her grandmother's boyfriend began abusing the 14-year-old girl by threatening her with the revolver and forcing her to have sex. Now she wanted to stop it and saw no other way out than to put an end to it all with the weapon she had been threatened with for three years.

It was half past two in the morning on November 3, 1984, when Lisa turned from Waters Avenue onto Rome Avenue. Despite her mood, she hummed to herself in the darkness. At the intersection, she passed a burgundy Dodge Magnum. She couldn't see it, but the driver noticed her in the rearview mirror. She was a pretty brunette, slim and in good shape. The man made a U-turn and passed the cyclist to study her again. He drove a little further and saw a van parked on the other side of the road. He turned into a dark parking lot of a church, jumped out of the car, crossed Rome Avenue on foot, and hid behind the van.

A few moments later, Lisa McVey saw a figure leap forward onto the road by a parked van. It took only a fraction of a second. The man grabbed her by the hair and forced her off her bicycle, which overturned a little further down the road. She screamed, but the stranger pressed a handgun to her neck.

"I'll kill you if you don't keep quiet!" he hissed in her ear.

The young woman had no doubt he meant every word. He forced her across Rome Avenue to a church parking lot, where he shoved her into a burgundy-colored car. Pointing a gun at her, he ordered her to take off her clothes.

"Do whatever you want, just don't kill me," she pleaded with the stranger.

He reached out and touched her. "Nice breasts," he grunted.

Then he unzipped his pants and forced her to perform oral sex. It was dark inside the car, but he commanded her to close her eyes. She kept them shut as the attacker turned the ignition and hit the gas. After he ejaculated, he pushed her back onto the reclined passenger seat, and while steering with one hand, he groped her with the other.

After some time, the car came to a stop. The man blindfolded Lisa and helped her put on her shirt and pants. He left her underwear, socks, and shoes behind in the car. Together, they entered through a main door and walked up two flights of stairs. Lisa could feel a handrail on both sides and, through the bottom of her blindfold, noticed that the stairs were covered in red carpet.

At the time, she didn't know his name, but it was Robert Joe Long. Since 1981, he had raped at least 50 women across Florida. Earlier that year, he escalated his crimes, and by now, Tampa police had already discovered the bodies of seven women.

Robert Joe Long holds a special place in my memory because he was the first of "my" serial killers to write to me after I had sent out a questionnaire as part of my master's thesis. I still remember vividly the moment I opened my mailbox and saw an envelope with American stamps and a postmark from a US prison. Inside the envelope were several sheets of lavender-blue paper. It quickly became clear that Robert Joe Long hadn't filled out the questionnaire. Instead, he seemed obsessed with smiley faces, whose expressions grew increasingly disturbing as the letter progressed. On one of the pages, he had even drawn the outline of an enormous hand. He repeatedly used the word "SNAP," like the sound of a twig breaking, or a neck snapping. He wanted to make a deal with me. If I wanted answers to my questions, I would have to send him photos of myself, posing in specific ways.

"After 20 years in a cage surrounded by men, I'm sure you can guess what interests me most about you, Florence," he wrote.

I couldn't help wondering whether his specific requests for the photos had something to do with the way his victims had been placed.

Robert Joe Long was born on October 14, 1953, in West Virginia. He was born with an extra X chromosome, a variation of Klinefelter's syndrome, which, among other things, leads to elevated levels of the female hormone, estrogen, in the body. This meant he developed breasts, for which he was severely bullied at school. As a teenager, he underwent surgery to remove some of the breast tissue.

The bullying fueled an intense rage against femininity, a rage that was only intensified by experiences with an extremely boundary-crossing mother. His parents divorced when Robert Joe Long was two years old. Overnight, his mother packed a suitcase and took her son to Florida. During the day, they were inseparable; in the evenings and at night, she worked as a bartender and waitress, leaving him in the care of strangers. She insisted he sleep in her bed well into his teenage years, even when she was also there. He witnessed her bringing strange men home at night and having sex with them while he was in the same room. When she got a job at a bar that required her to wear short, low-cut dresses, Robert Joe Long began to verbally abuse her with extremely vulgar language, even though she tried to explain that the clothing would earn her good tips.

His hatred and anger were initially directed at animals. He also discovered quite early how masturbation could alleviate the frustrations he carried. He performed poorly in school and soon began a series of petty crimes like theft wich escalated into burglary. Additionally, having grown into a large, robust young man, he frequently got into fights.

However, it seemed Robert Joe Long was getting his life on track when, at 19, he joined the army. There, he had the opportunity to train as a highly specialized electrician. At the same time, he married his high school sweetheart, with whom he had two children. Unfortunately, it didn't last long.

One day, while on his motorcycle, he was hit by a car, sustaining serious injuries to one leg and his head. His wife quickly noticed a change in him. His desire for sex became abnormal, and he started masturbating four to five times a day. His outbursts of anger became even more sudden and pronounced. He had to leave the army and went through a series of different jobs. After several incidents of inappropriate behavior, including toward the children's babysitter, his wife filed for divorce in 1980. By then, she had also been the victim of several violent assaults herself, including one where Robert Joe Long choked her and slammed her head into the wall, then threatened to kill her if she told the emergency room what had happened.

Less than a year later, Robert Joe Long committed what is believed to be his first rape in a series of at least 50. He became notorious under the nickname "The Classified Ad Rapist" because he found his rape victims through classified ads, similar to what would be found in local free ad papers. He targeted ads from women selling items and showed up at their addresses after convincing them he was a potential buyer. After ensuring the women were home alone, he asked to use the restroom, where he retrieved his tools: a knife and rope. After tying up his victims, he raped them, and since he was already there, he robbed them of their valuables. One particular assault led to a criminal case where he was initially convicted, but he was acquitted on appeal. Afterward, he moved from the area to Tampa, where he also kidnapped Lisa McVey.

On Mother's Day in 1984, two boys were playing in a field with cows on the outskirts of town, near a main road. They launched a homemade parachute into the sky and chased after it to catch it. At one point, the wind caught it, and before the boys could reach it, it drifted down into the grass. When the boys arrived, they were both close to throwing up. Their toy lay right next to a female body teeming with maggots.

Investigators immediately realized they were dealing with something out of the ordinary. Even though decomposition had begun, it was clear she had been subjected to an extremely violent assault. After tying and raping her, the perpetrator had strangled her with a rope. But he wasn't satisfied with just killing her; he had also "displayed" the body. Her legs were spread so wide that the distance between her feet was greater than her height, and the autopsy showed that the killer had broken her hip to make the position possible.

We've previously discussed rituals and signatures in this book, and to me, it's abundantly clear that for Robert Joe Long, this was about more than just the killing itself. When a woman is displayed in such a manner, which is completely unnecessary for the act of killing her, it strongly suggests that the perpetrator harbors immense hatred. This hatred could be directed at women in general, but the victims might also serve as surrogates for a specific person toward whom the killer's rage is truly aimed.

It is crucial to emphasize, of course, that at that time, the police had no idea there was a serial killer loose in Tampa. However, the officers had no doubt this was not an "ordinary" homicide case they were trying to solve, so they contacted the FBI at this early stage. Fortunately, they weren't entirely without clues. The most important were a tire print and a red textile fiber, which most likely came from the carpets used in cars.

Leading up to November of that year, police found no fewer than eight victims of the serial killer whose identity they still didn't know. Although there were some differences in the murders, most of the women were strangled, but Robert Joe Long had also used firearms and a knife, it was relatively easy for investigators to link the crimes. In part, there were technical clues like the tire print and the red fibers that reappeared at crime scenes again and again. In addition, they recognized the killer's behavior. The bodies were found in isolated locations where they had lain for a long time before being discovered, and many of them were displayed in the same way as at the first crime scene. In my opinion, there is nothing to suggest that the poses Robert Joe Long left the dead in were an attempt to shock those who might find the bodies.

It was about himself and his fantasy and what the women represented. The women themselves are crucial, because even though they differed in age, ethnicity, and appearance, they still had something in common. Most of them were marginalized women. Five were prostitutes, two were strippers, and most were addicted to drugs. These were women with hard lives. They moved and lived, if they even had a home, in the same low-income area of Tampa and were in some way connected to the city's sleazier nightlife, which also told investigators that the perpetrator must have frequented that part of town. One of the victims stood out: the third. She was 23 years old and worked in a factory. She lived in a trailer park with her family, but she also often walked alone when she needed to get away from the crowded mobile homes. Witnesses said she was a trusting person and that she regularly accepted rides from strangers when she had been out walking and needed to go home.

Victimology, the study of victims, is an important tool for both investigators and profilers for linking different crimes to each other. But, as with the other components of the method, victimology cannot stand alone. The victims of serial murderers or serial rapists can tell us a lot about the perpetrator. Everything the perpetrator does is about himself, and when he sees his victim, he projects something of his inner self onto them.

Looking at Robert Joe Long's killings, his victims were vulnerable women who were relatively easy targets due to the environment they inhabited. The murders didn't necessarily require extensive planning, because most of the victims were accustomed to voluntarily accompanying strange men. So, if I had been part of the investigation, I would have pointed the police toward an impulsive person who was familiar with the part of Tampa's nightlife where alcohol, drugs, stripping, and prostitution overlapped.

It was completely different in Dennis Rader's case. His victims belonged to the middle class and lived in "nice" neighborhoods, where neighbors, especially stay-at-home women, of whom there were many at the time, kept an eye on strange cars and suspicious behavior. This presented a much greater challenge for Dennis Rader, as his choice of victims carried a very high risk of discovery. He couldn't be impulsive; instead, he got a power rush from planning and stalking potential victims for days, weeks, and months. Long's and Rader's victims thus tell us about perpetrators who, although both bound and killed their victims, were nevertheless vastly different.

Regarding the women Robert Joe Long murdered, it is important to note that three of them were not sex workers or strippers. However, family and friends still described them as vulnerable, partly due to their state of mind, and partly due to their night and evening work, which meant they had to move around alone on deserted streets. This also tells me something about their killer.

In my work, as a psychologist, I have encountered both violent persons and the persons who are targets of their aggression, and it is quite clear that some persons with these tendencies have an ability to find persons who will have difficulty fighting back. It is not as if control, violence, and stalking happen overnight. These persons know how to manipulate others by taking small steps, perhaps starting with developing an intimacy that slowly escalates, so the person gradually become isolated from family and friends. If they try to resist, it can lead to violence. Even if they leave the abusive person, it's not unusual for them to find themselves in another violent relationship. In psychology, this is called repetition compulsion, repeating past experiences. This means that if someone has experienced violence, whether psychological, physical, or other trauma in childhood, there is a risk of repeating that pattern in their own life. A low sense of self-worth is also significant, leading a person to believe they isn't worth more and deserves a person who treats them that way.

The signals that we see that violent men pick up on, are also seen in cases of serial rape and murder, and this can tell us something about the perpetrators. In Robert Joe Long's case, where he managed to lure three women who didn't routinely accompany strange men, I would have considered whether the perpetrator possessed the ability to identify already vulnerable women and that the the perpetrator might be in a relationship where control and violence were part of the dynamic. Of course, there are many examples where a man is not a serial killer but still exhibits such behavior. This information could have helped the police in a situation with multiple suspects, allowing them to check for instances of domestic disturbances or convictions for spousal abuse among them.

When using victimology as a tool, remember that every detail can be important, because you actually end up with a profile similar to the one you create for a perpetrator. You look at physical characteristics to see if victims share something in their appearance, or if it wasn't a factor for the killer. If the victims are "difficult," meaning they are physically strong, it suggests you're likely looking for someone who is either capable of overpowering them or threatening them with a weapon. If the victim themselves let the perpetrator in, it can also suggest that the deceased trusted the killer, even if they weren't acquainted. This could imply that the perpetrator acted with some form of authority, perhaps posing as a police officer, a salesperson, or a utility company employee.

Non-physical details can also be crucial. Between 2005 and 2009, police in India found the bodies of 20 women in various hotel rooms. All had died of cyanide poisoning. All the women were of marriageable age but came from poor families who couldn't afford a dowry, meaning they risked becoming old maids, which is considered highly shameful in India. The victims had another, more practical thing in common: they often took buses from the same bus stations. That young, unmarried women would go to a hotel with a man they were not married to seemed mysterious, and again, it was assumed they had trusted their killer, and perhaps even had a relationship with him. This proved to be correct.

The killer, nicknamed Cyanide Mohan, hung out at bus stations and sought out young, poor, unmarried women. He claimed to have a good government job and belonged to the same caste as the victims, then began to court them. Over time, he persuaded them to elope with him to get married. He told them a dowry didn't matter to him, but he asked them to bring all their jewelry for the wedding. The evening before, he would check into a hotel with his "chosen one" and lure them into having sex, since they were getting married the next day anyway. Afterward, he asked them to take a morning-after pill to prevent pregnancy, but the pill actually contained cyanide, which killed the women very quickly. Cyanide Mohan then fled with the jewelry and continued his courtship with other victims.

Victimology is important for a profiler because victim profiles can help answer the question: "Why this victim?" Serial murderers and serial rapists usually select their victims because they are needed to fulfill a specific fantasy, or because their appearance or behavior holds symbolic meaning for the perpetrator.

A very clear example is the Japanese serial rapist Joji Obara, who was sentenced to life in prison in 2000 after raping as many as 600 women and videotaping the assaults. His method was entirely dependent on the type of victims he chose.

In Japan, there's a tradition of "hostess clubs," which are bars and nightclubs where men pay to drink and talk with the club's hostesses. These hostesses often come from Europe, North America, Australia, and New Zealand, as tall, blonde women are particularly in demand. Men can also pay the women for dohan, a type of date where they go to a restaurant or the theater. As one might gather, there can be a fluid transition to sugar dating or actual prostitution. It's also not unusual for hostess clubs to have connections to organized crime. In the past, it was certainly not uncommon for foreign women to be residing illegally in Japan to earn money. They therefore always tried to avoid coming under the scrutiny of authorities. For Joji Obara, a wealthy playboy of Korean descent, tall, blonde women were irresistible, even though he was ashamed of his short stature and ethnicity and had even undergone surgery to make his eyes appear less Asian. He felt the world owed him what he wanted, and what he wanted, he took. In a diary, he had even written that he was entitled to "conquer" 500 women before turning 50.

For a long time, the police showed little interest in stories of missing women until the dismembered body of a young British woman was found under an old bathtub in a cave. Only then did the police finally begin to take the cases seriously. Several of the victims whom Joji Obara had drugged with Rohypnol in a drink after taking them home after a dohan were, naturally, terrified afterward and dared not report the assaults to the police. Without the full picture, especially of the environment in which the crimes took place, it was initially difficult for the police to identify the underlying pattern. And it also proved impossible to convict Obara for the murder of the British woman, even though he was charged with it.

The investigation involving victims' appearance, background, and behavior provides a clue as to why a victim was chosen, and what connection, often only in the serial offender's fantasy, exists between the victim and the perpetrator. This contributes to the creation of a profile of the person investigators are searching for. Robert Joe Long was probably unaware of it, but victimology would come to play a decisive role in enabling the police to stop him.

*

Lisa McVey felt the man push her into the apartment's bathroom. He pulled down her pants and attempted to rape her anally, but stopped when she winced. Instead, he dragged her into the bedroom, where he ordered her to lie on the floor. There, he raped her vaginally. Afterward, he again took her back to the bathroom, where he put her in the bath and gently washed her hair and body. Then he found a brush and a hairdryer and styled her hair.

"You have truly beautiful hair," he said, pushing her into the bedroom where they lay on his waterbed.

The room was completely dark, so he loosened her blindfold but loosely tied her ankles with a piece of fabric. The bed rippled as he lay down beside her, and she flinched when she felt something cold against her skin. He simply wanted to remind her that his revolver was still within reach. Later, he had her massage his lower back and one arm, explaining that he had a lot of heavy lifting at work. He asked what she felt like doing, and she echoed his words, hoping he would believe she was enjoying being with him. Perhaps it worked. At least she noticed that he repeatedly called her "babe," as if they were lovers. However, this didn't stop him from assaulting her again and again.

"Thank you," he said when he managed to penetrate her anally.

His breathing became heavy, but Lisa didn't dare trust that he was asleep, so she lay still beside him. Meanwhile, she tried to mentally imprint every detail she could remember since he had pulled her off her bicycle. When dawn came, he blindfolded her again.

"I don't know why I'm doing this, you're such a sweet girl," he mumbled, adding, "Maybe it's revenge. I just broke up with my girlfriend and I'm so sick of women walking all over me."

His mood swung between two extremes. As gentle as he could be, like when he fixed her hair, he could suddenly become equally aggressive. Despite this, Lisa tried to establish a connection with him, telling him about her sick father, whom she helped care for.

When evening came, he dressed her in his own shorts and a black sweater. This time, he didn't just blindfold her, but also bound and gagged her before leading her into the living room. The television was on, and she could hear an episode of the action series *Airwolf*, her favorite, until it was interrupted by breaking news: the announcer reported a kidnapping. Hers. The man quickly turned it off and instead asked if she was hungry. She heard him making sandwiches in the kitchen, and soon after, he brought her a plate and a soda. As she ate, she began to cry.

"What's wrong?" he asked.

"Nothing," she sniffled.

"Bullshit!" he said.

When he heard that she was upset about being tied, he loosened the bindings and led her back into the darkness of the bedroom.

"I wish we could have met another way," he said, licking her ear, nipping her neck, and kissing her.

But he didn't rape her again. "Just rest," he said.

At 2:30 in the morning, the alarm clock rang. While she kept her eyes closed, he dressed her. Her shirt was dirty, he said, and gave her the black sweater she had worn earlier instead.

"It's time for you to get out of here," he added, supporting her as they left the apartment, went down the stairs, and out to the car. As she got into the passenger seat, she hit her head on the doorframe.

"Sorry, babe," she heard him say.

He got into the driver's seat, kissed her, and blindfolded her again before starting the engine.

"Can I trust you not to run away?" he asked, explaining that he needed to withdraw money before they could buy gas for the car.

They drove for five or ten minutes before he parked and got out. Lisa thought about the revolver and remained seated, hearing an ATM dispensing money. Then they drove to a gas station just around the corner. As they continued, she spoke. About 10 minutes passed until she could sense they were driving onto the highway, and the man sped up. She just managed to glimpse two motels as the blindfold didn't cover her entire field of vision, and she also spotted the word "Magnum" on the car's dashboard. As she considered her options for escape, she could sense the man thinking frantically, and he asked her what she planned to say about him when she got home.

"Just say you were kidnapped by an armed man who borrowed you for a few hours," he said.

He turned the engine off and pulled into a parking lot on Rome Avenue, where she had cycled about 26 hours earlier. He didn't want to let her go; he wanted to keep her, he mumbled. He gave her a hug and a kiss and wished her father a swift recovery. Then, he told her to get out and stand with her blindfold on for a few minutes. He gathered her belongings and gave them to her before driving off.

"Take care!" was his farewell.

For me, Lisa's story is one of the most heartbreaking, terrifying, and sad. Professionally, it's also fascinating, as one is naturally left with the question: "Why did she survive her encounter with Robert Joe Long?"

As we've discussed, many serial killers hunt a specific type of victim. Robert Joe Long, as mentioned, primarily targeted women connected to strip clubs or the prostitution scene. This could partly be due to the fact that these women were easier to access, but often, a hatred of women can also be discerned when a serial killer specifically targets sex workers. There's no doubt that his complicated relationship with a boundary-crossing mother played a role. Strangling his victims and then displaying them reveals to me, at least, a hatred that might appear general on the surface but also seems very personal, even though he didn't know his victims beforehand.

Looking at the case through victimological lenses, Lisa already stood out by not belonging to the same environment as the other victims. She was also the youngest at just 17 years old. And then something happened in the encounter between the two. As she talked about herself, especially the story of her sick father, Robert Joe Long formed a pseudo-attachment with Lisa. This is a false connection that is solely about the perpetrator himself, and it can be broken in a split second if the victim doesn't do what the perpetrator expects, or if the victim triggers something in him. The chilling part is that only the perpetrator knows what can create pseudo-attachment between him and the victim; it's not something the victim can figure out.

He told her, among other things, that they might have dated if they had met in another way, and it is as if he imagined they were actually a couple. Lisa almost immediately chose to agree with him. She quickly sensed the pseudo-attachment and tried to give Robert Joe Long the impression that she, too, could see him as a boyfriend if circumstances had been different. The reason she was able to do this at all was because she was already a victim of sexual abuse, and she herself has stated that it was the coping strategies she was accustomed to that allowed her to remain calm despite the repeated rapes in the apartment.

It's important to mention that the tenderness and care shown by the perpetrator is not perceived that way by the victim. On the contrary, it can be yet another boundary-crossing behavior that leaves the victim deeply confused. This is also seen in other forms of abuse, such as when a pedophile does a lot of good for their victim to control and reassure them. It can also happen in intimate partner violence. An abusive partner doesn't commit abuse constantly, but the intermittent care they show helps make it easier to control their spouse or partner. In none of these examples does the care stem from a deep-seated desire to do good. Throughout, the perpetrator is engaged in committing their crime, and the chance of "success" increases because the false care helps to confuse and calm the victim, perhaps even makes the victim feel sympathy for the perpetrator. I have spoken with victims who were precisely confused and sympathized with their perpetrators. This can result in that too much time passes before it was possible to stop the abuse and provide vital help to the victims.

Lisa McVey is not the only one who has escaped with her life after a close encounter with a serial killer. On the evening of September 12, 1990, Robyn Oldenburg was packing an overnight bag when there was a loud knock on one of her windows. She flinched. Although she tried to convince herself she was being paranoid, she couldn't get the newspaper headlines out of her head. Over the summer, a serial killer, The East Side Killer, as the media had dubbed him, had been active in the Bellevue district of Seattle, Washington, in the northwestern USA.

When I look at the case today, three things particularly stand out: The killer was unusually violent. The first victim was not only strangled but also beaten and kicked so hard that her liver was destroyed. Victim number two had been struck in the head numerous times, and the third victim had been stabbed more than 200 times with a knife. The crimes were, to a great extent, characterized by overkill, which indicated a motive rooted in revenge or rage, though not necessarily directed at those specific women.

Similar to Robert Joe Long, this killer also liked to display his victims. The first woman was dumped in a dumpster near a burger joint, lying with her legs crossed and a pinecone in her hands. The perpetrator had raped her after she died. In the second case, the woman was murdered in her home while her 13-year-old daughter slept. She lay on her bed wearing only red high-heeled shoes. The killer had inserted a rifle into the woman's vagina, and she was positioned so that anyone entering the bedroom would see it first. The third victim was also murdered at home. She lay with folded hands, clutching a book titled *The Joy of Sex*, and had a dildo stuffed down her throat.

This isn't just horrific; to me, it's also clear that the perpetrator had an extreme need to communicate something through the crime scene. Serial killers often want to shock those who find the victims or mock the police by showing what they're capable of without being caught. But in this case, there was more to it. The crime scenes were so extreme and personal that my hypothesis would be that the victims were stand-ins for one or more women in the killer's life. He also had a compulsion to tell the world that these women were "whores," which he emphasized by inserting objects into them, even if they were not sex workers.

Here was a serial killer who killed in different ways, and while the poses were a crucial part of his fantasy, they weren't entirely identical. However, investigators were able to strengthen the link between the crimes by examining the victimology. The women were roughly the same age and generally attractive. All three enjoyed going out, and it turned out they often frequented the same bars and nightclubs. In one instance, the victim had left her bag at one of the nightclubs, and her car was in the parking lot outside. This meant that the police could advantageously focus on the places where the victims' paths had crossed, as it was highly probable that they had met their killer there.

This also suggested that the perpetrator wasn't the type to make women uneasy. On the contrary, he was likely charming enough to leave a bar or nightclub with a woman without needing to use force. Friends and acquaintances also reported that the three victims enjoyed flirting with men, only to reject them when the men thought things would go further. Of course, this should in no way be interpreted as the victims bearing the slightest blame for their fate. As a profiler, one must also investigate the victims' behavior, especially in serial murder cases where rejection can play a very significant role.

Robyn Oldenburg had been closely following the case in the newspapers and on TV. She herself enjoyed going out and knew several of the places the three women frequented. So, when she heard noise at the window again, she didn't hesitate for long before calling 911. Moments later, police arrived and confirmed that someone had been trying to break into Robyn Oldenburg's home. Not far from there, an officer stopped a car to ask the driver if he had seen anything in the area. To the officer's great surprise, he knew the man behind the wheel. It was 32-year-old George Russell, whom the officer knew from a bar where he had a side job as a bouncer. George Russell said that he hadn't noticed anything, but when a background check revealed he was wanted in connection with another case for impersonating a police officer, he was arrested.

George Russell was a handsome, athletic Black man whose parents divorced six months after he was born in 1958. His mother had no desire to have a child, and after some time, she left her son, leaving a note for the father, who reluctantly took care of him. However, it wasn´t long before George Russell had to move between different family members. When he was six years old, his mother returned to him. She had married a wealthy dentist, but both she and the dentist largely left the boy to take care of himself, focusing on the child they had together. In his teenage years, George Russell was again abandoned when his mother ran off again, and from then on, his grades in school began to decline until he dropped out. He joined a group of petty criminals and soon led a long series of burglaries and other forms of property crime.

Soon, his stepfather married a White woman who made no secret of her dislike for the teenage boy, demanding that the stepfather choose between her and his stepson. From then on, George Russell had no permanent home, but because he was very charming on the surface, he always managed to find shelter with friends and acquaintances. His charm even worked on law enforcement, who, in several cases, let him go after he had committed burglaries.

When he started going out, he quickly realized he had an easy rapport with the opposite sex, even though he apparently felt disgusted by some of them. His friends reported that he often spoke of the women he met in nightlife as "promiscuous whores," even though none of them were prostitutes. On the contrary, Bellevue was a predominantly White, affluent neighborhood with well-educated and career-minded residents.

It turned out that George Russell had frequented the same places as the murdered women. In several instances, witnesses stated that he had acted threateningly toward women who rejected him, including the three deceased victims. Tests also showed that his DNA matched the DNA traces technicians had found on and around the bodies, and in 1991, he received a life sentence.

Unfortunately, it's often the case that victims, like those in the "Eastside Killer" or "Charming Serial Killer" case, receive greater attention because they lived a so-called "normal life," were well-educated, and had careers. Statistically, this type of victim is rarely targeted by serial killers, who largely go after the far more vulnerable, such as prostitutes, homeless individuals, runaway youth, migrants, hitchhikers, and others who won't be missed as quickly as others. For this reason, victimology can also be controversy and has, over time, been accused of victim blaming, where blame for a crime is placed on the victims. And when there are also, especially in the past, but still to some extent today, examples of media and investigators responding faster when victims are considered "more important" than sex workers and strippers, I can certainly understand why such criticism arises. However, as I hope I've conveyed, victimology is another important tool for profilers. It is not about assigning blame but about figuring out why a person ended up becoming a victim, because the reason often reveals a lot about the perpetrator. The fact is, the risk of becoming a victim is greater in some environments than others, and therefore, it's crucial to understand the victims' lives if you want to search for their killers in the right place. This can be very sensitive when interviewing relatives who have to share information about prostitution, burglaries, gambling, and other unpleasant details that might be central to the investigators. It can be uncomfortable for the bereaved to talk about, and it's not unusual for them to be so traumatized by the event that they cannot bring themselves to say negative things about their loved ones. Understandably, they develop a strong need to only talk about the good aspects, which is a completely natural reaction. It's important for investigators to be aware of this and therefore also seek information elsewhere.

I have also heard about this problem from police officers in Denmark, especially in rape cases where the victim and perpetrator didn't know each other. Some of the investigators' questions may seem provocative when they concern clothing or alcohol habits, but in the case of a serial offender, every detail can prove significant for solving the crime. It is then extremely important that investigators are transparent and explain why they are asking certain questions, so the victim understands that it is not about them being blamed.

It's also important to state that victimology by no means always provides clear answers. As mentioned, sex workers are among the groups at greatest risk when a serial killer is at large, and there doesn't need to be more to the choice of victims than their easy accessibility. If serial killers could choose freely, so to speak, we would likely see victims from many other societal groups, but it's simply much more difficult and riskier to target a CEO's wife than a prostitute. It's also not unusual for a profiler to only see the deeper connection between the victims once the killer is caught, because the selection only makes sense to him—and only to the rest of us once we hear the story of his childhood and upbringing.

I'm quite sure Lisa McVey also thought a lot about what made Robert Joe Long choose her, because as an adult, she joined the police force, where today she works specifically on preventing and solving sexual offenses against women. In the parking lot in Tampa, she fell to her knees, crying and shaking for a long time, before managing to get back on her feet and walk home. From there, she called the police. She then told investigators her story, trying to remember every single detail she had imprinted on her mind. She described the red carpet, the burgundy car and the word "Magnum," the ATM, and the motels by the highway. She described the perpetrator's voice and smell, and that she had felt his mustache when he kissed her.

The police compiled a list of every resident in the county who owned a Dodge Magnum. When they compared that with a list of everyone who had withdrawn money from an ATM around 3 AM on November 4th, only one name appeared on both lists: Robert Joe Long. When he was arrested, he confessed to the kidnapping and rape of Lisa McVey but denied committing any murders. However, investigators confronted him with their evidence, especially the red fibers and tire tracks, and then the serial killer gave up. He made a deal with the prosecution, pleading guilty to the murders of the eight women whose bodies the police had found, as well as a long list of rapes. This allowed him to avoid the death penalty.

The police had not yet found the bodies of his last two victims, even though they knew Robert Joe Long was the perpetrator. Therefore, he had to go through another trial, and this time the prosecutor demanded the death penalty for one of the murders. The jury members agreed, and after 34 years on death row, he was executed by lethal injection on May 23, 2019.

CHAPTER 6: THE MADONNA-WHORE COMPLEX: THE MAP WITH THE 37 X's

In a sun-drenched August of 1982, two Anchorage, Alaska, police officers were enjoying their day off. They had sailed from the city into the vast, beautiful landscape for which the largest American state is so famous. They anchored near a sandbar at the bottom of a canyon, carved by glaciers thousands of years ago. Knik River was a popular spot for the city's many hunters, accessible only by boat or plane, despite being just 30-40 kilometers from the city.

The two colleagues grabbed their hunting rifles and ventured into the wilderness, hoping to bag a moose, but they had no luck. Late in the day, they began walking back to their boat. On a sandbar, something caught their attention: a boot sticking out of the sand. While not entirely unusual, the two experienced officers decided to investigate further. They were right to do so. In the sand, they found human bones and remnants of clothing. They immediately stepped back, noted as many details as possible, and hastily made their way out of the canyon to raise the alarm.

Soon, the sandbar was swarmed with investigators, forensic technicians, and photographers. After the body was removed, they began sifting the sand. Their efforts paid off: a single .223 caliber shell casing from a powerful rifle was found. In Anchorage, the medical examiner began the autopsy. The cause of death was three gunshot wounds. The discovery of some fabric strips indicated that the young woman might have been blindfolded when she was shot. The body had been in the sand for about a year, so it took two weeks to identify the remains. It was 23-year-old Sherry Morrow, last seen at the Cherry Bar, where she worked as a stripper.

About a year later, a crew was constructing a new road near the site where Sherry Morrow had been found. Suddenly, loud shouts erupted, and the work with the heavy machinery stopped. In front of an excavator lay a skull and several other bones, and the road workers immediately contacted the police. Here, too, a .223 caliber shell casing turned up. The deceased was a 31-year-old woman named Paula Goulding, who had come to Alaska to find work as a secretary but failed to secure an office position. Instead, she became a topless dancer at one of the city's bars.

It wasn't unusual for the bodies of missing persons to turn up in the wilderness. Hunters and hikers, especially those from out of town who lacked the locals' familiarity with the wilds, were often caught off guard by the weather, got lost, or were injured and died before anyone could help them. But that wasn't the story the two bodies of Sherry Morrow and Paula Goulding told. Strippers and secretaries didn't exactly fit the wilderness narrative.

This was also true for Eklutna-Annie, the body of another young woman found near Eklutna Road two years prior. Investigators gave her this name because they hadn't been able to identify her. However, it was determined she had been stabbed to death, likely with a large hunting knife. Around the same time, the body of 24-year-old Joanna Messina surfaced in a gravel pit near Seward, a couple of hours' drive south of Anchorage. She had come all the way from New York, attempting to start fresh, but met a grim fate near the campsite where she had settled.

Sherry Morrow and Paula Goulding, and perhaps Eklutna-Annie and, in a way, Joanna Messina, had come to Alaska to make money, not to hunt moose and bears. Many others did the same in the 1970s and 1980s, as Alaska was in the midst of an oil boom that caused Anchorage to grow at record speed, reminiscent of past gold rushes. Naturally, most newcomers were men who worked hard during the day and enjoyed spending their savings in the city's nightlife. Countless bars, strip clubs, and brothels sprang up, and drug dealing became a more common phenomenon. Strippers and sex workers followed soon, who eagerly helped lighten the workers' wallets. As was often the case in that industry, there was a high turnover. Women often disappeared and reappeared at the other end of the country, but some were never heard of again.

Investigators were faced with the bodies of four young women. Three were found in the wilderness near Anchorage, while the fourth was discovered several hours' drive south. At least two of the women had been strippers, while Joanna Messina stood out. According to witnesses, she had left her husband and children in New York, along with her loyal German Shepherd, to "find herself." She ended up in Alaska, where she first rented a space in a building owned by a local veterinarian, with whom she also had a relationship. When he kicked her out, she ended up at a nearby campsite before disappearing. Her dog was never found.

Even though all the bodies were dumped in nature, and therefore the crime scenes themselves weren't accessible, a profiler can still glean stories from the findings. Several of these locations were only accessible by foot, boat, or plane, indicating that the perpetrator not only had to be familiar with the area but also was accustomed to navigating the wilderness and had access to either a boat or a plane. The victims had been shot with projectiles from powerful hunting rifles, which also suggests that they were dealing with someone with more than a casual interest in hunting; otherwise, he could just as easily have used a revolver or pistol, which would have been much easier to handle.

I would also have assessed that the perpetrator must have been trustworthy, or not the type whom the women would have feared. Three of the victims had frequented the seedy side of Anchorage's nightlife, where strip clubs were often a stone's throw from outright prostitution, and it might not have been unusual for them to accompany a strange man. But there could also have been something about the perpetrator that made them feel safe. Perhaps he was small in stature, or perhaps he was a humble or shy type. When investigators interviewed Sherry Morrow's friends, they said she had dreams of becoming a model and was meeting a photographer when she disappeared. He could have been the killer, luring her by posing as a photographer, or perhaps he was genuinely skilled at photography.

The victims' connection to nightlife could also tell me something about the motive. We've discussed several times that strippers and prostitutes can be easier targets than young students and career women, but for many serial killers, there's more to it. A significant number of them harbor a fierce hatred toward women, and here we're not just talking about ordinary male chauvinists who believe women belong in the kitchen. This is a deep-seated rage against the female sex, often formed early in life and frequently traceable to a problematic relationship between mother and son.

With serial killers, one often sees what's called the Madonna-Whore complex, where some women are put on a pedestal as flawless goddesses, while others belong in the dirt of the gutter. It can be very difficult to have a problematic relationship with a mother who *should* be a goddess but doesn't act like one. Just think of Robert Joe Long, who experienced his mother's prostitution firsthand, or Edmund Kemper, whose mother locked him in the basement because she was sure he would abuse his sister. We've also met Charles Albright, who was first dressed in girls' clothing and later shadowed by his mother when he was on dates. Frankly, none of these three had a healthy relationship with their mothers.

For boys who grew up this way, difficulties with the opposite sex often continue into adolescence, where they try to repair the damaged relationship with their mothers when they meet girls their own age. This is, of course, not a good starting point for a relationship, and they therefore often experience rejection, which only confirms that the hatred they feel is justified. It gets even worse if their upbringing has made them seem strange in the eyes of others, leading to them being ostracized or even bullied at school. The anger and desire for revenge can grow stronger and stronger, and who is easier to direct that rage toward than sex workers? They, for troubled men, are the ultimate proof that women are merely objects to be used and are also easy to access.

I'm often asked why, for example, Robert Joe Long or Charles Albright didn't just kill their mothers, or murder some of the girls who had rejected them in school or high school, which might seem like the most logical course of action. However, that's not how a serial killer's mind typically works. While not unheard of, few actually take their mothers' lives due to the deep emotional attachment. The hatred for women often originates in their relationship with their mothers. This connection is rarely present between serial killers and their victims, who instead serve as surrogates. Edmund Kemper is one serial killer who actually did end up murdering his mother, but only after he had already killed six young women.

The phenomenon of displacing rage onto others who are not the true object of that anger was shockingly evident in Russia, Ukraine, and Uzbekistan over four bloody months from January to April 2015. On March 14, 2015, 42-year-old Bakhtijor Matjakubov was walking near the Polytechnic Institute metro station in Kyiv, the Ukrainian capital. There, he spotted a middle-aged woman selling flowers from a stall on the sidewalk. He paced back and forth until pedestrian traffic thinned, then entered the stall and stabbed the flower seller multiple times. The woman screamed loudly and begged for mercy, which seemingly made Bakhtijor Matjakubov reconsider his intention. Instead of killing her, he stole some jewelry from her bag and fled. The flower seller was extraordinarily lucky, as by that point, her assailant had at least six lives on his conscience.

On New Year's Day, Bakhtijor Matjakubov had been driving aimlessly around Moscow when, near one of the city's metro stations, he saw a 36-year-old woman who appeared to be looking for a ride. He stopped, and the woman got into the passenger seat. He asked if she was married and had children, and she lied, saying she was married with two children. This answer caused rage to boil in Bakhtijor Matjakubov's veins, as he found it morally reprehensible for a married woman to get into a stranger's car, and this sealed her fate. He drove out of the city to a desolate area, where he stabbed the woman to death, threw her body in a ditch, and covered it with a coat. He later remarked to an acquaintance that he was glad there was now "one less whore in Moscow." That night, he continued to the nearest airport and flew to Tashkent, the Uzbek capital. The very next day, he entered a pharmacy, where he raped a woman, who was strangled. Six days later, an employee at a tailor shop was targeted, after which he traveled to Samarkand and killed another woman. This time, he ended up decapitating the victim.

Bakhtijor Matjakubov is an interesting case because he stated that he had hated women since he was very young. His first murders occurred at very short intervals, and the crimes quickly escalated, so the killings of the shop employees were not only far riskier than the first murders but also more sadistic and brutal. He then entered a cooling-off period in February, during which he reportedly did not murder anyone. The urge returned in March when he took a bus to Kyiv. In a small wooded area near a metro station, he spotted a 47-year-old woman walking her dog and followed her. He asked her if the dog bit, and when the woman said no, he stabbed her twice in the chest. After she died, he dragged the body into a thicket, where he had sexual intercourse with it, then ripped out her earrings and fled. Just two days later, in a park, he stabbed a 77-year-old woman 20 times and then sexually desecrated the body, again, an example of extreme rage against female victims, as neither the numerous stab wounds nor the necrophilia were necessary if the sole aim was to kill.

After the March 14th assault on the flower seller, whom Bakhtijor Matjakubov allowed to live, the police in Ukraine realized they were hunting a serial offender. With a description and a composite sketch, the killer felt the heat. He returned to Moscow, where the murders continued, targeting women whose appearance or behavior, in his eyes, made them "whores." His last murder took place on April 9, 2015, when he killed a 26-year-old sales assistant in a sex shop because he believed it was immoral for a woman to work in such a business. By then, the police in the Russian capital were on his trail, and he fled back to Kyiv, where he planned to kill a woman who had invited him on a date. He didn't get the chance, however, as he was arrested on April 15, 2015. He didn't hide the fact that he would have continued killing had he not been stopped by the police, who also delved into the killer's past. He was born in 1973 into a family marked by violence. He quickly became very aggressive and temperamental. Family members recounted how, even as a child, he subjected his siblings to violence, and that over time, he also attacked his parents, with classmates at school often becoming victims, too. By his late teens, the violence escalated to rape, and he received several convictions over the next decades for both rape and a series of robberies.

In November 2014, he met a woman he moved in with, but he discovered she was simultaneously texting another man. Bakhtijor Matjakubov described how he felt "the ground open up beneath his feet" when he found out and felt a rage worse than ever before. He followed the woman to a train station where she was supposed to meet the other man, planning to kill them both, but he just couldn't bring himself to do it when it came down to it. He explained that for as long as he could remember, he had felt a deep hatred for women, and that it had worsened with age until he could no longer control it.

Bakhtijor Matjakubov's was caught because of the flower seller in Kyiv surviving and her encounter with him and being able to describe him to the police. Something similar also happened in the Alaska case.

On June 13, 1983, a truck driver in Anchorage got quite a shock when a young woman sprinted in front of his vehicle on Sixth Avenue, frantically waving him down. He slammed on the brakes, stopping with a jolt, and then realized the woman outside was handcuffed. He had no doubt what to do that she was in a panic, and he quickly opened the door and let her in. She told him to drive to a nearby motel, where she sprang out of the cab and disappeared into a room before the driver even had a chance to ask her what she'd been through. However, he was concerned and called the police, who soon tracked down the woman. She had moved to a room at another one of the city's cheap motels, where she was still struggling to free herself from the handcuffs. The woman was 17-year-old Cindy Paulson, who worked the streets of Anchorage. She explained that a man had offered her $200 for oral sex, but as soon as she got into the car, he threatened her with a revolver to come home with him. While he subjected her to torture, including being hung by her arms from a hook in the ceiling and raped her multiple times, she noticed countless hunting trophies hanging on the walls. Afterward, the man drove them to Merrill Field Airport, where he parked next to a small blue and white plane. Her assailant told her he had a cabin in the wilderness where he often took girls to "have fun." As the man prepared the plane, Cindy Paulson saw her chance to escape at the exact moment the truck driver passed by and could pick her up. The last thing she heard was the man yelling after her: "Stop, you bitch! Stop, or I'll kill you!"

Cindy Paulson was so visibly traumatized that the officers in the motel room had no doubt she had endured something horrific. When they took her to the airport, she unhesitatingly pointed out the plane, giving investigators a crucial lead. It became even easier when a security guard at the airport came forward, having noted the license plate number of the car Cindy Paulson had described.

Soon, a couple of officers were waiting in a car for Robert Hansen, a 44-year-old son of Danish immigrants from Iowa, who had arrived in Alaska in 1967. Like his father, he was a baker and had opened his own business in Anchorage, where many of the city's police officers enjoyed buying their pastries. He was known as a somewhat shy man who supported the community and kept to himself, mostly spending time with his wife and children when he wasn't out hunting. He was, however, quite skilled at hunting and had won numerous awards for the animals he had shot.

The baker stammered that he had no idea what the officers were talking about. He claimed he had been with a friend until the early hours and then driven to the airport because he needed to repair a plane seat for one of his friends. He immediately gave investigators permission to search his house and car, while some colleagues contacted Robert Hansen's friend, who confirmed they had been together at the critical time. Thus, the police couldn't do anything more, even though the house and car perfectly matched Cindy Paulson's descriptions.

The assault case was set aside, but a single detective named Greg Baker couldn't get it out of his head. Most others doubted the young sex worker's story, especially since Robert Hansen's alibi seemed to hold up. It was clear she had been in his home, but perhaps she just had a grudge against him. Despite his chief's orders, Greg Baker went to the state police, who were investigating the cases of the female bodies found in the wilderness, which now included more victims. He told them Cindy Paulson's story, and together they looked closer at Robert Hansen's past. It turned out the baker wasn't just the somewhat anonymous family man with a love for the outdoors he portrayed himself to be. His criminal record showed a string of thefts, a kidnapping, and the rape of a prostitute, in addition to the theft of a chainsaw from a hardware store. However, he had successfully convinced judges that he was an ordinary man who had simply gone astray, either avoiding punishment or being released early from prison due to good behavior. The detective and his state police colleagues had no doubt: Robert Hansen was the serial killer they were hunting, they just had no evidence.

In the Anchorage case, a significant challenge for investigators was that the bodies they found had been buried for a long time. This severely limited their ability to determine what happened leading up to the murders. However, Cindy Paulson was able to shed light on this. She told them about the torture she endured and how he seemed to view her as an object he could use as he pleased. The police also had an idea of what Robert Hansen had in mind when he drove to the airport with his captive, it was highly likely the avid hunter was after more than just bears and moose when he landed out in the wilderness. There was no direct evidence, but that was certainly what the officers suspected. In my view, it would also make sense for the women to be reduced to prey by a perpetrator who apparently harbored such intense rage against women.

A term often discussed when it comes to men's hatred of women is femicide. Femicide refers to the killing of women *because they are women*. It's a controversial concept, especially in recent years, becoming a significant part of the broader gender debate. This is partly because there isn't a widely accepted definition. Consequently, some debaters view every killing of a woman as femicide, regardless of the motive for the murder, thus framing the crime as part of a systematic oppression of women in a patriarchal society. For instance, I've heard researchers describe witch burnings in olden times as femicide, despite the fact that many of those accused of witchcraft and executed were actually men. There are also many who believe it's femicide if a husband kills his wife because he discovers she has a lover, or because he wants to collect her life insurance.

I don't see it that way. Femicide is a specific type of woman-killing, but not all killings of women are femicide. I agree with the definition that states femicide is a murder committed by a man or men against one or more women precisely because they are women. It's not about the individual woman; rather, it is their gender that ignites the killer's rage.

As a profiler, I might suspect femicide, or at least that misogyny played a role at crime scenes. This is true, for example, if the victims have been subjected to torture or humiliating treatment before or after death. We've already encountered the latter in cases where killers obscenely displayed bodies. The way the perpetrator kills can also point toward femicide. While a single gunshot to the head wouldn't immediately make me think in that direction, strangulation, especially with bare hands, would certainly make me consider it. If the perpetrator has raped or mutilated the body, and here I'm particularly referring to breasts and genitals, it would strengthen my suspicion. However, it's important to emphasize that misogyny doesn't have to be the only motive, and signs of femicide don't necessarily mean it's actually the case. In some instances, a sadistic killer's actions might be a result of circumstances unrelated to a more general hatred of women, which is why it's important that nothing in a profile is considered set in stone. To find some explanation for such intense hatred toward women, we must examine both the perpetrators' upbringing and the historical relationship between men and women. We don't have to go far back in time before women in our part of the world were considered second-class citizens or men's property, and in certain parts of the world, this is still the case. Men could more or less do as they pleased, while there were very narrow limits on what women could do.

From a psychological perspective, this type of serial offender often comes from families where the mother has been highly sexually boundary-crossing. This can involve her having many different men at home and engaging in sex with them without regard for the children. In some cases, there might also be incest. In many cases, these are mothers who behave coldly toward their children, giving them the impression that they are in the way and that she regrets having them. These are children who don't experience love and affirmation and often not even the opposite, because their mother is completely indifferent to them, and they also often experience their father being entirely subservient to her.

What children learn in childhood, they carry with them as they grow up. If your parents have a healthy and loving relationship characterized by respect, that's usually what you take with you, because life is fundamentally an apprenticeship. If the opposite is true, problems can arise. I often experience this with the children, adolescents, and adults I work with. If one doesn't process an unpleasant upbringing, history can repeats itself, and it's often easier to see from the outside. It's rare that people who grew up in such families can see it themselves, and without help, there's a high risk that they will repeat the past with their own children.

As mentioned, hatred of women can be an aspect of serial rapes and murders. This was particularly evident in a brutal case from the late 1990s.

In October 1997, a passerby made a horrifying discovery in Humboldt County, northern California. In an irrigation canal lay the body of a young woman, or rather, a female torso. Arms, legs, and head had been sawed off, and someone had cut off the victim's breasts. Forensic examiners found no fewer than 27 stab wounds all over the torso and buttocks, a clear expression of the perpetrator's rage. A long gash from the top of the chest to the bottom of the abdomen, along with the dismemberment, showed that the killer had absolutely no regard for the victim, who had been treated more or less like an animal in a slaughterhouse. While dismemberment doesn't necessarily mean anything more than an attempt to mask the victim's identity, in this case, it would rarely be necessary to remove the breasts. This type of mutilation, in my opinion, can point to other, even more fundamental and psychological motives, which can ultimately lead to more killings.

About a year later, two security guards were patrolling a stretch of the California Aqueduct, a system of canals and pipelines that carries water from the Sierra Nevada mountains to the southern part of the state. Near a pump house, one of them spotted something bobbing on the water's surface. To the guards' shock, it was the body of a woman. They immediately alerted the police, who pulled the body from the water. As the body lay on the canal bank, officers immediately saw that one of the woman's breasts was missing. The autopsy report was no less macabre. The medical examiner confirmed that the woman had been tied up, tortured, and raped. She had been hit on the head with a blunt object, though this was not the cause of death; she had been strangled, though the medical examiner concluded from marks on her neck that the perpetrator had attempted it multiple times before succeeding.

It wasn't difficult to link the two crimes due to the mutilation of the breasts; it was also possible that the same perpetrator had murdered two other women. This link wasn't about mutilation, as in those two other cases, the breasts hadn't been removed, however, they too were found in irrigation canals. And there was yet another link to at least the woman found near the pump house. While the first victim couldn't be identified, investigators quickly discovered that victim number two was a 29-year-old prostitute who often found her clients at a nearby rest stop, where witnesses had seen her get into a large, black truck. Witnesses told a similar story about two other victims, a 26-year-old and a 25-year-old, whose bodies were found in June and September 1998. They also showed signs of torture, rape, and several attempts at strangulation. There was little doubt that the police were hunting a serial killer

Although investigators didn't have many leads, the case was solved relatively quickly in a way that left many stunned.

On November 3, 1998, just over a week after the body was found near the pumping station, 36-year-old long-haul truck driver Wayne Adam Ford walked into the police station in Eureka, Humboldt County, with his brother, Rod. Weeping, he told the officers that he had murdered four women "I've hurt others, that's why you need to take care of me," he whimpered, then pulled a sealed plastic bag from his inner pocket. Inside was a bloody breast.

Wayne Adam Ford was born in 1961 in California into what appeared to be a normal nuclear family with a mother, father, and two children. However, it seems to have been an emotionally crippled family. His father was rarely home, and when he was, the boys could expect physical and psychological violence, which made them constantly fear him. His mother was described as cold and absent, and in 1971, she left the family to travel the world for the next six years, leaving the boys with their father.

Wayne Adam Ford dropped out of high school and joined the military, where he spent six years. During that time, he married and for the first time showed a dark side of himself, as he forced his wife into S&M play and bondage and exhibited an extraordinary fascination with breasts. This quickly became too much for her, and the marriage soon ended. Wayne Adam Ford was furious and began searching for his ex-wife, but when he couldn't find her, he took his anger out on a young sex worker, whom he, among other things, raped and bit on the breasts. However, the case never went to court.

The following year, he was arrested for violating animal welfare laws, which led to a brief prison sentence. When he was released, he married again, this time to a girl who was just 19. It was a turbulent marriage marked by violence and control. Nevertheless, the couple had a child, which only worsened the conflicts, as the relationship ended in divorce, and the boy's mother did everything she could to prevent Wayne Adam Ford from seeing his son. It was shortly thereafter that he murdered the first of the four women, a hitchhiker he spotted from his large, black truck.

When the case went to trial, the defense naturally brought up the killer's past as part of the explanation for why he murdered the four women. The lawyer also highlighted that back in 1984, while in the military, the accused was involved in a serious traffic accident that resulted in a severe head injury. He had been in a coma for several days, and afterward, people around him noticed a change in his personality.

The jury did not accept the defense's explanations. They focused on how brutal the murders had been, especially when the medical examiner, in his testimony, explained that marks and injuries on the victims indicated Wayne Adam Ford had strangled the women while raping them, then revived them to continue the assault. This was why it appeared as though the perpetrator had attempted to kill the victim's multiple times. They also based their decision on the fact that the accused knew what he was doing was wrong and could have contacted authorities much earlier. Therefore, it resulted in a death sentence. As of this writing, Wayne Adam Ford is on death row at San Quentin Prison in California.

Wayne Adam Ford was, incidentally, called "the conscientious serial killer" because he turned himself in to the police and wept as he recounted what he had done. It's unknown what he truly felt, but if we assume he was conscientious, perhaps he was able to see that he was completely misguided, yet he was clearly able to disregard that insight when committing his crimes. This has been seen before. We talk about fractured identity, which allows some serial killers to fragment their lives so that the killer's actions don't affect the life the family man, soccer coach, and nice neighbor otherwise lives. When they are finally confronted with what they've done, the shame emerges. This type of serial killer can be even harder to detect because they find it easier to live a normal life alongside their darker one. It's uncertain how deep this feeling goes, and whether the shame might be more connected to self-pity

Back in Alaska, investigators had no doubt they were dealing with a hateful perpetrator. They were also certain that the baker, Robert Hansen, was the man they were after. But they had no evidence. In an attempt to move the case forward, they turned to the FBI, where John E. Douglas agreed to help the police obtain a judge's permission to search the suspect's home. However, it was important to him that the officers not share their suspicions, but simply let him look at facts such as photos from the crime scenes, autopsy reports, and the victims' background stories.

John E. Douglas believed the killer had to be a White man around 40 years old, suffering from a severe inferiority complex and low self-esteem as a result of one or more rejections in the past, likely related to relationships with women. He was highly likely a respected member of the local community whom few would suspect, but it would nonetheless turn out that he had a lengthy criminal record with offenses that had become more serious over time. He also believed that the serial killer in Alaska was an experienced hunter, and that his interest in hunting had been established in childhood and adolescence because it was something he could do even while socially isolated. The FBI agent predicted that the killer would most likely take souvenirs from the victims, and that these souvenirs could probably be found in the perpetrator's home, because he would need to relive his murders in everyday life. Finally, he provided two very precise descriptions of the killer: He was certain that the individual stammered or had some form of speech impediment and suffered or had suffered from skin problems or another type of visible affliction, which could have been the cause of the rejections in the past.

The investigators in Anchorage could barely have crafted a better profile themselves, even with the knowledge they possessed. When they had visited Robert Hansen after hearing Cindy Paulson's explanation, they noticed that he stammered, and it was clear he had previously suffered from severe acne, which had left many scars on his face.

The police already knew that Robert Hansen had an unusually spotty criminal record, and it went back a long way. They particularly noted a case from 1960, when their main suspect was a 21-year-old, arrested for burning down a garage containing school buses. The buses belonged to the very school he had attended, making it easy to infer that Robert Hansen had done it as a form of revenge against the girls who had rejected him due to his stammer and acne.

The intense rage Robert Hansen felt didn't just stem from his school days. Life at home wasn't easy for him either. Even as a child, he had to get up at night to work in the family bakery, which meant he often fell asleep in school, where he already struggled academically. His father mocked his stutter and appearance and forced him to use his right hand, even though he was left-handed. This might not sound so severe, but when children are forced to do something completely unnatural for them, they lose faith in themselves. They develop low self-esteem, become insecure, and in some cases, can develop anxiety and/or depression. Robert Hansen's father was a very dominant man, and the son found no help from his mother, who was very submissive to his father. This may have contributed to Robert Hansen's anger toward the world developing into a hatred of women, especially as he was also repeatedly rejected by girls at school.

As he got older, he started stealing. Often, these were things of little monetary value, but it wasn't about the money. There's no doubt Robert Hansen was a kleptomaniac. This makes sense given his history, as it gave him a feeling of power that he otherwise hadn't experienced much as a child or young man. When he succeeded in getting away with it, it supported his fantasy of being untouchable and having the right to violate societal norms, suddenly, he was on top of the world. Kleptomania is seen in quite a few serial killers who also experience a sexual component to it. This was true for Robert Hansen, who later stated that he was close to orgasm when he stole, which, of course, couldn't have been known from his behavior alone.

His kleptomania coincided with the period around his second marriage. On the surface, it seemed happy, but the relationship also forced Robert Hansen to confront his dark desires even more. He described going to prostitutes to do things he couldn't ask his wife for, such as oral sex, because "nice girls" in his eyes didn't do such things. This reinforced the Madonna-Whore complex that already dominated his view of women, and for him, it helped justify his actions, as he believed strippers and prostitutes "deserved it."

Armed with the profile, the investigators went to the courts. It had never happened before that a judge had granted permission for a search based solely on a profile, and the police had been very specific about what they expected to find at Robert Hansen's home. They had received help from John E. Douglas, who, in addition to what the revolver Cindy Paulson had described and the .223 caliber used to shoot the women, also pointed to souvenirs like jewelry and driver's licenses to the police's satisfaction. The judge granted permission for the search.

On October 13, 1983, the Anchorage police moved in. Patrol cars arrived at the airport, Robert Hansen's home, and the bakery simultaneously. The suspect wasn't at any of the addresses but arrived shortly after at his workplace, from where he willingly accompanied the officers to the station. They placed him in an interrogation room filled with pictures, maps, and papers from the investigation.

Meanwhile, the other police officers were in full swing. They found nothing of interest in either the airplane or the bakery, but in the home, in a bedroom closet, they made a discovery that sent a chill down their spines. In a box, there was a map of the wilderness around Anchorage, marked with no fewer than 37 crosses in pen. Four of them matched the locations where four of the bodies had been found. In the attic, investigators found several weapons, including a revolver with a wooden grip, matching the weapon Cindy Paulson had described, and a .223 caliber hunting rifle. A box containing jewelry, driver's licenses, and ID cards also turned up.

Outside, some of the city's residents gathered to figure out what was happening at the baker's shop. One of them was a neighbor who was shocked when she learned what Robert Hansen was suspected of. She told one of the officers that her husband had previously told the police that he and Robert Hansen had been together when Cindy Paulson was abducted, but that this was not true. This matched another of John E. Douglas's predictions. He was certain that the neighbor and another friend had lied, and he recommended that the police bring them in for questioning and threaten them with legal action if it came out that they had obstructed the investigation. This helped. Both men admitted they had given Robert Hansen false alibis. They thought their friend had been involved in some trivial matter and had therefore chosen to help him. They had no idea, nor could they have imagined, that it concerned a whole series of murders.

Confronted with the overwhelming evidence and witness testimonies, Robert Hansen gave up. He informed the police that he was willing to confess to the murders of the four women whose bodies had already been found if he could serve his sentence outside of Alaska. He admitted that, in Alaska alone, he had committed over 30 rapes but had threatened the women into silence, arguing that no one would believe the word of a "whore" or a "stripper" anyway. He also confessed that he had lured several of the victims by pretending to be a photographer looking for models, only to handcuff them as soon as they got into his car. In his eyes, it was the women's own fault that things ended up as they did, partly because he was sure the prostitutes had raised their prices after sizing him up.

In 1984, Robert Hansen was sentenced to 461 years in prison for four murders, a long list of rapes, and several less serious crimes. In prison, he agreed to point out eight other graves based on the crosses on his map, but it is believed that he was responsible for at least 21 murders in total. If any of the other victims are found, it will be by chance, as the killer can no longer show where they are located. He died of natural causes at the age of 75 in 2014.

Even now, almost 40 years after the conviction, the profile developed at the time stands as one of the most famous. The prediction of Robert Hansen's speech impediment and skin problems still seems almost psychic. However, it wasn't so. John E. Douglas based his assumption on statistics. There are, in fact, several examples of serial killers with speech impediments and appearances that can, in one way or another, be off-putting to others. Furthermore, the FBI agent had just completed a profile on David Carpenter, a serial rapist and killer who became notorious as The Trailside Killer because he attacked hikers on trails in natural areas near San Francisco. In that case, he had also predicted that the killer had a speech impediment that made it difficult for him to communicate with the opposite sex. This proved to be accurate.

At that time, the FBI heavily relied on statistical probabilities and agents' own experience, which also made sense in these two other cases. However, as a profiler, one must be careful not to give too much weight to statistics, because the numbers, by their very nature, come from older cases. And stuttering is a good example of this. Today, a profiler would hardly be so specific because speech impediments and many other problems are handled in a completely different way now than in the past.

CHAPTER 7: WHEN WOMEN KILL: THE WRESTLER FROM MEXICO CITY

Maria de la Luz Gonzales Anaya was 64 years old when an unknown assailant attacked her in her apartment on November 22, 2002, and strangled her. She was beaten in the face multiple times before the killer ended her life and then stole money and jewelry. The murder was intensely covered by the Mexican press, and journalists speculated whether El Mataviejitas, "the little-old-lady killer," had struck again. It wasn't the first time an elderly single woman had been murdered in her own home in Mexico City.

The police categorically dismissed the idea of a serial killer in the capital. They believed the notion of a killer targeting older women was pure fabrication, solely intended to sell more newspapers. However, it became increasingly difficult to maintain that stance as more bodies were brought in for autopsy. The similarities were striking. The deceased women were all in their sixties, seventies, and eighties. This alone was enough to dominate headlines, as in Mexico, abuela (grandmother) holds an almost mythical status as the nation's moral focal point. That someone could murder grandmothers was utterly unheard of.

All the victims were single, and they didn't have much contact with their families. They were frail and all received welfare benefits from the municipality, and one of their few pleasures was walking in the parks near their homes. Some of the women had been assaulted before being killed, while others were solely strangled. In some cases, the killer had used their hands; in others, the murder weapon was rope or pantyhose. In a few instances, the perpetrator had gone further by inserting objects into the victim's post-mortem, but there were no signs of rape in any of the cases. The apartments had been ransacked, and wherever possible, the killer had stolen cash and jewelry, in addition to a number of worthless trinkets.

After Maria de la Luz Gonzales Anaya's death, the killings continued. It often took several days for bodies to be discovered because there were no external signs of forced entry. At a number of the crime scenes, investigators found partial fingerprints and managed to speak with several witnesses. The witnesses told the police they had seen a nurse lurking near the victims' apartments. She was described as tall, robust, and masculine. She wore makeup, apparently a wig, and seemed unusually broad-shouldered.

The investigators didn't put much stock in the eyewitness accounts. They stuck to the statistics, which told them the probability of them hunting a female serial killer was very low. Therefore, the eyewitnesses were either assumed to be mistaken or the mysterious nurse had nothing to do with the murders. After all, it wasn't unusual for elderly women living alone to need visits from a home nurse.

If the Mexican police had contacted me, I would have insisted on not fixating on the killer's gender from the start. Even though the crimes were very violent, and strangulation is a very personal and aggressive way to kill, it's crucial to maintain an open approach in your analysis. On one hand, it physically requires a lot of strength to strangle a person; on the other, it's also a very personal way to kill, where the perpetrator can feel the victim's life slipping away. Looking at the numbers, it's also exceedingly rare for female murderers to resort to strangulation. But that's the thing about profiling: you have to be very careful about being overly confident. It's crucial to only report what you are certain of. For instance, if there's semen at the crime scene, you can definitely say a man was present. It's important to constantly update the profile as you get more information or if you discover aspects of a crime that point in a different direction.

In the "abuelas" case in Mexico City, the victims seemingly let their killer into their homes. The question of whether elderly women would trust a stranger enough to grant entry is difficult to answer definitively, although it might be easier for a woman to gain such trust. If the perpetrator were male, he might have adopted a persona of authority or helpfulness to disarm the victims' fears. The insertion of objects into some victims revealed a profound need to humiliate and unleash rage upon these older women. This tactic is not uncommon; perpetrators who avoid direct sexual assault often use objects to convey a message of disdain, implying they won't "degrade" themselves by using their own bodies.

Regarding the motive, I'd be more confident in my assessment. While initially appearing to be robbery-murders, several aspects of the killer's behavior pointed in another direction. Most notably, the theft of worthless trinkets from the victims' homes was crucial. These items, though valueless, were significant to the killer. The act could be interpreted as taking souvenirs to preserve memories and feelings of the act, or as trophies to affirm a sense of dominance, much like a hunter displaying their kill. Such behavior is strongly associated with serial crimes. The murder method also points away from simple robbery. For perpetrators focused solely on theft, the killing is usually quick, often with firearms or heavy objects, to eliminate a witness and move on to the primary goal of enrichment. However, the Mexico City killer spent time building trust and then used strangulation, a prolonged method that takes three to six minutes and often involves a struggle. This deliberate choice of a drawn-out, personal method indicates it was a central part of the crime itself, not just a means to an end. Therefore, I would have no doubt that the police were mistaken in their initial dismissal of a serial killer. It makes me wonder how the case might have unfolded if investigators had seriously considered the eyewitness accounts. While female serial killers are rare, they do exist.

*

Between December 13, 1989, and November 19, 1990, the bodies of six men were discovered across Florida. The men, aged 40 to 62, had all been shot between two and seven times, and some were nude or partially nude. Their valuables were missing, and in multiple cases, their cars had been stolen. As a profiler, I wouldn't comment on gender unless absolutely certain, for example, if semen was found at the crime scene. In the Florida case, victimology also cautioned against prematurely determining the perpetrator's gender. It turned out most of the victims had something in common: they frequented prostitutes. Therefore, the killer could well have been a sex worker. This would, at least, explain why the victims felt safe enough to let a killer into their cars and drive to secluded locations.

By the summer of 1990, police got a crucial lead when one victim's car was abandoned after a traffic accident. A witness gave investigators a description of two women fleeing the scene, and police subsequently found several of the victims' belongings at various pawnshops. On one receipt, a fingerprint matched a fingerprint found in the abandoned car. The owner of the fingerprints was already in the system, having a prior criminal record. Her name was Aileen Wuornos, and she was arrested at a bar on Florida's east coast.

To call Aileen Wuornos's upbringing hard would be a massive understatement. She was born in 1956 when her mother was just 16 years old. Her father was convicted of raping a seven-year-old girl and committed suicide in prison in 1969. When Aileen Wuornos was four, her mother abandoned her and her one-year-older brother, and they went to live with their maternal grandparents, both of whom were alcoholics. Aileen Wuornos accused her grandfather of abuse and sexual assault. By age 11, she began selling sexual favors at school for cigarettes, drugs, and food, and at 14, she became pregnant after being raped by one of her grandfather's friends. The child was immediately adopted after birth, and the following year, she was thrown out of her home after her grandmother died due to alcoholism. To survive, Aileen Wuornos turned to prostitution and settled in an old car in a nearby forest. From then on, she accumulated countless entries on her criminal record for drunk driving, assault, illegal possession of weapons, and robberies. She was also involved in a case where she used a gun to rob $200 from a man in whose car she was.

In 1986, 30-year-old Aileen Wuornos began a relationship with a woman six years younger. They moved in together and lived off the money the former earned as a sex worker. The two were questioned the following year in connection with a violent assault involving a beer bottle. Aileen Wuornos' girlfriend, Tyria Moore, made an immunity deal with the police. As part of this agreement, she helped facilitate a confession from Aileen Wuornos during a recorded phone conversation, in which Aileen Wuornos admitted to the killings. The recording and a wealth of forensic evidence led to a death sentence for Aileen Wuornos. Throughout the legal process, Aileen Wuornos changed her story multiple times. Initially, she insisted the men had attempted to rape her and that she shot them in self-defense. Later, she claimed only the first victim had forced her into sex.

Aileen Wuornos's life story bears a striking resemblance to those of male serial killers. She was sexually abused, involved in arson at age six, and began working as a prostitute in her teens. It's not entirely clear whether her primary motive was financial gain or an act of revenge against men in general, but there's no doubt she harbored a significant hatred towards men, similar to the misogyny often seen in male serial killers. This hatred likely stemmed from her abuse and her experiences as a prostitute. For me, the motive is central to classifying Aileen Wuornos. If she were acting out a fantasy primarily driven by revenge against men, she'd fit the definition of a serial killer. However, if her main goal was to eliminate witnesses to robberies, then she'd be classified as a robbery-murderer. Her actions also bear similarities to spree killing, where a murderer kills multiple people in different locations without cooling-off periods. Perhaps Aileen Wuornos was, in reality, a combination of these different types of multiple murderers.

*

Gwendolyn Graham, a 23-year-old nursing assistant, moved from Texas and began working at the Alpine Manor nursing home. There, she met 24-year-old Catherine Wood, and their friendship quickly blossomed into a romantic relationship. It's important to note that the account of "The Lethal Lovers" is largely based on Catherine Wood's testimony, given after she made an immunity deal with the police to testify against Gwendolyn Graham in exchange for a less severe charge. This makes it challenging to fully understand the dynamic between the two women.

The couple shared a significant sexual appetite, and Gwendolyn Graham introduced her new girlfriend to the world of BDSM (Bondage, Dominance, Sadism, Masochism), including experiments with asphyxiation, which is sometimes believed to heighten pleasure. At some point, these fantasies escalated to include murder, and the two developed what they called their "murder game." The objective was to murder six nursing home residents, but to make it more challenging, their first names had to begin with the letters M-U-R-D-E-R. The couple targeted residents with Alzheimer's disease, as they rarely comprehended what was happening and were often physically frail. The first victim was a middle-aged woman. According to Catherine Wood, it was Gwendolyn Graham who strangled her by covering her mouth and nose with a washcloth while Wood stood guard at the door.

Four more murders followed, though they soon abandoned their letter game as it became too difficult to match names. Often, the two women became so aroused that they would find a room to have sex, and the same occurred when they later prepared the bodies for burial. Over time, they grew so overconfident that they told colleagues what they had done, claiming it further intensified their sexual arousal, but their confessions weren't taken seriously; instead, many found their humor highly inappropriate. The idea behind the murders was to forge an unbreakable bond between them, but this didn't last. When Catherine Wood, again, by her own account, wanted to stop, Gwendolyn Graham returned to Texas with a new girlfriend and began working in a newborn unit at a hospital. Catherine Wood later explained she feared what her ex-girlfriend might do and confessed her involvement to her ex-husband. He went to the police, and soon after, several bodies were exhumed for autopsy. However, there was no conclusive evidence that they had been murdered, which isn't unusual with the strangulation method the women used. Therefore, the case hinged on Catherine Wood's testimony.

Catherine Wood claimed her ex-girlfriend, as the dominant partner, had initiated and carried out the murders, while she herself merely stood guard and was a victim of severe manipulation. Gwendolyn Graham's new girlfriend also testified, admitting that Gwendolyn Graham had confessed to five murders. Gwendolyn Graham received five life sentences, while Catherine Wood was sentenced to 20-40 years in prison and was released in 2020. Perhaps she got off lightly. A later book, at least, presented a quite different picture of Catherine Wood as a manipulative, power-hungry woman who reveled in ruining others' lives and was the one who planned the murders, involving Gwendolyn Graham as insurance against being abandoned. "The Lethal Lovers" is not only an example of female serial killers but also part of a unique "club" of murderous couples, which will be explored in the next chapter.

*

On a warm summer day in Mexico City, a knock came at the door of 83-year-old Ignacia Puebla. The old woman went to answer it. Outside stood an unusually tall woman for Mexican standards. She was robust, almost muscular, with very short hair. She showed an ID card and explained she was from the municipal elder care department, working with a welfare program Ignacia Puebla was part of, which provided free medical care and public transportation. The old woman let the municipal employee in, and they went into the living room. The employee seemed astonished to see that Ignacia Puebla was not alone; one of the old lady's sons, who had recently broken his leg, was recovering on the sofa. She, dressed in a nurse's uniform, offered to look at his X-ray and then took his blood pressure. As she was pumping the cuff, another son entered the apartment, and the nurse excused herself and hurried out the door. Later, the family realized the woman had stolen money from the apartment, and police managed to get a usable fingerprint from the X-ray she had touched

However, the police still refused to accept the idea of a female serial killer. They believed a woman simply couldn't possess the strength required to strangle the elderly women, some of whom were quite robust. If the eyewitness descriptions were accurate, there had to be another explanation. Investigators in Mexico City sought help from colleagues in Paris, where a serial killer had terrorized the Montmartre district between 1984 and 1987, attacking, strangling, and robbing between 18 and 21 elderly women. The culprit, Thierry Paulin, was a young, homosexual man who performed as a drag queen and disguised himself as a woman when committing his crimes. He had confessed to the murders but died of AIDS-related illnesses before his trial could begin. This story became a mantra for the Mexican investigators, who began focusing on the city's LGBT community, particularly transgender sex workers. Three months after the mysterious municipal nurse's visit to Ignacia Puebla, a large contingent of officers launched a massive raid, arresting approximately 50 transgender women. Not a single one matched the police's description, and none of their fingerprints matched those found at the crime scenes, forcing investigators to reluctantly release them all.

Not long after the mass arrests, on the afternoon of January 25, 2006, a 25-year-old man was returning home from his job as a waiter at a local restaurant. He had rented a room from an elderly woman, and seeing the door to her part of the apartment open, he decided to greet her before going to his own room. As he stepped inside, he was nearly knocked over as a figure pushed past him and ran down the stairs. The person was tall and muscular, wearing black trousers and a red sweater. The young man hesitated, then called out to his landlady. There was no answer. He stepped inside and entered the living room. The old woman lay on her back on the tiles. Her hands were clenched into fists, she was bleeding from wounds on her head, and a stethoscope was wrapped so tightly around her neck that her face was blue.

The tenant spun around and sprinted out into the street. He looked around and saw the figure in black trousers and a red sweater heading north. He started running and simultaneously spotted two police officers who happened to be patrolling the area. Together, they chased the suspicious person. When they caught up, a woman turned towards them and swung at them with the bags she was carrying. She was arrested, and the officers went through the contents of her bags. Inside were, among other things, a list of elderly women receiving welfare benefits, a fake ID card from the health administration, and a stethoscope. When investigators searched her home, they found several of the small items stolen from the victims and a collection of newspaper clippings about the murders, despite the arrested individual being illiterate.

The woman apprehended by Mexican police was 48-year-old Juana Barraza, who perfectly embodied the description often given to female serial killers: "Quiet killers."

As previously noted, female serial killers are relatively rare, with men committing roughly 90% of serial murders, depending on the definition and methodology. However, when women do engage in such crimes, they often remain undetected for longer periods. This is largely because most people find it difficult to believe that women are capable of such violence. This inherent bias explains why Mexico City police so persistently believed the killer was male. While male serial killers are often apprehended relatively quickly within months or a few years, women, on average, remain at large for eight years from their first murder and tend to claim more victims than men (averaging 8-14 for women versus 8-11 for men). One explanation is that female serial killers are typically more cautious, leaving fewer clues, and often select victims and methods that don't immediately suggest foul play. This was evident with "The Lethal Lovers," where the nursing home residents' murders went unnoticed until one of the women confessed. While there was no such doubt in Mexico City once the pattern was clear, the police's insistence on a male perpetrator undoubtedly prolonged the investigation, perhaps unnecessarily, had they paid more attention to eyewitness accounts. It's worth noting that the media's moniker for the killer shifted from "El Mataviejitas" to "La Mataviejitas" once the suspect's female identity became known.

Fundamentally, I believe that both men and women share the same core motive for killing: power and control. Both genders also find psychological gratification in the act of murder. While sex plays a more prominent role for male killers, it's crucial to remember that when the motive isn't sexual, but rather about exerting power and degradation, similar dynamics are observed in women, particularly when they murder to enrich themselves, as money itself is a form of power. Consequently, an economic motive is frequently observed among female multiple murderers. Revenge or hatred towards a specific person or group is a shared motive across both genders, as seen in the case of Aileen Wuornos. However, serial killers often have multiple overlapping motives, as was the case with Juana Barraza, which we'll explore shortly. Finally, there are differences in weapon choices. While both genders may use firearms, men are far more likely to strangle their victims due to their generally greater physical strength. Knife usage is also seen in both genders, but men often inflict significantly more stab wounds than women. When it comes to poisoning, this is predominantly the domain of female murderers. A US study of homicides between 1980 and 2008 ("Homicide trends in the United States") shows that while 60.5% of all poisoners in this period were men and 39.5% were women, this is contextualized by the fact that most murders are committed by men overall. When examining individual cases, male murderers use poison in only about 0.3% of their killings, whereas women use poison in approximately 2.5% of theirs. Poisonings are notoriously difficult to detect, requiring chemical analyses of substances like blood for revelation, and are only pursued if there's a suspicion that a death wasn't due to natural causes.

A significant aspect of female perpetrators' behavior is their victim selection. While men often "hunt," spending weeks or months stalking and planning the deaths of chosen victims like Dennis Rader, women far more frequently kill individuals they already know in some capacity. Some target close relations, often termed "black widows," while others seek out victims who are dependent on them, typically due to physical or mental frailty. Let's examine a couple of examples.

Nannie Doss appeared to be a sweet, elderly woman. She smiled and laughed often, and enjoyed spending time with her grandchildren. Yet, she was also constantly searching for the perfect, romantic man, and when that quest failed, she killed her chosen partner.

The story of "The Giggling Grandmother" begins in 1905, when she was born into a poor farming family in Alabama. Her father was strict, controlling, and violent, denying his children schooling and forbidding his daughters from wearing makeup, nice clothes, or attending social events. At age seven, Nannie

Doss suffered a head injury in a train accident, and subsequently, much like Robert Joe Long after his motorcycle accident, she endured headaches, blackouts, and depression. She sought refuge in romance novels and personal ads, daydreaming of Prince Charming.

She married at just 16 to a young man she had known for only four months. Her husband had an unusually close relationship with his mother, who moved in with the newlyweds. Unfortunately, for Nannie Doss, her mother-in-law's personality mirrored her father's, and for the six years the marriage lasted, she was subjected to similar physical and psychological abuse. Shortly before the divorce, two of their four daughters died, despite seemingly being healthy beforehand. Nannie Doss's ex-husband left with one of the remaining daughters, while she kept the youngest.

A year later, she remarried. This time, she had met a violent alcoholic through a personal ad, who initially wrote her romantic letters, which she answered with suggestive messages and photos. Despite the violence and abuse, the relationship lasted 16 years. During that period, two of Nannie Doss's grandchildren died. First, a baby boy died shortly after birth. Nannie Doss's daughter believed she saw her mother stick a hatpin into the newborn's head, but this was dismissed as hallucinations caused by strong anesthesia during childbirth. Doctors, however, could not explain why the baby died. Two years later, Nannie Doss had such a fierce argument with her daughter that the daughter temporarily moved to her father's home, leaving her son with Nannie. He died there on July 7, 1945. Doctors stated the cause of death was suffocation, but couldn't explain how it occurred. Two months later, Nannie Doss collected the grandchild's life insurance payout of $500.

Next, her husband died after she put rat poison in his whiskey, but the official explanation was food poisoning. His widow used the life insurance money to buy a nearby property. Later, she found another match through personal ads. This man, however, didn't live up to Nannie Doss's expectations and died when she poisoned his dinner. Fortunately, for her, he was an alcoholic, and on the death certificate, doctors noted his heart failed due to his addiction.

Nannie Doss soon began another relationship. Before she discovered her new love was unfaithful, first her mother, whom she had agreed to care for after a fall, and then her sister, whose health was otherwise robust, both died. After the two women were buried, Nannie Doss focused on her new man. In 1954, she married for the last time. He was neither an alcoholic nor a violent type, yet she prepared a prune cake with poison that sent him to the hospital. He survived but died at home about a month later when his wife gave him a poisoned cup of coffee. This time, the doctor who had treated Nannie Doss's fifth and final husband became suspicious, especially since she could now collect yet another life insurance payout. When the doctor performed an autopsy and found large amounts of arsenic in the deceased's tissue, Nannie Doss was arrested.

She confessed to the murders of four husbands but denied any involvement in the deaths of her family members. She earned her moniker, "The Giggling Granny," because she giggled every time she recounted to investigators or journalists how she had killed her husbands, as can be seen in many of the black-and-white photos taken of her during her confession and subsequent trial. She denied that the murders were about the money she received. Instead, she blamed the head injury she sustained as a child and the romance novels that had led to unrealistic expectations. "I was looking for the perfect man, the great romance of life," she said.

Nannie Doss died in prison at the age of 59 in 1965. In the 1950s and earlier, it was relatively easy to camouflage poisonings as natural deaths. However, in today's world, with longer lifespans and significant advancements in medicine to combat diseases, it has become much harder for "black widows" like Nannie Doss to get away with their crimes. Nevertheless, other environments still offer better opportunities for a killer to hide their misdeeds, such as hospitals and nursing homes, where deaths are not inherently suspicious.

On Friday, September 17, 1982, Petti McClellan arrived at a newly opened pediatric clinic in Kerrville, Texas. Her eight-month-old daughter, Chelsea, had been born prematurely with underdeveloped lungs, making her frequently ill. Now, she had a lingering cold, and her mother wanted a doctor to examine her, just to be on the safe side. While Petti McClellan spoke with the doctor, Nurse Genene Jones took the baby to another room to play. Shortly after, the nurse raised the alarm: little Chelsea was no longer breathing. She immediately began CPR, and with an oxygen mask, the tiny patient was rushed to the nearby Sid Peterson Hospital, where her life was successfully saved. Chelsea's grateful parents widely praised the quick-thinking nurse who had recently been hired at the clinic.

About a year later, mother and daughter returned for a vaccination. Shortly after Genene Jones gave the first injection, the girl became breathless. It looked like she was having some kind of seizure, and her mother asked the nurse to stop, but Jones gave the child another injection. Now, her breathing stopped completely, and the small body began to twitch until it went limp. Again, an ambulance rushed them to the hospital, and en route, her breathing was revived. Genene Jones carried the little girl inside, where doctors took over until it was safe to transfer her to a specialized unit by ambulance. The nurse and the girl's doctor accompanied them, and en route, they again started life-saving efforts when their patient stopped breathing. This time, it was in vain. Chelsea McClellan was dead. Genene Jones cried as she and the doctor washed the small body and wrapped it in a blanket before the parents received their deceased child. After their farewells, the nurse carried the girl to the hospital's chapel while the doctor ordered an autopsy. Something wasn't right. Chelsea McClellan had recovered from her premature birth and was only at the clinic for a vaccination. What had happened was in every way unusual.

About a week after the funeral, Petti McClellan visited her daughter's grave and found Genene Jones kneeling at the grave's edge, sobbing and repeating Chelsea's name. Petti McClellan found the behavior odd and stared at the nurse, who quickly left. Meanwhile, a doctor at the hospital had looked into Genene Jones's previous workplace, a pediatric ward in San Antonio, nearly 100 kilometers away. Contacts there told him a chilling story. Several of her colleagues had noticed a period of unusually high patient deaths—usually in the evenings, when Genene Jones was on duty. They even began calling it the "death shift."

The hospital wanted to sweep the story under the rug, if there was anything to it, and initiated a round of nurse firings, officially due to restructuring. This is why Genene Jones had sought work at the Kerrville pediatric clinic. Several cases at her previous workplace were investigated, and the doctor at the San Antonio hospital asked his colleague at the Kerrville clinic about a powerful muscle relaxant, succinylcholine, suspected of being involved in the deaths. The succinylcholine at the Kerrville clinic was missing, but suddenly, Genene Jones announced she had found the bottle. When the doctor examined it, she noticed two needle punctures in the rubber stopper covering the top. The bottle was almost full, but a closer analysis showed that a large portion of the contents was saline solution. She could only guess how many times someone had used the potent medication.

Thus, the case began to unfold. Eight cases involving children with similar symptoms who survived with Genene Jones's help were investigated, and Chelsea McClellan's body was exhumed. A test then showed she had succinylcholine in her system. Meanwhile, both the press and investigators began to delve into the nurse's past. She was born in 1950 and adopted at a young age by a wealthy family in San Antonio. Her father ran several nightclubs but struggled with a gambling addiction, and the family soon went bankrupt, after which her father tried several other business ventures.

As a child, Genene Jones felt overlooked. She believed her parents didn't care for her and described herself as the family's black sheep. She began to feign illness to gain attention and sympathy from adults while trying to dominate other children. The result was the opposite; she was bullied, especially for being overweight. Teachers described her as a manipulative liar. She only felt close to her brother, two years younger, and his death from a homemade firecracker exploding in his face deeply affected her. When her father died young from cancer and her mother began to drink, Genene Jones married a high school dropout. Her husband soon fled into the army when he discovered she wasn't pregnant at all, a lie she had told to get him to agree to the marriage, and she soon became unfaithful with a number of different men. She decided to become a cosmetologist, but when her second brother died of cancer, she feared what could happen if she worked with chemicals in makeup, cream, and hair dyes for the rest of her life, and therefore began studying nursing. Acquaintances later said she viewed the profession as almost sacred, and she developed a habit of always diagnosing people in her social circle. Colleagues also noted that although she was skilled, her behavior was strange. When young patients were dying, she seemed almost ecstatic when she helped save their lives, and when she failed, she grieved as if the children were her own.

It was also noted that she often tried to exert authority over others that wasn't hers and would become angry if things didn't go her way. This is where I start to recognize the profile of a killer belonging to the "angel of death" category. These are individuals who view themselves as almost divine, unable to reconcile with the fact that to the rest of the world, they appear quite mediocre. In their roles as doctors, nurses, or caregivers, they feel on par with God, and there's something intoxicating about the power of holding life and death in their hands. For a subgroup of "angels of death," the killing itself isn't necessarily the most important aspect, but rather the opportunity to save the dying and then receive the honor bestowed upon them. It seems this was also the case for Genene Jones, who saved numerous children who were close to death.

The case proved difficult for the prosecution. Although the number of child deaths was high, no one had witnessed the nurse administering injections. Therefore, they focused on Chelsea McClellan's case, where they had the succinylcholine test, the punctures in the bottle, and Jones's bizarre behavior at the cemetery. The verdict in 1985 was 99 years in prison, but due to specific rules, she was eligible for parole in 2018. Subsequently, she was charged with five other murders, with the possibility of the death penalty. This led Genene Jones to accept a plea bargain: she pleaded guilty to one murder, and the remaining charges were dropped. The sentence was life imprisonment, and she will be eligible for parole no earlier than when she turns 87.

As is evident, female serial killers are rare but by no means unknown. In many aspects, they differ from their male counterparts, particularly concerning victim selection. The question, of course, is how much physical strength plays a role here. Women can be just as sadistic as men, but there are limits to their physical capacity to kill. Personally, I have no doubt that there would be an equal distribution of male and female serial killers if they possessed the same physical strength as men, or if women were, on average, stronger. And we would also see women targeting men in the same way if men and women were equally strong. The evil mind is by no means exclusive to men. However, these differences mean that it can be relatively easy for a profiler to assess whether a male or female perpetrator is more likely. This was simply not the case in the "La Mataviejitas" case. Almost everyone—perhaps except for the eyewitnesses—found it hard to believe their own eyes when newspapers and TV stations showed pictures of Juana Barraza. But when one examines her background and compares it with, for example, Robert Joe Long's, it becomes quite clear that she fits the typical serial killer profile well.

Juana Barraza was born in 1957, when her mother was still a teenager. Her mother already suffered from severe alcoholism at that time and made a living as a domestic worker and sex worker. Her children were often left alone, and as the eldest, it became Juana Barraza's responsibility to care for her younger siblings. They often slept on the bare ground, had to find food in trash cans, and were not allowed to attend school, which meant Juana Barraza remained illiterate throughout her life. She was regularly subjected to physical and psychological violence, and several times it was so brutal that she lay bathed in her own blood. However, she had a stepfather whom she loved very much.

When Juana Barraza was a teenager, her mother sold her to a 62-year-old man for alcohol. With him, she was imprisoned, beaten, tied up, and raped, and over time, he rented her out to other men in the area. She became pregnant at just 13 and went through a series of abortions before becoming a mother for the first time five years later. During her stay with the older man, the young woman constantly hoped her mother would come and rescue her, but what she didn't know was that her mother had told the rest of the family that her daughter had run off with the older gentleman. Several years passed before her uncles found her and her son. When her mother died a few months later from her addiction, she felt absolutely nothing, as she herself recounted.

Several violent relationships and more children followed, and things didn't improve when Juana Barraza's stepfather died young from cancer. At 24, her son was murdered by street robbers, and she later described his death as the saddest moment of her life. To support her children, Juana Barraza performed various household chores in her neighborhood, and when money was tight, she shoplifted food from stores and the market.

Concurrently, she embarked on a remarkable career in lucha libre, the Mexican version of show wrestling, where participants perform in superhero and supervillain costumes. Here, she called herself "La Dama del Silencio" (The Lady of Silence), reflecting her quiet, introverted nature. However, this was hard to discern when she performed in her pink spandex suit with a large pink butterfly mask covering her face. She was popular, but even though she toured Mexico, each match only earned her about $ 23, which was not enough to support her and four hungry children at home. Her petty thefts escalated into larger burglaries and break-ins, providing a livelihood for her family until 2001, when a severe injury threatened paralysis if she continued wrestling.

The true number of elderly women Juana Barraza killed may never be known. She confessed to the final murder, where she was caught in the act, and was convicted for 16 others, where her fingerprints were found at the scene, but she may have been responsible for up to 49 victims. Speculation surrounding her motives was rife. Some believed she sought excitement after her wrestling career ended. Others linked her killings to her menstrual cycle or the full moon, suggesting increased aggression, or even her preference for red clothing as a sign of female rage. Barraza herself, however, was unequivocal. She expressed no remorse and frankly admitted to the police her hatred of elderly women, noting they were from the same generation as her mother. "I know it's not an excuse, and I don't deserve forgiveness from God or man," she stated. "When I saw those old ladies, I felt a violent rage, which grew stronger when they thought they were worth more than me, or believed they could humiliate me because they had money." Today, she is serving a sentence of no less than 759 years in prison, with parole eligibility not before she turns 100.

There's no doubt that Juana Barraza was a deeply traumatized individual, and these traumas manifested in her crimes. This is not offered as an excuse, as she was fully aware of her actions and the grief she inflicted on the victims' families. However, it enhances our understanding of the profound consequences that childhood experiences can have on the most vulnerable children in society. Trauma can lead to difficulties in coping with past abuse. The reactions that should ideally be directed at the original perpetrators are suppressed, only to be later displaced onto others who symbolize the initial abusers. This pattern is common among many serial killers who cannot manage their emotions and thus fail to react appropriately. For many children who grow up with such traumas, aggression can become the only means of gaining security in a world they perceive as having turned against them. For Juana Barraza, the elderly women became symbols of the mother she couldn't avenge because she was already deceased, and because it was emotionally too difficult for her to confront that specific pain. In other cases, revenge against a mother figure might be impossible because she still holds too much power over the adult, necessitating the selection of a surrogate.

For me, La Mataviejitas is particularly fascinating because she exhibits traits of both female and male serial killers. One final observation worth noting is the hubris exhibited by some male perpetrators, such as Dennis Rader, who sent letters to the press to ensure he received recognition for his crimes. This sense of invulnerability was also evident in Juana Barraza, and on that note, we conclude her story.

There are a few examples of female serial killers, like Juana Barraza, where the killer's gender could be a point of confusion. As mentioned, women often employ more discreet methods and do not achieve the same "popularity" as male serial killers in the media. The study of female serial killers is an underprioritized area, leading to significant uncertainty about the true number of murders committed by women. I agree with researchers and law enforcement officials who believe the actual figures are far higher than we currently acknowledge. Women take longer to be discovered when they murder, and they are more adept at concealing their tracks. This is perhaps exacerbated by the fact that they are not typically on our mental radar for such crimes. Precisely for this reason, we must gain more knowledge about them, especially their childhoods and upbringings. While we have extensive knowledge about male perpetrators, robust data on female serial killers remains scarce. Case studies reveal that female serial killers also often have extensive histories of childhood abuse and problematic family structures. We don't yet fully understand why women often murder differently from men, but aside from the methods, there are many similarities between the genders: women are also manipulative, immoral, impulsive, charming, lacking in conscience, and possess normal to above-average intelligence. Furthermore, we are beginning to see some female serial killers who target unknown victims, suggesting it's time we approach them with the same seriousness as their male counterparts.

We've explored male and female serial killers individually, and now it's time to delve into what happens when men and women join forces to become killer couples.

CHAPTER 8: SINISTER PARTNERSHIPS: THE HEAD IN THE CHEST

Late in the evening of June 26, 1980, a resident pulled into an alley near Hoffman Street in north Los Angeles, not far from the Hollywood Walk of Fame. As he parked behind his apartment building, something blocked his way. In the glow of his headlights, he spotted what looked like a treasure chest from a pirate movie. He stepped out and approached the chest, opening the lid curiously. On top lay a piece of clothing, which he lifted. Beneath it, he found a woman's severed head, wrapped in jeans and a pink T-shirt emblazoned with "Daddy's Girl." The lips were slightly parted, and if he wasn't mistaken, the head appeared to be made up with makeup. The man recoiled as if shocked, then sprinted past the parking spaces, up the stairs to his apartment, and called the police.

It didn't take long to identify the deceased. Five days earlier, in Studio City, about a kilometer from where the chest was found, passersby had discovered the headless body of a 20-year-old woman named Exxie Wilson. She had come to the city from Arkansas to work as a prostitute on Sunset Strip, an area infamous for its seedy nightlife. Her body had been discarded in a dumpster with no apparent signs of violence, but after the head's discovery, police now knew she had been shot in the head at close range. That same morning, officers had been called to a steak restaurant where an employee, taking out the trash, found another body: 24-year-old Karen Jones, who, like Exxie Wilson, was a streetwalker. Forensic examiners found a 25-caliber projectile in her head. Acquaintances revealed that the two women were friends and occasionally worked together.

Investigators were now certain: a serial killer was active around Sunset Strip. Earlier that month, two stepsisters, 15-year-old Gina Marano and 16-year-old Cynthia Chandler, had vanished on their way to meet friends. The girls had run away from home before and enjoyed partying with other rootless youths on Sunset Strip, so initially, their family hoped they'd simply found new friends. This hope was shattered on June 12 when the teenagers' bodies appeared near a park. Both had been shot in the head with a .25 caliber pistol, just like the other women. Ballistic examinations confirmed that all victims had been shot with the same gun.

The killings continued. As newspapers sensationalized the story of Exxie Wilson's head, which was found to have been frozen for a period before applying make up, a group of hunters discovered the mummified body of a girl in the San Fernando Valley on the outskirts of the city. It was identified as 17-year-old Marnette Comer, who had run away from home and been selling sex on Sunset Strip. She was last seen on June 1 and had been dead for at least three weeks. The cause of death was a gunshot wound to the head, and the weapon was a .25 caliber pistol.

Then, something puzzling occurred. On August 9, a group of residents from Barbara Ann Street, near the alley where the chest with Exxie Wilson's head was found, called police about an overwhelming stench coming from a van that had been parked there for almost a week. The back doors were opened, and several investigators nearly vomited. The interior, with its plush red upholstery reminiscent of hourly-rate motel rooms, was splattered with blood everywhere. On the floor lay a man on his stomach, wearing cowboy boots. His jeans and red underwear were pulled down around his ankles. The hot summer days had caused the body to swell and turn bluish-black, but countless stab wounds from a knife were still visible, and the perpetrator had inflicted deep lacerations on the man's buttocks, with damage to his anus. Near the driver's seat, investigators found a .25 caliber shell casing, but the body had no gunshot wounds. It also had no head.

It's understandable that investigators initially struggled to solve this case. The bodies of the young women were discarded, meaning police lacked access to the original crime scenes, complicating both forensic work and profiling efforts. However, certain probabilities could be established. Firstly, the killer managed to murder some of the victims in pairs, which is relatively rare. This suggests either an individual perpetrator with exceptional control over their victims, armed with a pistol, or the presence of two perpetrators. It's also evident to me that the perpetrator(s) knew which victims would be easy to lure. As mentioned, several of the women were runaways and sex workers, accustomed to getting into a car with a stranger. Yet, the siblings were also lured without perceiving a threat, which could be attributed to hitchhiking still being relatively common at the time. The presence of a woman in the car could have further put them at ease.

Secondly, there are the bodies themselves. One or two bullets to the head, often fired from behind, indicating no eye contact between the women and the shooter. This suggests an almost "expeditious" approach to the killing. In contrast, the perpetrator(s) spent a considerable amount of time with the deceased. While there were no signs of rape, semen was found in several victims, strongly pointing towards necrophilia. Necrophiles are sexually aroused by dead bodies. Very few who fantasize about this also desire to kill, which is why a disproportionate number of individuals with this paraphilia are found in professions that bring them into contact with corpses, such as roles in hospitals, nursing homes, funeral homes, cemeteries, or crematories.

There are also instances of necrophiles who act out their fantasies with prostitutes who use makeup and remain still, mimicking death. While our understanding of why some individuals become necrophilic is limited, a psychological hypothesis suggests it stems from a profound difficulty in relating to living individuals. This was evident in Jeffrey Dahmer, who murdered 17 young men between 1978 and 1991. As a homosexual man, he craved human connection but was unable to establish it with living men. Instead, he attempted to create "living dead" by injecting chemicals into victims' brains, seeking individuals who would belong to him entirely. Beyond necrophilia, he also resorted to cannibalism to make the young men part of himself and kept body parts to create an "altar" honoring his relationship with them. For necrophiles, it becomes psychologically possible to form an attachment without needing to relate to the other person, precisely because that person is deceased. Most of us don't consider this, but for some, forming and developing human relationships is extremely stressful and mentally exhausting. They struggle to form friendships and romantic connections and often have significant difficulties engaging sexually with others, which makes this hypothesis reasonable. However, it's crucial to emphasize that sexual contact with a corpse isn't necessarily an expression of necrophilia; it can also be about post-mortem humiliation or venting rage, and differentiating between these motives at a crime scene can be challenging.

What remains clear, however, is that time was spent with the bodies post-mortem. This was especially true for the young woman's head. As noted, technicians determined it had been frozen, and makeup was applied afterward. While it would be difficult to draw definitive conclusions from the situation alone, it was clear that whoever applied the makeup seemed to have prior experience. This doesn't exclude a male perpetrator, but it certainly could have been a woman. Police also couldn't determine if other actions had been taken with the head, but Edmund Kemper, whom we encountered earlier, engaged in sexual acts with his mother's severed head. The fact that the perpetrator(s) "played" with the head is undeniable; if the goal was to prevent identification of the murdered individual, allowing the head to resurface makes no sense. This was unequivocally the act of someone utterly devoid of empathy for the victim, who instead used the head to shock others by placing it in a chest for discovery by an innocent party.

Decapitation is, thankfully, a rare behavior, and a profiler would have to consider if the two crimes could be linked, especially given the .25 caliber shell casing found at the male victim's scene. However, several factors suggested a different perpetrator. First, the victim was a middle-aged man, whereas the previous victims were young girls and women. Second, the crime scene itself indicated chaos. While police lacked access to the previous crime scenes, the murders of the women seemed relatively "simple," one or more shots to the head. Here, the killer had gone berserk with a knife, leaving blood spatter throughout the van, and the victim had been stabbed so many times that it clearly conveyed an intense rage expressed on the spot. I would have been particularly intrigued by the injuries to the man's buttocks and around the anus, especially since his jeans and underwear were pulled down to his ankles. Could this indicate a homosexual encounter gone horribly wrong? Did the victim and perpetrator know each other? This type of mutilation, in my view, feels very personal and vengeful. Again, this isn't a conclusion, but it would have been a strong hypothesis.

If this were indeed a murder within the same series as the women's killings, I would have advised investigators to consider if they were dealing with a killer couple, where one partner murdered the women while the other killed the man. However, the link between the decapitated man and the young women was not strong, and with Los Angeles's murder rate hitting record highs during those years, it's understandable that police didn't initially view the killings as part of a single series.

Police quickly identified the man as Jack Murray, a 45-year-old who saw himself as a country music star but was often described as a discount version of Tom Jones. He frequently performed at a nearby bar, Little Nashville, and was notorious for having numerous girlfriends in addition to his wife.

A couple of days after the discovery of the headless man, the phone rang at the police station. Detective Kilgore answered. On the other end was a theatrical female voice, sounding as if she'd watched too many police procedural shows and courtroom dramas. She asked if he knew about the Sunset Strip murders and if he'd heard the name "Claudia" before.

A "Claudia" had previously called another police station, suspecting her boyfriend of the murders. He had repeatedly come home with bloody clothes and a bloody knife, and she had described how two young girls, the stepsisters, had been shot in the head, and one had been sexually abused after she died. Claudia hadn't revealed her boyfriend's name because she was scared. If she was right, she might be the next victim; if she was wrong, it would cost her the relationship. She had hung up then, but now, it seemed, she was back.

"Do you want to get your perpetrator today?" she asked.

"Uh, sure," Kilgore stammered.

"Okay, how much do you know about the case details?" the woman asked, sounding like an actress in a B-movie.

She continued to describe how Marnette Comer and the two stepsisters had been killed. "The next one on the list was shot with a different gun. We dumped her in some bushes near the Saugus-Newhall area by a creek. I don't know if you've found her...."

Kilgore realized Claudia was talking about a victim who hadn't yet been discovered. "It's possible, there are so many," he said.

"Oh, so you don't know about her!" the voice on the phone concluded.

Kilgore changed the subject, asking why she wanted to expose her boyfriend. Claudia said she was tired of being treated like dirt, and things had been getting worse lately, with everything seeming to fall apart.

"I actually killed someone on my own," she confessed, describing a decapitated body in a van. "He's going to keep going and going and going, and I can't take it anymore, I'm losing my mind!" she added.

Kilgore wondered if Claudia, if her story held true, regretted what she had done.

"To be honest, it's fun to kill people, and if I were allowed to go free, I'd probably do it again. I have to say, and I know it sounds sick, it sounds psychopathic, and I really don't think I'm a psychopath, but it's fun in a way. Like riding a rollercoaster!" she continued.

Then, she began planning the police's next steps. She knew both she and her boyfriend needed to be arrested, but she wanted to give her boyfriend, "Doug," a chance to get off work first. The "Claudia" who had called a few weeks earlier had first called her boyfriend "Don," but then stuck to the name "John." John was Jack Murray's real first name, but whether it was just a coincidence was unknown. She suggested that she and the investigators could meet for lunch at a diner near her boyfriend's workplace, and then described herself and her clothing so officers could recognize her. She also gave Kilgore her address, which he immediately checked.

"But please don't come here, let me do things my way," she said.

Kilgore played along.

"How about 2 o'clock? That works for me—unless you'd rather meet earlier?"

The woman hadn't hung up yet when officers pounded on the front door of her apartment. Her real name was Carol Bundy. If people who knew the 37-year-old nurse were to describe her in one word, it would be "awkward." She was short and plump, wore glasses with lenses as thick as bottle bottoms, and dressed in clothes that made her look 20 years older. And she tended to cling to people who gave her the slightest attention, especially men. She also often seemed theatrical in her behavior, as if she had only learned late in life how to react in different situations, so no one was surprised when she first screamed and then almost fainted at Little Nashville when news of Jack Murray's death spread. It was as if she had no filter, and several of her colleagues at the hospital avoided her because she often told tall tales or confided in them about her sex life in overly salacious detail. On one night shift, things had gone completely wrong when she recounted how she had shot a man and cut off his head, and her colleagues alerted the police. However, Carol Bundy had managed to take the stairs down while officers were coming up in the elevators, giving her time to get home, where she began gathering evidence for the police before she called: a projectile that her boyfriend Doug had said went through Gina Marano's head and a pair of panties. A bikini bottom belonging to Marnette Comer. A pair of red high-heeled shoes and a heart-patterned blouse that came from the woman whose body had been dumped by a creek and whom police had not yet located.

Concurrently, other police officers arrived at a factory not far from Carol Bundy's apartment. The heatwave continued. Not a breath of wind stirred, and the flag on the factory roof hung limply down its pole. At 11:30 AM, a whistle blew for lunch break, and men in overalls streamed out of the gate. Among them was Carol Bundy's boyfriend, 31-year-old Douglas Clark. In the caretaker's shed, he extended his arm to shake hands with one of the officers and immediately caught sight of handcuffs in the policeman's other hand.

"Is that really necessary?" he asked.

"I think so," the officer replied.

The police cars drove to the parking lot at Carol Bundy's apartment, where several patrol cars were already present. The arrested man tried to explain to the investigators that Carol Bundy was insane, but they didn't answer him. Instead, they got out and left him handcuffed in the car. From there, he could see the officers approach the apartment door.

"She has a shotgun, that's going to be a massacre!" he shouted.

Instead of threatening with a shotgun, Carol Bundy opened the door and waved the underwear she had found. She handed over the projectile and led two investigators into Douglas Clark's room, where she gave them a photo album. It contained pictures of Douglas Clark having sex with one of the neighbors' 11-year-old daughters, but it was Jack Murray she had in mind:

"I killed Jack all by myself because he was an asshole who deserved to die!"

The relationship between Carol Bundy and Douglas Clark was incredibly turbulent. In 1979, Bundy left her abusive husband with their two children and moved into an apartment. She quickly developed an intense infatuation with the building's superintendent, John Murray, the country singer from Little Nashville. Murray assisted her with various tasks in her apartment. He helped her secure welfare benefits she was entitled to due to severely impaired vision in both eyes, a condition later correctable by surgery. They began an affair, and when Murray refused to divorce his wife, Bundy even offered his wife money to leave him. This plan backfired, leading John Murray to ask Carol Bundy to move out, which didn't stop her from virtually stalking him.

Concurrently, Carol Bundy met a new man at Little Nashville: Douglas Clark. He called himself "the king of one-night stands" and was skilled at seducing mature, lonely women who could support him, giving him time for his true passion: underage girls. Carol Bundy fell head over heels for him on their first night together and immediately let him move into her apartment. She constantly feared he would leave her, so she allowed him to do as he pleased, even inviting other girlfriends home. She even helped him groom the neighbor's daughter and was the one who took the pictures in the album she later showed to the police when she was arrested.

What we can say with reasonable certainty about The Sunset Strip Killers is limited, as both Carol Bundy and Douglas Clark were pathological liars who constantly changed their stories to suit their immediate goals. However, certain traits frequently reappear in other killer couples. It's not unusual for partners, whether of the same or opposite sex, to commit murders together. Often, one partner leans toward psychopathy, exhibiting cold, calculating, and manipulative behaviors, though it's also not unheard of for the dominant role to shift. The dominant instigator takes the lead, making it easier for the other party to go along with horrific acts. The submissive partner is typically more disturbed and chaotic, often having experienced a history of abuse during childhood. It's common for teachers or classmates to describe boundary-crossing behavior in such individuals from an early age.

These two personality types are often drawn to each other because they unconsciously recognize traits in one another. The dominant partner naturally seeks someone they can control, which makes sense. However, the submissive partner, despite often experiencing a traumatic upbringing, seeks someone to submit to. This might sound strange, but for them, it makes sense. If you've been subjected to abuse, seeking the familiar or handing over all responsibility to another can provide a sense of security and recognition. Individuals with such upbringings often struggle to navigate life, and it can bring them peace not to have to make decisions themselves, even if it means repeating patterns from their childhood that traumatized them. When it comes to couples who commit assaults, rapes, or murders together, the submissive partner may also see it as a way to exact revenge through the dominant party.

In this regard, there isn't a vast difference in motives when couples become involved in such crimes as serial killers, as when there is only a single perpetrator. It's still about exerting power and control and fulfilling some psychological need, which often varies from one individual to another.

*

From the summer of 1963 to Christmas 1964, four children aged 10 to 16 disappeared from small towns east of

Manchester, England. Thousands of volunteers helped search for the missing, and countless flyers were distributed, but to no avail. The children had vanished without a trace.

The truth only emerged in the autumn of 1965 when police received a frantic call from a young couple. The call came from a phone booth in the town of Hyde, where the young man making the call, David Smith, and his girlfriend had armed themselves with a screwdriver and a knife, which they only put down when a patrol car arrived to take them to the station. There, David Smith recounted that earlier that day, he had been asked to come over to his girlfriend's sister and brother-in-law, a couple in their twenties named Myra Hindley and Ian Brady. Shortly after he arrived, he had heard a series of horrific screams from the living room, where he had seen Ian Brady kill a young man with an axe. Afterward, he had helped the couple wrap the body in plastic and drag it up to a room on the first floor of the apartment, and he had promised to return the next day to assist in the disposal of the deceased. He added that he had only helped because he was afraid that Ian Brady would otherwise have murdered him as well.

The chilling story of what later became known as The Moors Murders began when Myra Hindley secured a secretarial position in 1961 at the same company where Ian Brady worked in accounting. She was immediately captivated by him and wrote passionately about him in her diary, but a whole year passed before he invited her to the cinema. Not to see the new James Bond film or a romance, but a film about the Nuremberg Trials, which concerned Nazi crimes. This was due to his early fascination with Nazism and Nietzsche's ideas of the Übermensch. Their relationship became a "match made in hell."

Myra Hindley was born in 1945 and, from the age of five, grew up with her grandparents because her parents didn't have room for both her and her younger sister. Her father had fought in World War II, had a severe alcohol addiction, and regularly erupted in violent rages that affected both his wife and daughter. He quickly taught his eldest daughter that violence was the solution to life's problems. One day, when she came home and reported that a boy her age had scratched her, she was given the choice between beating the boy or being beaten with a belt herself. Later, after years of abuse, she turned on her father and beat him, demonstrating that she had learned her lessons well.

At 15, she lost her best friend. He had invited her to swim, but she couldn't go, and when the boy drowned, despite her being a skilled swimmer, she convinced herself that she was to blame for his death. This accident significantly shaped Myra Hindley's personality. The fear of being responsible for others' deaths is traumatizing, and it can lead one to avoid close attachments to other people, because of fear for abandonment. Her father's unpredictability and her mother's submissiveness did nothing to bring calm to her life; quite the opposite. She often tried to form attachments with those who didn't want her, experiencing rejection repeatedly and thus entering relationships that recreated the insecurity she knew from childhood.

Myra had only herself to rely on. As an adult, she tried to regain control, but it was as if her chaotic self could never achieve that calm. Instead, the chaos grew increasingly pervasive. Acquaintances later recounted that she was difficult to get to know. When she started taking judo, other participants noticed she was more violent than others, often holding various grips longer than necessary. For people suffering from survivor's guilt, the aim is to heal the grief. This can happen by shifting the blame onto others or by making others victims, which becomes even more complicated in a case involving a young woman whose relationship with death has become completely distorted.

Ian Brady's upbringing is by now a recognizable pattern. Four years older than Myra Hindley, he was born to a single mother but was adopted at four months old. His mother visited him regularly but never revealed her true identity. He was a difficult child. When he became angry and didn't get his way, he would bang his head on the floor until his parents gave in, and trouble would always surround him. He even started carrying a knife before his teenage years. He was intelligent but performed poorly in school, where he was also bullied for being odd and a "sissy" when it came to sports. At age nine, he went camping on the moors with his family. At night, he snuck out into the moonlight and gazed over the vast expanses, later recounting an overwhelming feeling of superiority, believing everyone else around him was nothing but maggots.

Soon after, animal cruelty began. He stoned dogs, decapitated rabbits, and set a live cat on fire, and at school, he became increasingly brutal toward younger children. His rage over not getting his way continued, as did his habit of banging his head against walls or floors. This behavior should cause concern when observed in children and adolescents, as it suggests an inability to manage anger effectively. Particularly concerning is that Ian Brady directed his rage both outward and inward. After a series of criminal offenses and a prison stay, he moved in with his biological mother and her husband. Although his stepfather found him work at a greengrocer's, his criminal path continued until he taught himself bookkeeping in prison, which led to a job at the firm where Myra Hindley was hired.

Just like Ian Brady, she was a recluse, and she soon spent all her time with him, adopting his fascination with Nazism. Regularly, the two would read aloud to each other from books that detailed all the horrifying specifics of Hitler and his crimes against humanity. Among their reading was also the work of Marquis de Sade, the 18th-century French author who wrote violence-glorifying pornographic texts while imprisoned. Periodically, Ian Brady would break up with Myra Hindley, but he always took her back, thereby binding her even more strongly to him.

She would do anything for him and began, among other things, to bleach her hair to resemble a true Aryan. She also agreed to have a series of erotic photos taken. He told her about his criminal past, and together they began planning bank robberies; these never materialized, but Ian Brady wanted to see how far his girlfriend was willing to go. As time passed, he confided more and more of his fantasies to her, which included both pedophilia and thoughts of committing the perfect murder. Concurrently, Myra Hindley's character changed, becoming far more outgoing than she had been, and she was almost ecstatic when she and Ian Brady moved in together in the summer of 1963.

One day in July, Myra Hindley got behind the wheel of the couple's car. Ian Brady followed on his motorcycle. As they approached a small girl on the sidewalk, Ian Brady flashed his headlights. Myra Hindley, however, continued, and when they saw a slightly older girl walking alone on the street, he flashed his headlights again. This time, she stopped. Sixteen-year-old Pauline Reade that lived next door to the two and was one of Myra Hindley's younger sister's friends. Therefore, it was no problem getting the teenager into the car when she was told that Myra Hindley had lost a pair of expensive gloves on the moors and needed help finding them. Ian Brady followed them, and according to Myra Hindley, he and the girl went out to search while she remained in the car. After half an hour, she got out. A short distance from the road, in the low vegetation, lay the dying Pauline Reade with her throat slit and her clothes disheveled. Myra Hindley was certain that Ian Brady had also raped the girl. They buried the body on the moors and drove home, where they saw family members searching for her.

The next two victims were also lured into the car by Myra Hindley at the market, where she asked for help carrying some boxes. The two 12-year-old boys, John Kilbride and Keith Bennett, were driven out onto the moors, where Ian Brady raped them, strangled them, and buried them. There is strong evidence that the couple became more emboldened after these three murders. At a traveling fair, they spotted 10-year-old Lesley Ann Downey, whom they lured after dropping some items right in front of her. This time, the trip wasn't to the moors but back to their apartment. There, the little girl was photographed naked, bound, and gagged before being raped and strangled. The couple was arrested after the axe murder of 17-year-old Edward Evans, whom Ian Brady had picked up at a gay bar in Manchester. Afterward, he claimed he merely intended to assault a "homo" and steal his money, but much suggests that Ian Brady himself was bisexual or homosexual, and that the two had consensual sex before the murder.

Initially, police did not suspect Myra Hindley of anything more than complicity, but when David Smith mentioned hearing about a suitcase in a locker at a station, the case took a different turn. There, they found the photos of Lesley Ann Downey and a chilling tape recording of her last 13 minutes alive, which revealed that Myra Hindley had been far more involved than she had initially indicated. In the couple's apartment, investigators also found a notebook with John Kilbride's name in it and a large number of photos from the moors, where three of the bodies were subsequently found.

Both Myra Hindley, who was called "Britain's most evil woman," and Ian Brady were sentenced to life imprisonment, as the death penalty was abolished while their case was in court. In 1987, both confessed to the last two murders and helped police locate one of the graves. Of her crimes, Myra Hindley herself said: "I should have been hanged. I deserved it. My guilt was worse than Brady's because I lured the children, and they would never have gotten into the car if I hadn't played my part. I have always considered myself worse than Brady."

Had it not been for David Smith's testimony, it is an open question whether the British killer couple would have been exposed. There were no bodies, and the crime scene on the moors would have been a nightmare for forensic technicians. For a profiler, it would also have been a difficult case. I might have been able to mention something about the trust between the children and the perpetrator, which could have potentially raised suspicions that a woman might also have been present. However, children have certainly gone with strange men before. Geographical profiling was not yet a structured method back then, but it had long been understood that killers were often to be found in the area where a murder had been committed, so that could presumably have given a hint toward the small towns west of Manchester, but there was otherwise not much to go on.

From an early age, Myra Hindley had been deeply fascinated by dead animals and accidents. She was accustomed to violence and wasn't afraid to inflict it or otherwise harm others; it had been a part of her life from the very beginning. She also later said that she was fascinated by what Ian Brady had in mind and that she "needed to investigate" what it would be like to kill a human being. There were several signs that she fantasized about murder, and she regularly told stories so gruesome that friends and colleagues distanced themselves from her. The murders were the ultimate way to bond with Ian Brady and achieve the attachment she constantly sought.

*

In the early 1990s, Canada was shaken by a case reminiscent of The Moors Murders in England thirty years earlier. June 29, 1991, was a beautiful, sunny day that many locals enjoyed on and around Lake Gibson near Niagara Falls, on the border between Canada and the USA. One of them was a man out in his canoe, while another fished from the shore. Both received the shock of their lives when they spotted body parts floating in the water. Police were alerted, and soon after, the lake was drained. At the bottom lay seven cement blocks. They had clearly been thrown into the water before the cement dried, as several were disintegrating, but in a few, body parts were still embedded. A single, larger cement block lay at the water's edge. It quickly became clear that the victim was 14-year-old Leslie Mahaffy, who had disappeared two weeks earlier. The autopsy report confirmed that the young girl had been subjected to extensive violence before she died and was highly likely to have been strangled.

Police were facing a difficult case, but as a profiler, one could still deduce a good deal, even if Lake Gibson wasn't the primary crime scene. First and foremost, there were the cement blocks. They were heavy, which could mean multiple people were involved in throwing them into the water, or that the perpetrator had access to a recovery vehicle or similar equipment. The latter was unlikely, however, as the largest block lay at the water's edge, clearly too heavy to have been thrown. Next, there was the body itself. Dismembering a body is not something one simply does. It's messy, and it requires a particular kind of psychology to bring oneself to perform the act at all. This tells me that the person or persons involved were unusually cold-blooded, there was not the slightest respect or compassion for the deceased, and one could hypothesize that this was not their first crime, as dismemberment would have been a very significant leap to take for a first-timer. There could also be an element of planning involved in the act, as not everyone has cement lying around at home. Conversely, one might think of tradespeople or contractors with access to the material. Another possibility was that the killer or killers subsequently bought the cement, which would imply they had spent some time with the body before it was dumped in the lake.

It was a summer overshadowed by fear in the Canadian province of Ontario, where a serial rapist had terrorized the Scarborough district of Toronto since 1987. Up to 20, perhaps more, women had already been assaulted, with no indication that the perpetrator would stop. The assaults consistently occurred from behind, so victims couldn't see the perpetrator, who threatened to cut their throats if they turned around. Often, the rapes took place in the front or backyards of the victims' homes, while their families were inside. The rapist became increasingly violent, starting to insert branches or stones into the women after the assaults, and also began taking souvenirs from his victims, a clear example of escalation, which often suggests that more and more is needed to satisfy the serial offender's fantasy. Police managed to collect DNA material, but analysis was a new and slow technology at the time, and no results were yet available.

Not far from Gibson Lake in Niagara-on-the-Lake, on the same day the body parts in the lake were discovered, Karla Homolka and Paul Bernardo took their seats in a carriage moments after exchanging their vows. Twenty-year-old Karla Homolka had found the dream prince she had always desired: tall, handsome, athletic, and financially secure. Together, they resembled models from contemporary fashion magazines, and in time, they would earn the nicknames "Barbie & Ken Killers," although I prefer "The School Girl Killers," because they specifically targeted schoolgirls. On the glossy surface and in Karla Homolka's imagination, the wedding celebration was a dream, but for many of the guests, and especially her parents, it was a sorrowful affair.

About six months prior, on Christmas Eve itself, the family's youngest daughter, Tammy, died from what doctors reported as alcohol poisoning after drinking with Karla Homolka and her boyfriend. That, however, was far from the whole truth. Paul Bernardo had long had an eye on the 15-year-old girl, and Karla Homolka decided to fulfill his wish. She brought a sedative home from the veterinary clinic where she worked and put it in her younger sister's drink. When Tammy fell asleep, Paul Bernardo raped her while Karla Homolka watched, until the teenager began to vomit. Shortly after, she stopped breathing. The couple called emergency services, but only after they had cleaned up, dressed Tammy, and put her to bed in her basement room. Outwardly, the two mourned with family and friends, but it wasn't long before Karla Homolka wrote to a friend that she was tired of her parents continually grieving the loss of their youngest daughter. Weren't they aware that their eldest was getting married? The couple grew tired of the atmosphere in her parents' home and soon moved into their own house. And it was here that Leslie Mahaffy met her end.

Paul Bernardo had spotted Leslie Mahaffy one night outside her home. She had a tendency to come home late in the evenings, and this time, her parents had made good on a threat to lock the door, leaving her to spend the night by the front door. Paul Bernardo managed to blindfold the girl and force her into the car, then drove home to Karla Homolka with their new "toy," as he called her. Leslie Mahaffy was raped and tortured for hours before the couple noticed that her blindfold was slipping; this likely sealed her fate. Karla Homolka later claimed Paul Bernardo had strangled her, while he maintained that Karla Homolka had given the girl an overdose of veterinary medication. They placed the body in the basement, where it lay the following day when Karla Homolka's parents came for dinner. Only after that was it dismembered and encased in cement, which Paul Bernardo bought for the apartment.

People who met Paul Bernardo got the impression of an intelligent and well-behaved young man, a real mother-in-law's dream. But behind that smooth exterior hid a person with serious problems. As a child, he was already caught peeping, and he behaved inappropriately toward others early on. At 16, he learned that his father was not his biological father, but that he was the result of an affair his mother had had. Subsequently, he was called a "whore's child" and a "bastard," which created an intense rage against his mother. His voyeurism was "inherited", as his stepfather had the same tendency, and it was not uncommon for parents in the local area to forbid their children from playing with the Bernardo family's son. As he grew older, he behaved both humiliatingly and violently toward his girlfriends and found pleasure in sadomasochism. It must therefore have been close to a miracle for him to meet a girl who, behind an equally smooth exterior, harbored the same dark desires.

There are descriptions of Karla Homolka's father as a violent alcoholic who beat both his wife and children, which stands in sharp contrast to her own account of a normal and good upbringing in an average nuclear family in the solid middle class. She was intelligent but not particularly diligent in school, and as a teenager, she flirted with the occult. What set her apart from so many other phases young people can go through was that she combined it with a strange fascination with animals, which, among other things, became apparent when she dug up a dead pet but later she became a veterinary assistant. Acquaintances described her as a sadist, and she was very dominant, tough, and controlling in her girl group, which she ruled with a firm hand by bullying others and keeping them down or out. This need for dominance often stems from very low self-esteem or traumas that the dominant person has been subjected to. The trauma is transferred to another person on whom one can vent their anger when it's not possible to do so with the original source of the trauma. As a psychologist, I have spoken with many of these "tough cookies," and after long periods of therapy, something traumatizing from the past always emerges.

It can take a long time for them to articulate and share their experiences with others, and many go to their graves without sharing them, but it is very important to talk about them if one is to address the issues they represent. It is, therefore, also my hypothesis that there is a trauma in Karla Homolka's past due to her fascination with death in general. Death and the occult suggest to me that she was living out a form of inner tension, but I don't know what it was based on. Another, or both, possibility is that she was one of the rather rare female psychopaths and thus was born without the ability to empathize with others.

The two fed each other's pathologies, and therefore their actions likely became far worse than if they had not met each other. There was not just one, but two fantasies to live out. Paul Bernardo undoubtedly had the urge to kill, but it became easier to carry out when he met Karla Homolka, so they could be two in the crimes.

About a year after the discovery of the cement blocks in Lake Gibson, passersby found the body of a young girl discarded in a ditch along a rural road. She was identified as 15-year-old Kristen French, who had been abducted in broad daylight from a parking lot outside a church, an incident witnessed by several people. Many had seen a young blonde woman holding a map as if she were lost. When Kristen French asked if she could help, the woman and a young man forced the teenager into a car. The autopsy showed that she had been subjected to extensive violence and rapes before being strangled. It was also clear that the girl's hair had been cut and her body washed before it was dumped. The washing was likely to erase various traces on the girl's body, while the hair cutting was either to hinder identification or to keep a souvenir. It has been seen before that serial killers have used hair or even skin to create figures to remind them of the murder.

On December 27, 1992, Karla Homolka went to the police to report Paul Bernardo, not for kidnapping, torture, rape, or murder, but for domestic violence. Quite coincidentally, the report coincided with the result of the DNA analysis of the samples Paul Bernardo had provided in connection with the investigation of the Scarborough rapes. The conclusion was clear: he was the man behind the assaults. In those days, Karla Homolka confided in her uncle and aunt, who encouraged her to go to the police. There, she told how, due to the violence Paul Bernardo had subjected her to, she had been completely under his control and had not dared to do anything but what she was told. There wasn't much concrete evidence against him, so the prosecution made a deal with Karla Homolka: if she would testify against Paul Bernardo in court, she would only be charged with negligent manslaughter and would receive a sentence of 12 years in prison. She accepted, and it was a clever move, as the agreement was binding.

It turned out that Paul Bernardo possessed videotapes that his defense attorney was also aware of. They had believed they could use the tapes in court to incriminate Karla Homolka and shift some of the blame from Bernardo. Two of the tapes contained gruesome recordings of severe sexual assaults on Leslie Mahaffy and Kristen French. On these, one could see how the two young women were forced to perform in pornography, including praising Paul Bernardo for his sexual prowess. And one could see and hear that Karla Homolka actively participated in both torture and rape. It also emerged that even when she was alone with Kristen French for about an hour while Paul Bernardo went out to get food, she didn't lift a finger to help the girl.

Paul Bernardo was, as expected, sentenced to life imprisonment without the possibility of parole, while his former wife got away with 12 years, which caused outrage across Canada. Today, Karla Homolka is a free woman, married, and has children.

The School Girl Killers are a prime example of what can happen when two or more individuals commit crimes together: there's a tendency for things to get worse. Firstly, Paul Bernardo's actions escalated from rape to murder after he met Karla Homolka. This might have happened anyway, but something in their relationship may have made it easier for him to take that next step. Secondly, there was an escalation of the crimes the two committed together. The rape of Karla Homolka's sister was terrible enough, but her death might have been an accident due to the sedative they used. However, there's no doubt that murder was the ultimate goal for the two unknown teenage girls the couple killed, and the autopsy reports also show that the torture intensified between the second and third murders.

You see the same pattern in other crimes; for instance, the risk of a fatal outcome increases if two or more criminals commit armed robberies. It's as if they fuel each other, challenging one another. It's the same mechanism at play when a biker puts on his vest and behaves entirely differently within the group than when he's alone.

Another detail I notice when studying the case more closely is the role distribution between the two. Often, the woman is labeled as the submissive and compliant one, and this is what Karla Homolka played on when she made her deal with the prosecution. However, I'm not convinced that the situation wasn't reversed. Paul Bernardo had a chaotic upbringing, while Karla Homolka was the cold and composed one who, in sexual recordings, "performed" as her younger sister in her clothes shortly after her death to excite him. Paul Bernardo was obsessed with blondes, and most of his rape victims were blonde, while the two unknown teenage girls the couple murdered were brunettes. This doesn't necessarily mean anything, but I don't think one can dismiss the idea that Karla Homolka also had a say here. And truthfully, we don't know which of the two actually committed the murders, as they blamed each other for the atrocities.

There are several explanations for what causes a couple to evolve into a killer couple, but much lies in the dynamic between the two. As we saw in the cases of The Lethal Lovers (who killed nursing home residents) and The Sunset Strip Killers (Carol Bundy and Douglas Clark), they likely fit the typical role distribution of a dominant and a submissive partner. Generally, the dominant personality takes the initiative, but this isn't something that happens on a third date. However, they typically look for signs of a potential accomplice from the beginning. More or less unconsciously, they seek a person who has a psychological need to be controlled and directed, which is often seen in cases of domestic violence.

However, a gradual escalation occurs over time. This is sometimes seen in sexual games, which can be part of a healthy relationship, but then the dominant partner takes a step further by perhaps involving another person whom the couple shares. It can also involve exchanging fantasies, which initially remain just that, fantasies. There are also examples of serial killers who have involved their partner by watching horror movies, where the conversation turns to how the two could commit a murder without being discovered, just for fun, of course. Most people would immediately reject such ideas, but if they don't, the dominant partner can continue. Concurrently, they often ensure they control and isolate their partner from family and friends, so the submissive becomes completely dependent on the dominant and almost fears being unable to live without the other there to make decisions. Choking games and role-playing can escalate into rape games, which can lead to arrangements with prostitutes, and from there, things can escalate, as they did for Karla Homolka and Paul Bernardo.

A similar pattern emerged in Carol Bundy's relationship with Douglas Clark, where bizarre sex games escalated to the abuse of a neighbor's daughter, then to the mistreatment of sex workers, and ultimately to murder. This continued until Carol Bundy finally broke down and contacted the police.

Douglas Clark's trial echoed with a booming sound that puzzled the jury members. Judge Torres explained that Douglas Clark had been sent to an adjoining room to cool off, but could still hear what was being said. The booming against the wall resumed. "As you can hear, he can confirm it," the judge remarked, much to the amusement of everyone present.

The judge ordered the proceedings to continue, but was again interrupted by the noise.

Carol Bundy had struck a special deal with the prosecution and was now acting as the prosecution's star witness against Douglas, who had fired his lawyers and was representing himself. It went poorly, to say the least. He frequently got lost in irrelevant details, which sometimes even worsened his case, and he constantly argued with the judge, who, as punishment, had revoked some of his privileges related to his detention. The judge repeatedly tried to persuade him to hand over his defense to professionals, as it was clear that Douglas Clark, alone, didn't understand that he was losing control of both the case and himself.

Later that day, the judge allowed the accused back into the courtroom, handcuffed. He had had enough. As Douglas Clark unleashed a torrent of curses towards Judge Torres, a muscular bailiff approached him and fitted him with a leather muzzle. This didn't stop the accused from kicking the furniture, prompting two other bailiffs to strap Douglas Clark to his chair. Despite the muzzle and a cloth napkin in his mouth, the audience could still understand the meaning of what he tried to shout: "Fuck you, judge!"

The Unraveling of Douglas Clark and Carol Bundy

The trial clearly reflected Douglas Clark's personality. He was dominant, manipulative, and saw himself as an infallible superman. Looking at his history, there isn't much out of the ordinary, but a couple of details stand out. His father worked in the navy, so the family moved frequently, living in no less than 37 different countries. This, of course, can make it difficult for a child or young person to form attachments to others. His youth was marked by rootlessness, and he developed an early heavy consumption of alcohol and women.

Looking at Carol Bundy, however, many traits will now be recognizable to a reader of this book. Her mother had dreamed of a little princess, but got a tomboyish, plump, severely nearsighted, and clumsy girl. At one point, when Carol Bundy was little, her mother locked her out of the house and said, "You don't live here anymore and I'm not your mother." For long periods, she turned her back on her own daughter—especially when another daughter was born who met all of her mother's expectations. Things didn't improve at school, where the other students heavily bullied Carol Bundy. Both her parents were alcoholics, and when her mother died, her father made her take over her mother's role, even in the bedroom. Carol Bundy was 13 then. She stated that she and her younger sister were told to decide between themselves who would first sleep with their alcoholic father, and they drew lots. Initially, her younger sister had to go in while Carol Bundy covered her ears to avoid hearing her cry.

As a teenager, she was often seen walking around naked and would masturbate in the presence of others. She craved the attention and recognition she felt she got from it, and then she also started selling sex for candy, food, and money. Her father's alcoholism worsened, and he became violent toward his daughters. At one point, he threatened them with a rifle and shot their cat, leaving blood everywhere in the kitchen. He told the girls he had considered killing both them and himself. At 17, she ran away and got together with a 56-year-old alcoholic who forced her into prostitution to earn money. Subsequent relationships were also marked by abuse, violence, and boundless behavior.

There's no doubt that the many traumas she experienced at such a young age left their mark, and that her many relationships with men stemmed from a hunt for recognition and love that, in her case, had become completely distorted. It's also not surprising that she had an extremely hard time with rejection, which explains her acceptance of Douglas Clark's bizarre behavior, partly involving her in the abuse of the neighbor girl and partly taking her on hunts for young women he could kill. It also makes sense that the murder of Jack Murray was so violent because he had shortly before tried to break up with her. The intense rage she felt was clearly evident in the overkill that met investigators in the van. She herself stated that she took the head home to Douglas Clark to proudly tell him that she had now murdered on her own, but that he instead became enraged at her for, among other things, having left the shell casing in the vehicle. For her, it must have been another violent rejection, which may help explain why she decided to confide in her colleagues at work and then call the police.

We will likely never know exactly what happened when The Sunset Strip Killers were active. Police found the pistols used in the murders at Douglas Clark's workplace, but otherwise, technical evidence was scarce. For example, investigators could not find traces of semen on Exxie Williams' head, even though Carol Bundy claimed Douglas Clark had engaged in sexual intercourse with it. Semen was found on a couple of the other victims, but analyses showed it did not match his blood type. It did, however, match Jack Murray's. Conversely, traces of blood were found in a garage belonging to Douglas Clark, a garage where, according to Carol Bundy, Douglas Clark had "amused himself" with the bodies of the two stepsisters. I have no doubt that Douglas Clark deserves to be behind bars, at least for having abused a then 11-year-old girl, and I am also quite sure that he was involved in one or more murders. But considering his and Carol Bundy's histories and the few technical pieces of evidence, I cannot rule out that Carol Bundy, and Jack Murray, may have been far more involved than she let on. Carol Bundy was convicted of the murder of Jack Murray and of a young sex worker who has never been identified, but whom she, according to her own statement, helped select and shoot. She received 25 years in prison for the first murder and 27 years for the second, and she died in prison at the age of 61 in 2003.

Douglas Clark remains on death row in California onto 2018, where he died of cardiovascular disease on October 11, 223 at the age of 75. He is one of the serial killers I have corresponded with and he was in my examination for my thesis in 2004. In his letters, he protests his innocence, but I have no doubt that he committed murder. The question, however, is whether justice would have been better served if he and Carol Bundy had swapped places. This will never come to light. Even though Douglas Clark writes page after page about how Carol Bundy was the only one who killed anyone, we can still gain something from the letters, as they reveal a great deal about the personality disorders that he and most other serial killers and serial rapists possess, which we will examine in more detail in the next chapter. Knowledge of personality disorders can indeed also be an important tool in investigative work, especially when it comes to interrogation methods and the presentation of evidence in trials.

CHAPTER 9: A DISTURBED INDIVIDUAL: THE SERIAL KILLER WHO INSPIRED THE MOVIE *SCREAM*

Danny Rolling loved his dog more than anything on earth. It never failed him, and whenever he needed to confide in someone, it was his four-legged friend who listened. That's why the little boy's heart was broken, sitting with the dying dog in his arms in the family home in Shreveport, in the northwestern corner of Louisiana, close to the Texas border.

Danny Rolling and his younger brother were scared, not just because of what their father had done to the dog. They were always scared. Their father, who supposedly had some horrific experiences in the Korean War in the early 1950s, had become enraged when his very young wife became pregnant in 1953. He had no desire to have children and assaulted her several times before their first son, Danny Rolling, was born the following year. From birth, the father showered Danny Rolling with curses and swear words, and when he didn't crawl "correctly," his father grabbed him by one leg and swung him into the wall. The same thing happened when his mother became pregnant just three months after Danny Rolling's birth; the father threw Danny Rolling headfirst onto the floor. Both he and his younger brother were regularly tied up, and a couple of times a week, they were punished when their father grabbed his belt and beat them with the buckle, without them ever understanding why. Their mother consistently started giving them dinner before he came home from his job as a police officer, because he believed the sons breathed "wrong" at the dinner table and therefore had to feel it if they couldn't correct themselves. He categorically refused to hug his sons, believing that such sentimentality would turn them into sissies, and he forbade his wife from holding birthday parties for them or planning family vacations.

Therefore, it came as a great surprise when he one day came home with a puppy he had found in connection with a work assignment. The dog became the one Danny Rolling turned to when there was no one else to talk to. He had already given up on his mother, who at that time had attempted to shoot herself in a suicide attempt that failed. She had, admittedly, left her husband with the children several times, but each time returned to the threats, fear, and violence.

"Look away, it's not really happening," his mother said again and again when his father went berserk.

It became clear to Danny Rolling quite early on that his mother seemingly wouldn't protect him and his brother. At school, they couldn't help him either. Even though his grades got worse and worse, and he was sent to the school psychologist several times, nothing happened that changed things at home. It didn't get any better when his father, almost daily, let his eldest son know how useless he was at everything. Danny Rolling himself didn't know it, but the psychologists had written in some papers about him that he "suffered from an inferiority complex with a tendency towards aggression and weak impulse control." They recommended regular therapy, but it never materialized. He sought refuge in art and music to create his own world for himself and the dog, where they could be together while being moved around when his mother regularly tried to leave his father. By the age of six or seven, he thought about harming others and was at one point discovered with an iron in his hand, mumbling something about murdering "the boss." In time, he would develop into a peeping tom. Initially, he wished to observe completely ordinary families, which he wished could be his, but later, with a sexual component, where he masturbated while either stalking or looking at women.

It was one of the countless times they had returned home that Danny Rolling's father unleashed his anger on the dog. Before his son's eyes, he tortured the dog, which Danny Rolling now held in his arms as the dog died. And it only got worse. A few years later, Danny Rolling could hear his parents shouting at each other. There was nothing unusual about that. He walked through the house and into the bathroom, where the argument was taking place. He arrived just in time to see his mother grab his father's razor blade and cut her wrists. As blood sprayed out, she managed to push his father out and close and lock the door. His father hammered on the door and continued the argument, while Danny Rolling, in the bathroom, could only watch as his mother bled. However, they managed to get his mother hospitalized in time. Instead, the anger his father had directed at his mother was unleashed on Danny Rolling, who began to flee into the world of music when he played his guitar. In his room, he sang his prayers to God, but his thoughts began to fill with sadistic fantasies, nourished by the alcohol he had started drinking whenever he could get away with it. At that time, Danny Rolling was 11 years old.

Calling Danny Rolling's upbringing chaotic would be a severe understatement, and it's hardly surprising that many years later, he was diagnosed with several personality disorders, something we will be focusing on in this chapter. I've encountered various types in my work as a psychologist for over 20 years. In recent years, I've actually observed an increasing number of children and adolescents with nascent personality disorders. I discovered when I began studying serial killers that their upbringings bore striking resemblances to those I saw in many of the children and adolescents I treated. And like them, the vast majority of serial killers also had one or more personality disorders.

I should quickly add that I naturally don't expect "my" children and adolescents to grow up to be serial killers; fortunately, that's an extremely rare phenomenon. I far more often see them turn anger and grief inward, developing eating disorders, compulsive behaviors, anxiety, depression, or self-harm. Some react outwardly, developing temper problems and risking becoming violent, and then there are a few who have thoughts of harming other people. The central point for them, and in connection with serial killers, is that childhood has a great impact on the people we become as adults. It would be strange if it didn't. If you grow up with parents who are addicted to alcohol or drugs and prioritize their addiction above all else, and if they are also violent towards their children, who may even be subjected to sexual abuse, it doesn't take a university degree to know that it will affect the children for the rest of their lives. This is not an excuse for the horrible crimes serial killers have committed, but it is part of the explanation for how they can treat others in such a terrible way. At the same time, knowledge of personality disorders is an important part of a profiler's work because it's another tool that can help explain an offender's behavior. As we'll see, there can be differences in what a crime scene looks like and what the killer does, depending on their personality type. An analysis of the personality can also be significant in both the interrogation room and the courtroom once the perpetrator is caught. We'll also touch upon that in this chapter.

But first, let's look at what personality disorders actually are. It's important to emphasize that these are not mental illnesses like, for example, schizophrenia. The vast majority of serial killers are perfectly aware that killing is wrong; they simply don't care. There are examples of serial killers who are mentally ill and, for instance, kill because they believe they are vampires or because demons demand that they murder. They are usually caught quickly because they are unable or uninterested in erasing their tracks. As we delve into a number of different personality disorders, it's important to note that some of the traits are normal in themselves, but it's the combination and degree of the traits that are significant for diagnosing the disorders. Just because you have some of these traits doesn't mean you have a personality disorder. A diagnosis is not given unless one meets a set of criteria, which can vary depending on whether one uses the European or American classification system. In this book, I use the American system because most of the serial killers I've dealt with have been diagnosed in the USA. Furthermore, a diagnosis is not even considered unless the affected person has problems in their daily life, and it negatively impacts those around them. This is a research area that receives a lot of attention, and much has happened in personality disorder research in recent years.

When I started university, few doubted that environment, that is, upbringing, was the basis for the formation of our personality, because it's not fully formed until we turn 18. Today, however, there's a consensus that there are both a hereditary component and environmental influences when it comes to the development of personality disorders. This means that one can be genetically predisposed to a disorder, but it will often require a series of experiences in childhood for it to eventually develop into a definite diagnosis.

Let's first look at the personality disorder that most ordinary people probably know: antisocial personality disorder. It is widespread among serial killers, or at least traits thereof, including Danny Rolling. However, very few, if any, have only that diagnosis. On the surface, people with antisocial personality disorder can appear charming, and they are often articulate. But the positive traits exist only on the surface. They feel no guilt or shame, and they have impaired empathy. They can put on a show so their surroundings fall for their charm, but in reality, it's difficult for them to understand other people's feelings. With impaired empathy, they have no loyalty to people, and thus, the attachment that is one of the prerequisites for not harming other people does not arise. You can get a sense of how psychopaths behave when you write or talk to serial killers, who very rarely use metaphors. They are extremely concrete and can have difficulty generating narratives that come from within, in their language. My hypothesis is that they use language very concretely because they are so goal-oriented in their thoughts. When Dennis Rader referred to his victims as "projects," it was because he was unable to imagine them as human beings. If you ask a serial killer if he feels sorry for the victims' families, he will most often not understand the question; it's simply not part of a psychopath's way of thinking.

When reading or hearing about serial killers, you will encounter both psychopaths and sociopaths, and the two terms are often used as synonyms, but there is broad agreement on understanding the difference as follows: Psychopathy is something innate, and I have only encountered it a few times in my professional work. In adults with psychopathy, you will be able to trace the traits far back in time to their early childhood, which applies to many serial killers whose behavior has been completely askew almost from the beginning. Sociopaths', on the other hand, problematic behavior can be traced to events in their environment. Their lives can be chaotic and marked by abuse from the start, but they can also live a relatively normal childhood up to a certain age, where something traumatic then happens that harms the child. This was the case for Danny Rolling, who, as a result of his father's mistreatment, developed a violent rage against both his father and mother, who, in his eyes, should have saved her children. It was that anger that, with considerable certainty, developed into the sadistic fantasies he was already grappling with at age 11.

Another disorder that is common among serial killers, and which is probably known to many fans of crime series and true crime, is narcissistic personality disorder. The narcissistic personality structure is characterized by an exaggerated self-absorption, and people who have this diagnosis are afraid of not being seen and recognized because their self-esteem relies on others' validation. It typically manifests as a strong need for attention, admiration, and a tendency to appear arrogant and self-absorbed, while in reality, they overestimate themselves. Similar to antisocial individuals, narcissists often exhibit impaired empathy and a belief that they are so much more valuable than others that they have the right to live by their own rules.

We have encountered several individuals with narcissistic personality disorder here in this book. Take Dennis Rader, for whom the recognition for his murders was so central that he even wrote to newspapers and investigators to get them to use the alias he had invented: BTK. I have also experienced this extreme form of narcissism in my correspondence with Douglas Clark—one of The Sunset Strip Killers—who was convinced that he was a world-class lawyer and therefore would defend himself in court, which contributed to him receiving a death sentence. He has constantly protested his innocence, but he could not resist the attention that interested me in his case. The solution for him was to let me know, in his letters, that he was one of the world's leading experts on serial killers, as he has met many of them in prison. The question, of course, is whether he is writing about the others or whether he is actually describing himself in the letters to me. Ted Bundy did something similar, referring to himself in interviews in the third person so that he could always claim he was only speaking hypothetically, while also getting the opportunity to be in the spotlight.

In his letters, Douglas Clark repeatedly referred to Ted Bundy, who was on death row in the same prison, and he also claimed that Carol Bundy wanted to imitate Ted Bundy's murders. With his knowledge of Ted Bundy and other serial killers, he believed he could help me with my empirical study. I naturally think that his knowledge comes from himself, but in our correspondence, that's not what's important, because the way he writes gives me a lot of knowledge about his personality. Douglas Clark, like Dennis Rader, sees himself as a kind of superman, but in reality, their narcissism and that of others covers an extremely low self-esteem, and it covers experiences that are difficult for them to handle.

It can actually be very painful to be a narcissist, because occasionally, they see the truth in the mirror. In their own minds, they are infallible, but they constantly fail. Many of those I treat are immensely sad people because they constantly feel that the world misunderstands them and doesn't perceive them as the geniuses they feel they are. And when it dawns on them that others don't see them as they see themselves, serial killers truly become dangerous. If they are fired, as was the case with Dennis Rader, or rejected by, most often, a woman, their self-image cracks for a while, and then you see the extreme rage that makes them so violent. When they succeed in regaining power and control through a murder, they can restore their self-image for a period until the cool-down period comes to an end.

The third personality disorder we will look at, and which we have also encountered here in this book, is called borderline personality disorder. A person with a borderline diagnosis typically reacts very impulsively and without thought for the consequences of their actions. They can be unpredictable and have very large mood swings. They typically have difficulty controlling their emotional outbursts and can therefore appear aggressive and angry. It is also quite typical that people with borderline personality disorder have an undifferentiated view of the world. They often have intense but chaotic relationships with other people, while also fearing rejection and being downright anxious about being left alone. One of the most painful aspects for people with this diagnosis is that they have an uncertain sense of who they are and what they want. I have great compassion for those I have treated, because they are so characterized by a feeling of inner emptiness that makes them doubt who they really are, whether they even have a self or an inner core that the rest of us take for granted.

In the case of Aileen Wuornos, who shot and killed seven men, the diagnosis was quite clear when she was interrogated about the murders. In her case, the personality disorder couldn't be discerned from the crime scenes, as she "simply" shot the men. However, I can clearly sense it when I observe her behavior. She is very disturbed in her demeanor, and she constantly changes her explanation, even though it only strengthens the suspicion against her: first, she did it, then it was self-defense, then it was revenge. She also changes character rapidly. One moment she sits calmly and tells her story, the next she's acting out. Borderline is also one of the diagnoses Danny Rolling received. Psychiatrists and psychologists concluded that he had a tendency to rapidly change temper, especially under pressure, and that he craved a form of control in his life, which he lost as a very young child when he could never figure out what had triggered his father's rage. This search for control is often seen in serial killers, for example, with Dennis Rader, who literally took control of his victims by cunningly binding them.

A rarer variant among serial killers is dependent personality disorder. As we have discussed several times, serial killings and serial rapes are primarily about power and control. Perpetrators usually know how to initiate, plan, and carry out their crimes without being discovered, and in many cases, they behave dominantly. For the dependent individual, it's the opposite. These are people who are extremely unself-reliant, self-effacing, and helpless. They have an exaggerated fear of standing on their own two feet and are intensely anxious about being abandoned. They often let others take responsibility for significant areas of their lives, find it very difficult to say no, and easily give in to others' wishes, just as they rarely express their own needs or make demands on people they are dependent on. This is a disorder I have seen in people who are or have been in violent relationships where the partner has subjected them to almost total control. It's also here that I encounter cases of compulsive repetition, where women go from one violent relationship to another because, in a way incomprehensible to many, it gives them a sense of security, it's what they know, and they cannot imagine ever being able to cope alone.

This doesn't immediately sound like a serial killer, but when it comes to killer couples, the submissive partner will often have a dependent personality disorder. An example could be Myra Hindley, who helped Ian Brady rape and kill five children in northern England. While one can genuinely speculate whether Karla Homolka wasn't the dominant one when the School Girl Killers terrorized Canada, I have no such doubt regarding The Moors Murders, because it became quite clear that Myra Hindley did not participate in the murders in the same way as Karla Homolka. The question in my mind, then, is whether Myra Hindley would have become a serial killer if she hadn't met Ian Brady.

The next personality disorder we will look at is histrionic personality disorder, but before we do, let's go back to August 26, 1990, and the American university city of Gainesville, Florida, which had just been ranked 13th on the list of the best cities to live in the USA.

It was four in the afternoon on a warm, sunny summer day, and police officer Ray Barber was just about to clock out when he received two calls from the station, coincidentally concerning the same address: Williamsburg Village Apartments. The first was a complaint about a resident playing loud music; the second concerned a building manager who needed assistance. For Ray Barber, it was business as usual. In a city with so many students, neither call was unusual, and he assumed he could handle both on his way home.

When he arrived, he parked at the entrance to the complex's courtyard. He got out and was greeted by the building manager, who told him he had a visit from a pair of nervous parents who wanted him to unlock their daughter's apartment door because they couldn't reach her. The manager didn't want to take on the responsibility alone. There was still no cause for concern. In Gainesville, young people constantly made spontaneous decisions about parties and outings and forgot to inform their parents. But when the parents told him that they had an appointment with their daughter, 17-year-old Christina Powell, and that no one had seen her since the morning of the previous day, Ray Barber had a strange feeling inside. The feeling increased when the mother and father added that Christina Powell's roommate, Sonja Larson, of the same age, had not called her mother the day before, which they had agreed to do.

Ray Barber, along with the building manager and the residents' association president, went up the stairs to the apartment. The parents followed. The building manager unlocked the door and let the officer enter. He and the residents' association president followed. On a sofa, they spotted a young woman. It looked bad. The residents' association president turned on her heel, while the building manager pushed past her and rushed past the parents on the stairs.

"Oh, God!" he shouted, before vomiting on the asphalt.

Ray Barber immediately called for backup, and soon after, blue flashing lights from police cars and ambulances illuminated the courtyard, where residents gathered. Meanwhile, investigators and technicians began their work. Christina Powell was naked. Her clothes were cut into pieces and lay beside her. She had been stabbed five times in the back, but the killer had turned her over and spread her legs so that her pelvis was the first thing people saw when they entered the apartment. As a particularly barbaric detail, the perpetrator had cut off the young woman's nipples. Her hair was spread out like a fan. The contents of her bag were scattered around, as if the perpetrator had turned it upside down, and a technician found a picture of Christina Powell and her boyfriend, with the boyfriend's image torn away. In another room, they found the body of Sonja Larson. She, too, had been stabbed, but it was clear that she had fought violently, and the killer had stabbed her in the front of her torso. There were no signs that he had rummaged through her belongings.

Outside, officers began questioning the other residents. A neighbor recalled hearing someone taking a shower in the girls' apartment early Friday morning, while George Michael's song *Faith* was playing loudly. Then, he had heard a thumping sound. He had assumed that the girls, who had just started university, had begun hanging pictures.

Just then, a young woman parked her car and got out. She walked toward the apartment but was stopped by a uniformed officer who asked for her name. The officer called over a plainclothes colleague and showed her the woman's name in his notebook, after which the two whispered a few short sentences to each other. The young woman was taken to a local crisis center, where she was told that her two roommates had been murdered. She nearly fainted when she realized what could have happened if she hadn't been away that weekend.

Neither the police nor the technicians were finished at Williamsburg Village Apartments when Gail Barber, Ray Barber's wife, a police officer at the Alachua County Sheriff's Office, was asked to stop by Christa Hoyt's apartment. The 18-year-old woman was a clerk at the station, but she hadn't shown up for her night shift, and she wasn't answering her phone. Gail Barber knew Christa Hoyt well. She was diligent and almost never sick, and it wasn't like her to be absent without notice. She thought of the two murdered students her husband had found, but dismissed the thought. What was the likelihood that a married couple, within such a short interval in a peaceful city like Gainesville, would be the first at these types of crime scenes?

Together with her colleague, Keith O'Hara, Gail Barber drove to Christa Hoyt's place. They got out of the patrol car and walked to the front door, knocking. It was completely silent inside. They knocked again and tried the doorknob. The door was locked. Just then, the complex's building manager came out of his apartment. Together, the three went around to the other side of the building. The building manager knew something was wrong because the fence around the backyard was damaged. The two officers continued through the backyard. It lay deserted in the darkness. They walked over to the apartment's glass sliding door. That too was locked. They noticed that the curtain didn't reach all the way to the floor, so they knelt down and turned on their flashlights. Inside the room, a slumped figure sat on the bed. The person was wearing socks and shoes. They could see a little blood on the floor. They moved the light beams upwards, and then they saw it: the figure had no head.

As reinforcements sped through the city, Gail Barber and Keith O'Hara noticed water running inside the apartment. They alerted their colleagues as soon as they arrived, thinking the killer might still be inside. Once fully assembled, the front door was forced open, and armed police secured the residence. Water was indeed running in the bathroom, but the perpetrator was not there. Instead, they noticed bloodstains on the shower stall floor. The first thing they saw when they entered the bedroom was Christa Hoyt's head, staring at them with lifeless eyes. The head was placed on a shelf, making it appear as if it were observing its own body, and the hair was spread out like a fan. It quickly became clear to the officers that the killer had dragged the shelf in from another room. The 18-year-old clerk's clothes lay in the bedroom and had clearly been cut open. She had been stabbed several times in the back. One of the stabs was so deep that the knife had gone through her heart. Afterward, the killer had cut open the body from the sternum to the pubic bone, exposing the intestines. Just as with Christina Powell, the killer had also cut off Christa Hoyt's nipples.

The cause of death was obviously the many stab wounds, but the medical examiner could also tell investigators that both Christina Powell and Christa Hoyt had been raped. The perpetrator had also washed both women's genitals with soap and water, although it was still possible to find semen in both victims.

We've previously discussed how challenging it can be to get a crime scene to tell a story if the perpetrator hasn't left much behind. That's not the case here, in an incident I studied during one of my trainings. Additionally, I've watched 50 hours of trial footage. Here, the challenge is more about where to begin. The investigators and I quickly concluded that the same perpetrator must have been responsible, as the probability of two killers being at large in a small city with fewer than a hundred thousand inhabitants, both cutting off their victims' nipples, is very small. Furthermore, there was the way two of the victims were displayed, both in terms of shock value and the fact that their hair was arranged in a fan shape. At both crime scenes, water had been running in the bathrooms, suggesting that the perpetrator had taken a shower, just as he had washed two of the victims, and note that I'm focusing on Christina Powell and Christa Hoyt. They were both stabbed in the back, both raped, and subsequently washed. This was not the case with Sonja Larson. On the contrary, she was stabbed in the chest and left in her room. In the BTK case, we discussed how Dennis Rader's target victim in the Otero family was Josephine, the daughter, because he spent by far the most time with her. This is the same behavior one can observe with the two roommates in Williamsburg Village Apartments. I would be quite certain that Christina Powell was the one who fit into the killer's fantasy, while Sonja Larson "simply" needed to be removed so the perpetrator could concentrate on what he was in the apartment to do.

And there's more to the story. As mentioned, Christina Powell and Christa Hoyt were stabbed in the back, as if the killer didn't want to look them in the eyes when he killed them, but it was apparently no problem in Sonja Larson's case. This made me wonder if there was a special connection between the killer and the two primary targets, and if they might have been surrogates for another woman.

The display of Christina Powell's and Christa Hoyt's bodies is also central. As we've noted before, this can be an expression of a desire to shock, but it can also mean that the killer harbored intense rage, perhaps against women, perhaps against someone in their close family. There's no doubt that The Gainesville Ripper, as he was dubbed, targeted specific victims. His primary targets were not stabbed in the torso, which must have held significance for his actions. They were also not stabbed as many times as Sonja Larson, who simply needed to be quickly eliminated. The washings might seem odd. Had I not seen the crime scene photos and read the autopsy reports, it would have been difficult to say anything about the perpetrator, but with access to the sources, it's clear that it wasn't just about removing evidence. There's a certain gentleness at play and something psychological that the killer was acting out.

Committing murder is not a simple matter. A number of the serial killers I've communicated with have told me this themselves. Afterward, it can be emotionally difficult to cope with what one has done, especially for those who have difficulty regulating emotions due to their personality. The washings in the Gainesville case could have been an attempt to cope with the murders, but at that point, that would only be a hypothesis.

Another remarkable behavior I notice is the fact that the killer bathed in the women's apartments. Investigations also showed that he had eaten there. This is actually not that unusual. Here in Denmark, Marcel Lychau Hansen called the "Amager Man" drank milk at one of the crime scenes, and Dennis Rader made a habit of drinking a glass of water, washing it, and putting it back, which for him was a power trip because he was the only one in the world who knew about it. Again, it's about power and control. They showed that the crime scene was theirs, that they had conquered it, and that they could do whatever they pleased. At the same time, it was a way for them to prolong the experience, because they had done something that only they knew about. Even though it's quite possible they were also hungry, thirsty, or needed to clean up, it was primarily a psychological game they were playing.

The perpetrator clearly spent a long time at the crime scene, and despite what was happening, no one heard anything that would have prompted them to raise an alarm. This tells me that the killer had pretty good control over what he was doing. In the first instance, he even had control over two women at once, without them being able to call for help. The autopsy showed traces of duct tape on the victims' mouths, and in Christina Powell's and Christa Hoyt's cases, tape had also been used on their wrists and ankles. Their killer was, therefore, prepared. It also turned out that he had broken open the doors with the same tool, a screwdriver. And then there's the appearance of the primary targets. It could be a coincidence, but they were both small and slender and had long, brown hair and generally resembled each other a lot. All of this tells me that they were hardly chosen at random. I would have advised investigators, in mapping the victims' last days, to be open to the possibility that the killer had followed them, and that witnesses might have noticed it. I would also mention that he might have experience with investigative work, as he had removed the duct tape from the bodies and taken it with him, so he didn't risk fingerprints being found on it afterward. It's not because I thought he had to be an investigator himself, but he might have a job related to the police, have officers in his social circle, or just read a lot of true crime.

In this case, I would also offer an assessment of the personality. That the perpetrator was highly likely a sociopath or antisocial which is almost self-evident. Firstly, the vast majority of serial killers exhibit traits of that personality disorder. Secondly, the crime scenes and the behavior within them strongly reflect something pathological and psychological being acted out, as well as a search for power and control. More interesting is what the perpetrator tried to communicate by displaying the bodies, because even for a serial killer, what investigators in Gainesville witnessed was extreme. This leads my thoughts towards what is called a histrionic personality disorder. "Histrionic" means "dramatic" or "theatrical," and it is precisely drama and a constant search for attention that characterize the disorder.

There are superficial emotions and exaggerated emotional expressions, which often lead to significant challenges and conflicts in relation to social rules and norms. The disorder often gets in the way, making it very difficult for people who suffer from it to achieve deep, meaningful relationships with other people. They are therefore also easily influenced, easily hurt, and often react by creating a lot of drama. Their behavior is often egocentric, as they are excessively preoccupied with appearance, their own attractiveness, and a longing for recognition. The urge for drama truly manifested itself at the crime scenes in Gainesville, where the killer clearly needed to be overly dramatic. It was as if it couldn't be wild enough. It wasn't enough to pose the bodies; the nipples had to be cut off, too. It wasn't enough to display the severed head; the body also had to be cut open. I have heard police officers tell of histrionic crime scenes several times, where bodies are displayed, and the two apartments in Gainesville certainly lived up to that. This is not to say, of course, that one becomes a serial killer or in any other way dangerous simply because one has a personality disorder.

That a man is diagnosed with histrionic personality disorder is by no means unknown, but the disorder is most prevalent in women, and we have a very good example from Denmark, from Nykøbing Falster Hospital. On January 1, 2015, nurse Christina Aistrup Hansen was arrested, suspected of having killed four elderly patients with overdoses of morphine and sedative diazepam. Psychiatrists concluded that the 31-year-old woman had a histrionic personality disorder. They began questioning the nurse's colleagues, and it quickly became apparent that most had noticed the propensity for drama and attention that characterizes the personality. Several of them had begun calling particularly dramatic shifts with deaths, cardiac arrests, and massive bleeding "Christina Hansen shifts"—somewhat like in the case from the children's clinic in Kerrville, Texas, where nurse Genene Jones's shifts were nicknamed "the death shift." Many developed a strained relationship with the Danish nurse, and some began to suspect her because it was a little too often her who discovered when patients had cardiac arrest and could thus provide them with life-saving first aid. If people around her hadn't heard about the episodes, she made sure they knew. To a colleague, she once sent a text message saying: "I just killed someone."

This could, of course, have been gallows humor jargon between colleagues, but the urge for attention also appeared on Facebook, where, shortly before her arrest, when four patients had died during one night shift, she wrote that it would be possible to make a movie about her experiences at work. Witnesses painted a picture of a proactive and very self-aware type who enjoyed being in charge and occasionally believed she was more skilled than the doctors when it came to choosing the right treatment.

During the case, prosecutor Michael Boolsen told the court: "The defendant has arranged herself as the lead in a bizarre play where the patients are her extras... She has used her nursing expertise in a deeply perverted way, driven by her histrionic personality disorder."

At the city court, Christina Aistrup Hansen was sentenced to life imprisonment, but the verdict was overturned in the High Court because the judges did not find it proven that the overdoses alone were the cause of the patients' deaths. The nurse was therefore found guilty of four attempted murders and received a sentence of 12 years in prison.

*

In Gainesville, panic spread like wildfire. Hundreds of students dropped out of university and returned home, while many others formed "sleepover pacts" where 5, 10, or even 15 people would gather and take turns sleeping so someone could keep watch. The situation worsened when two more bodies were discovered on August 28, 1990, at the Gatorwood Apartments complex. This crime scene eerily resembled the first, with one crucial difference: one of the victims was a young man. He had clearly fought hard against the killer, who had stabbed him numerous times from the front. Once he was subdued, the perpetrator focused on the female student, who was raped and then stabbed in the back. Her genitals had also been washed, and her hair was fanned out, leaving no doubt that The Gainesville Ripper was responsible for these latest deaths as well.

The media went into a frenzy. Day after day, the gruesome details of the case dominated headlines, and immense pressure mounted on investigators. With relief, they soon announced that a tip had led them to a prime suspect. He was an odd young man who had been expelled from Gatorwood Apartments for fighting and for his habit of showing up unannounced in strangers' apartments. He had a history of violence towards his grandmother and was known to carry a knife. Furthermore, his face was disfigured from a traffic accident, seemingly fitting the public's perception of a serial killer. The only problem was the complete lack of evidence, even after a thorough search of his home. However, the murders *did* stop after his detainment, so police intensified their efforts to find evidence that could convict him. Even when it was revealed that his blood type didn't match the semen found at the crime scenes, he remained behind bars.

Yet, there was another reason why the horrific killings had ceased. It was at this crucial point that a woman from Shreveport decided to call the police. She had been torn by doubt, but now she could no longer remain silent. "Folks, I think you should take a closer look at a guy named Danny Rolling," she urged.

She and her husband had come to know him through their church. He often visited them, but over time, they both felt an unsettling presence about him and had gradually let their contact fade. When the woman read about the Gainesville murders, she was reminded of an unsolved triple homicide in Shreveport, where a young mother, her son, and her father had been stabbed to death. She wasn't alone in this suspicion. Investigators from Gainesville had already been to Shreveport and had no doubt. The killer had focused on the young mother, who had been bound with duct tape, raped, and killed with stab wounds to the back. Her body had been obscenely displayed, and her genitals had been washed, though not with soap and water, but with vinegar. Too many details matched for it to be a mere coincidence: The Gainesville Ripper's reign of terror had begun in Shreveport.

As investigators delved deeper into Danny Rolling's past, their suspicions were only strengthened. His childhood, as described earlier, had been a living hell, leading to a chaotic and deeply troubled adolescence. His alcohol abuse was compounded by heavy marijuana use, and he dropped out of high school. He enlisted in the military like his father, but was quickly discharged, confirming his father's constant taunts that he was useless. For a period, he lived with his grandfather and became involved with the Pentecostal Church. He prayed for a girlfriend, and in church, he met a young woman whom he married. They became parents to a daughter, and Danny Rolling held several jobs to support his small family. However, the pressure proved too much. His substance abuse resumed, he struggled to keep jobs, he left the church, and he subjected his wife to violent assaults. They divorced after three years of marriage. A series of suicide attempts followed, and he began a relationship with a 17-year-old girl while simultaneously committing numerous armed robberies that led to lengthy prison sentences.

In 1984, he stalked a young girl and subsequently broke into her home with the intent to rape her. Instead, he broke down in tears. The two talked. She made him coffee, and they sang together. According to Danny Rolling, they eventually had sex;

whether it was consensual is unlikely to ever be known, and she drove him home, after which he fled, fearing she would alert the police. He continued his transient existence, living alternately with family and friends across the country, before once again ending up behind bars for a supermarket robbery. Upon his release, he managed to find a job at a restaurant in Shreveport, but a conflict with his boss, when he threatened to shoot him and the chef, led to his dismissal. That same day, the mother, her son, and her father were murdered. A few months later, Danny Rolling got into a fight with his father and shot him in the stomach and head. His father survived, but Danny Rolling fled again, embracing the nomadic life that had become his norm. He continued to rob supermarkets, even asking one witness to pray for him, before continuing towards Gainesville, where he settled in a tent in a wooded area near Christina Powell and Sonja Larson's apartment.

When the woman from Shreveport hung up the phone, police didn't have to search long for Danny Rolling; he was already in jail for another armed robbery. He had been arrested in a small tent camp in a wooded area near Christa Hoyt's apartment, and there, officers had confiscated a screwdriver, a knife, a cassette recorder, and some audiotapes, which were now in storage. Investigators retrieved the items and discovered that Danny Rolling was a surprisingly skilled country singer who wrote his own melodies and lyrics, which he recorded on tape. On one of them, they could hear his own words:

"Mysterious rider, what is your name?
You are a killer, a homeless person gone insane."

On another tape, he mentioned hunting deer and described how he killed them. No one who listened to the voice doubted that he was talking about a completely different kind of prey.

After his arrest, Danny Rolling's personality became his biggest enemy. People with trait of histrionic personality disorder, wich Rolling had together with narcissistic traits, according to Dr. Harry Krop, the defense psychologyst, are often highly self-centered and crave attention and drama to mask their deep-seated insecurity. The Gainesville Ripper found it difficult to keep silent about his actions. He quickly confided in a couple of his fellow inmates, though the nature of his confessions often shifted with his volatile moods—another hallmark of his personality. One moment, he seemed ashamed of his deeds and needed to unburden himself; the next, he would boast to others. In both scenarios, the central motivation for him was attention. This proved to be his downfall, as several inmates relayed his confessions to investigators, significantly aiding the interrogations.

When it comes to interrogating serial killers and rapists, information about personality disorder, play a vital role, as the approach to different personality disorders is crucial. For criminals like Danny Rolling or nurse Christina Aistrup Hansen, it can be relatively straightforward because they often, in one way or another, reveal or hint at their crimes. However, this is far from always the case. Many perpetrators are meticulous planners who go to great lengths to leave no traces, and most have no interest in divulging their secrets. Often, they only admit what they know the police can prove beyond a reasonable doubt, while they internalize the rest, reliving it in their fantasies during incarceration. This is another form of power display, reaffirming their control over aspects of their crimes. That's why investigators need to understand the suspect's personality and how to encourage them to open up. With individuals like the "Amager Man," who is serving a life sentence for two murders and six rapes, attempting to build a strong rapport might not even be possible, let alone productive.

A prime example of effective profiling in interrogation is the case of Robert Hansen, the Alaskan baker who kidnapped, raped, and hunted strippers and prostitutes in the wilderness outside Anchorage. As mentioned, John E. Douglas developed a remarkably accurate profile that led to a search warrant. He also advised local police on how to interrogate the serial killer. Hansen's crimes stemmed from extreme low self-esteem and a desire for power and revenge against women. Douglas believed the culprit would feel very powerful and in control upon arrest. Therefore, he recommended that investigators fill the interrogation room with maps, pictures, and reports to give Robert Hansen the impression that they knew even more than they actually did. He advised them to leave Hansen alone in the room for a considerable time, allowing the deep-seated insecurity that plagued him to surface. Investigators were told that Robert Hansen viewed the interrogation as a game, aiming to beat the system on its own turf. This meant he would most likely confess to murders that could be linked to him with technical evidence, while denying everything else. If they wanted the baker to admit to more crimes, they had to avoid condemning him. Instead, they were to show genuine interest in him and his motives, and generally act as if they enjoyed listening to his story.

This approach yielded results, particularly when they pretended to be deeply impressed by his planning and the measures he took to avoid capture. The combination of listening, asking with interest, and then letting the full weight of the evidence bear down on Robert Hansen had a clear effect, as recounted by one of the public prosecutors, Frank Rothschild, much later in an interview with *Newsweek*: "It worked! As we were doing it, I looked at Hansen across the table, and I watched a wild transformation from the mild baker Bob, who was a pretty small guy. He wasn't physically imposing. And he wore glasses and seemed like such a little nerd. But suddenly his neck turned bright red, and the hairs on his neck stood up, and he transformed into the man who had killed all those women. Right before our eyes, he really got angry."

Following this, Robert Hansen demanded to speak with his lawyers, after which he entered into an agreement that resulted in a life sentence in exchange for his confession to four murders and a long list of rapes.

Before the trial, Danny Rolling was examined by two psychologists and a psychiatrist. He received the primary diagnosis of borderline personality disorder, which, as previously mentioned, is characterized by a lack of control, rapid changes in temperament, and intense rage. Individuals with this diagnosis often struggle to form attachments with others. Furthermore, they concluded that he had antisocial personality disorder and trait from histrionic personality disorder and narcissistic personality disorder, which we discussed earlier in connection with the almost exaggerated way the primary victims were displayed. It should hopefully also be clear that there was thus a link between the behavior at the crime scenes and Danny Rolling's personality disorders. Looking back at his childhood and upbringing, this is hardly surprising. Things went wrong for him right from the start. No one who experiences that degree of violence, fear, and abuse emerges unscathed, and certainly not without help. In my opinion, there is no doubt that the murders of Danny Rolling were revenge: revenge on his father and his abuse and his mother's failure, revenge on the society that failed to help him, and revenge on those who managed to live good lives when he couldn't. Interrogations of several of Danny Rolling's former girlfriends also explained the mysterious washings. The women stated that Danny Rolling washed them in the same manner, but precisely why he did so, only he knew, if he was even aware of the reason for the behavior himself.

Before meeting the judge and jury in Gainesville, Danny Rolling decided to plead guilty to the eight murders. Therefore, the jury's task was not to determine whether to recommend a sentence of life imprisonment or death. Here, the murderer's upbringing and personality disorders played a significant role. The defense called numerous witnesses who had known Danny Rolling as a child and were aware of what he had endured. The courtroom was very quiet when it was his mother's turn. She was too ill with cancer to appear in court, so her testimony had been recorded on videotape and shown to the jury, who considered it during their deliberations in the following days. In this case, the brutality, wickedness, and consideration for the victims' families weighed most heavily. It had, among other things, emerged that Danny Rolling, after having bound Christina Powell with duct tape, had told her in detail what he would do to Sonja Larson before returning to her.

The jury recommended a death sentence, and the judge chose to follow their advice. Danny Rolling was executed by lethal injection on October 25, 2006, but his case is unlikely to be forgotten anytime soon. In 1996, the horror film Scream premiered and revitalized the then-somewhat dated slasher genre. Filmmaker Kevin Williamson stated that he was inspired by the Gainesville murders, and it proved to be a successful decision for him, as the film became a blockbuster and was followed by six more in the series, a 7 Scream film is on the way and will be released in 2026.

CHAPTER10: WHERE ARE THE DANISH SERIAL KILLERS? THE STORY ABOUT THE HITCHHIKER SLAYER

On January 19, 1977, two hikers ventured onto the small trails in the Refuge Canyon nature area near Santa Barbara, a couple of hours' drive north of Los Angeles, California. The canyon was a popular destination for the many students in the Isla Vista area, home to the University of California, Santa Barbara, and even in winter, many enjoyed the beautiful, mountainous landscape. The two hikers, however, had an experience they could well have done without. Close to a bend in the main road, they spotted an almost naked woman lying as if she had been almost thrown from the road. As they got closer, it was clear that she had been shot in the head. Nearby lay some bloody paper napkins of the type often found in restaurants, but they saw no clothes or other belongings. The hikers rushed to the nearest phone, from which they raised the alarm, and shortly after, several police cars and an ambulance arrived.

The young woman was quickly identified when investigators found her backpack a short distance away. It was 21-year-old psychology student Patricia Laney, who had been reported missing the day before. She was a known face in the student community, where she performed theater and busked when she wasn't engaged as an activist in the important issues of the time. She had last been seen at a busy intersection, where she had been handing out flyers warning against hitchhiking, as several young women had recently disappeared from the area. A friend was supposed to pick her up so they could go together to rehearsals for a play they were both in, but he was delayed, and when he arrived, Patricia Laney was gone. The medical examiner confirmed that the student had been shot once at close range with a .22 caliber pistol, and there were strong indications that the body had been abused.

The shock among the students had barely settled before the police found another body of a young female student just a kilometer from the first discovery site. This time, it was 21-year-old Jaqueline Rook, who had disappeared on November 20 the previous year. Like so many other carefree students who did not own a car in an area with poor public transport, she had hitchhiked at a central intersection near the university because she planned a shopping trip. Unfortunately for investigators, the body was so decomposed that there were not many clues to go on. However, the medical examiner confirmed that Jaqueline Rook had been shot once in the head and that there were signs of sexual abuse.

The female students remembered all too well the year before, when the police had finally caught Edmund Kemper, who, in Santa Cruz, near San Francisco, had murdered and mutilated at least six female students whom he had offered a lift. Now it seemed as if the case was repeating itself in Isla Vista. The area was otherwise known as a peaceful place, where students were still influenced by hippie ideals and valued their creative expression in the form of theater, art, and activism as much as their studies. This was apparently no longer to be the case, and many began to talk about an outside madman who was now hunting blonde female students. The police had noticed the latter, as several of the missing remarkably resembled each other. But whether it was a stranger was an open question, because Refuge Canyon was not a place one would know about if one was not local. Most traffic went via the coastal road, while the road through the nature area led to the quirky town of Solvang, founded by Danish immigrants.

Just like the police back then, I would also focus on the similarity between the dead and missing young women. One thing is that they resembled each other, which young students often do when it comes to clothing, hairstyle, and light hair, but they also had behavior in common: they hitchhiked. It was quite normal back then, although after the Edmund Kemper case, warning lights had started to flash. This could mean that the young women did not feel threatened by the perpetrator when they accepted a lift. I would consider whether he was also part of the student community, or at least could be age-wise, and whether he could somehow appear insecure or harmless.

On May 22, 1977, the body of yet another young woman was found, this time in a desolate area near a canyon. She, too, had disappeared from Isla Vista and, like Patricia Laney, had been shot in the head at close range with a .22 caliber pistol. Thus, the three murders could be linked with considerable certainty based on the victims' appearance, behavior, and the way they had been killed.

I would also strongly delve into the fact that the perpetrator was apparently necrophilic. As we have discussed before, necrophilia can, on the one hand, be a way to humiliate victims after death, but it can also be a sign of a person with psychological problems, such as extremely low self-esteem, who, due to countless rejections, has given up forming normal, healthy relationships with the opposite sex. Or the same sex, if they are homosexual. In this case, I would focus on the latter reason for the necrophilic tendencies, because the killings were so "simple." In many of the other cases we have looked at, the killings are much more theatrical. Often, there are various forms of torture, repeated rapes, bondage, and usually strangulation at the end, but for The Hitchhiker Slayer, as the perpetrator was nicknamed, the act of killing itself was probably not the most important thing—otherwise, he would not have been satisfied with a single shot. It is almost as if it just had to be over so he could abuse the bodies before discarding them without hiding or displaying them. In other words, the bodies were what mattered to him. He could have strangled them to avoid a lot of blood, but that was apparently not part of his fantasy, so it could also be a perpetrator who was fascinated by what a firearm can do. He had something in his hands that could decide life or death in fractions of a second, and that must have given him a tremendous power rush.

Compared to many other serial killings, there was nothing sophisticated about what The Hitchhiker Slayer did. This might also have told investigators something about his age, especially considering that he possibly had some knowledge of the student environment, either because he lived nearby, had been a student, or perhaps had been isolated or humiliated by students. Something certainly indicated that he managed to blend unnoticed into the environment. As we shall see later, he was not a university student, but he was definitely local, as he came from Solvang, a forty-five-minute drive northwest of Isla Vista through the area where several of the bodies were found.

Speaking of Solvang, one of the questions I most often get when I give lectures in Denmark is whether there are Danish serial killers. It depends a bit on how one defines a serial killer. According to the FBI, a serial killer is a person who kills at least two people in separate events with a cooling-off period, but in my opinion it is also extremely important to include the killer's motive. If you use the narrow definition, a contract killer would, by definition, be a serial killer, and so would a gang member who kills rivals from another group in two different clashes. In this way, one misses the special characteristic of the serial killers we have dealt with here in the book, and who are the type one almost always meets in films and TV series. As a criminal profiler, and also for the people from the FBI-profilers I have spoken with, it is crucial to add motive to the definition, because when one talks about serial killers, one is talking about killers who indeed kill several people in events that are separated in time and have a cooling-of period, but the motive is to kill or the interaction with the victims before, meanwhile and after the murder. They are not out to earn money or take revenge on the specific victim; they have a fantasy that is so strong that they, in their own perception, must murder to find a form of release, until the urge again becomes too strong or stop.

This is the reason why I do not consider Dagmar Overby, who is often mentioned by attendees at my lectures, to be a serial killer. Dagmar Overby was a Danish woman who, until her arrest in 1920, killed up to 20 infants. At that time, it was not unusual for single and poor women who had become mothers to advertise in newspapers for someone who, for payment, could take over the child and possibly arrange for an adoption in a time when such things were largely unregulated. For Dagmar Overby, it was an easy way, for her, to earn money, and since she couldn't be bothered with the children, she killed them in various ways shortly after taking them in. She was only discovered when one of the young mothers regretted it and wanted her child back. When Dagmar Overby came up with a lot of excuses, the woman went to the police, who found the child's burned bones in the apartment's stove, after which the "Angel Maker," as she was called, was arrested. In court, she was initially sentenced to death as one of the last women in Danish history, but the sentence was commuted to life imprisonment. Dagmar Overby has, in many places, been called Denmark's worst serial killer, but it is a label I disagree with, because her murders were not based on some fantasy she tried to live out. For her, the motive was money, while the murders were a practical measure that made it easier to increase earnings. Dagmar Overby was, incidentally, not alone in this type of murder at that time, when "angel makers" existed around the world. In Sweden, Hilda Nilsson was sentenced to death in 1917 for having murdered eight infants in the same way as her Danish counterpart. In 1896, Amelia Dyer in London was hanged for six child murders, although she was suspected of several hundred.

Another killer who is often brought up when I give lectures is Peter Lundin, who in 2001 was sentenced to life imprisonment for the murders of his girlfriend, of and on, Marianne and her two sons, aged 10 and 12 years old. Back in 1991 in USA, Lundin killed his mother, and thus, he has committed several murders in connection with two different crimes, but that does not make him a serial killer. The motive is the difference. Peter Lundin's victims were all close to him, and he killed them as a result of a personal conflict with them; it was not about some fantasy he wanted to live out. The home was characterized by alcohol abuse and a bad relationship between mother and son, and she was, according to Peter Lundin, killed in connection with a fit of rage. Many years later, he and Marianne were at a party, with her two sons, where a violent quarrel arose. They got into a fight, and the physical altercations continued at home, where he killed her and her two sons. Her sons died, either because Lundin wanted to prevent them from testifying against him, or because they came to their mother's aid, which is often seen when men, who are not the children's biological fathers, are violent. In other words, these were typical affect killing in both cases.

In fact, I believe that in Denmark we have only had one single serial killer that we know of in the year 2023 where this book was written, and he was apprehended back in 1976. On the afternoon of April 20, a young mechanic's apprentice went down to the basement of a residential block on Skelvangsvej in Randers. Here, he found 15-year-old Connie Lund Koue in a large pool of blood. The police were alerted, and they quickly established that the teenager had been attacked in the laundry room, but blood traces showed that she had initially managed to escape. The killer had caught up with her and stabbed her 33 times with a knife before cutting her throat, a sign of a perpetrator filled with rage and seeking an outlet for his aggression. Connie was incredibly still alive when the police arrived, but died shortly after at the hospital.

Investigators began questioning the residents of the building, including 25-year-old Claus Kai Berggren, a newcomer known as "The Copenhagener." He admitted that he had been in the basement that morning to repair his moped and had, at that time, greeted the victim and her sister. When a couple of the other residents stated that "The Copenhagener" had passed them earlier in the day and said that there was a dead girl in the basement, almost before the emergency vehicles had arrived, the police's suspicion was seriously aroused. It was strengthened when they noticed abrasions on the man's face and a wound on his finger, so they searched the apartment.

The suspect's wife, who was otherwise hospitalized at Rigshospitalet in Copenhagen due to birth complications, was brought to Randers, and she confirmed that a cucumber knife was missing from a kitchen drawer. The police subsequently found it taped to the underside of a table during the interrogations. Investigators remembered the unsolved murder of eight-year-old Conny Jacobsen in the stairwell of

Fensmarksgade 41 in Nørrebro, Copenhagen, five years earlier. The girl had been playing on the street with some other children when a young man approached her and said that a lady in the stairwell wanted to talk to her. Just inside the door, the man stabbed Conny Jacobsen more than 20 times before cutting her throat. In Randers, the police found that Claus Kai Berggren had also been questioned in that case, but that some friends had given him an alibi, as they were all at a nearby pub from where they had heard and seen the flashing blue lights on their way to Fensmarksgade. In 1976, investigators reviewed the case again, and it dawned on them that there had been two emergency calls in Nørrebro that day Conny Jacobsen was murdered, and it was the "wrong" one that Claus Kai Berggren's friends had heard.

After a few days, he confessed to both murders. He also stated that after his engagement party in early 1971, he had raped one of his wife's friends in the basement of the property. He had subsequently threatened her with a knife, and she had therefore refrained from reporting the assault. The young woman's name was Connie Petersen. He often thought of her, and a whole year later, he sought out the apartment where she lived with her mother. The mother said that her daughter was not home, which caused anger to well up in Claus Kai Berggren, who stabbed the woman in the arm several times. Connie Petersen, who was home, came to her mother's rescue, and Claus Kai Berggren also tried to stab her, but, for inexplicable reasons, suddenly fled. He was sentenced to a short prison term and then moved with his wife and their child to Randers, where he had been offered a study place. It was here that the trap snapped shut, and the "Conny Killer," as he was later called, received a life sentence.

I've looked into the case and read the letter he wrote to the forensic psychiatrists involved. It's eerily similar to letters I've received from serial killers around the world. Like most others, Claus Kai Berggren began fantasizing about torturing and abusing women as a teenager, which always made him want to masturbate. After his arrest, he blamed his alcohol abuse, but it was most likely an excuse, as the urge to kill was present very early in his life. His life was characterized by chaos and heavy alcohol consumption, often resulting in violence against his wife, whom he, among other things, choked, and he stalked a woman on the street in Copenhagen at least once.

Looking at his upbringing, there are also several similarities between Claus Kai Berggren and the serial killers we've encountered in this book. Even as a child, he struggled to get along with other children. He was introverted and compulsive, and unusually aggressive towards others at school. He also stammered, at times so severely that he could be difficult to understand. We've encountered this phenomenon earlier in the book in the case of Robert Hansen in Alaska, and it has been observed in numerous other serial killers. Of course, stammering doesn't make someone a serial killer, but especially in the past, stammering could be a sign of distress. In the 1980s and earlier, children who stammered were often bullied at school, and many also had difficulties at home. Among stammering serial killers, it's observed that they perceive their stammer as part of the rejection they experienced at home, much like left-handed people were forced to use their right hand in olden times. We still don't know exactly why some people stammer, but it's very likely that hereditary, biological, linguistic, and psychological factors are involved. Fortunately, today we understand how to help children with the problem. However, this insight didn't benefit Claus Kai Berggren.

His parents regularly engaged in theft, and some of the stolen goods were given to their son as gifts. He began stealing things of no particular value, which suggests a form of kleptomania. This is also seen in many serial killers and is usually a kind of power display, intended to show that they can do as they please and that society's rules don't apply to them. Much later, forensic psychiatrists concluded that the "Conny Killer" lived with constant inner tension and early fantasies of self-assertion and dominance, but at the same time was characterized by vulnerability, insecurity, and an inability to engage emotionally and insight into other people's feelings. All of this led to enormous internal pressure that he sought to release. They also described him as extraordinarily dangerous, yet he was paroled in 1990. However, he was back behind bars after about six months when he was violent towards his then-girlfriend and her daughter and attempted to lure young girls to secret meetings. In 1998, he was paroled again, but the result was the same, and in 2002, Claus Kai Berggren died at the age of 50 from pancreatic cancer. It is said that attempted murders count when it comes to serial killers, so in the "Conny Killer's" case, there are three victims, and when I read the case files and what he himself wrote, I have no doubt: Claus Kai Berggren was a Danish serial killer on Danish soil.

*

On April 18, 1979, 21-year-old Thor Nis Christiansen was cruising in his car down Hollywood Boulevard, where neon lights glowed and tourists strolled, taking pictures of the famous stars on the pavement, reading the names of renowned actors and directors. Los Angeles, as always, buzzed with life, even after dark, for while the famous street was a family mecca by day, the evenings and nights belonged to bars, strip shows, and men seeking a date.

Thor Nis Christiansen had found a girlfriend. One day, he had offered a hitchhiker a ride, and the chemistry between the two young people was so good that they quickly moved into an apartment near the university in Isla Vista. But that didn't stop him from embarking on adventures in the car he cherished more than anything else he owned.

On a sidewalk, he spotted a 24-year-old sex worker named Lydia Preston. He pulled over to the curb and rolled down the window. He explained to her that he was a visiting construction worker and could use some company. Lydia Preston sized him up. He was a tall, muscular guy with very light hair and a thin mustache, making him look like a typical Scandinavian or a surfer from the Californian beaches. Had she met him in early 1977, she would have seen a severely overweight young man weighing 125 kilos (275 pounds). A guy with greasy skin and greasy hair due to a diet of fast food, alcohol, and hashish. At that time, he had moved from California to Oregon, and although no one in his family or among his few friends knew what he had been doing there, exercise and a change of diet must have played a role.

The customer and the prostitute agreed on a price, and she got into the passenger seat. She knew of a nearby hotel where they could rent a room by the hour, which Thor Nis Christiansen agreed to, which is why Lydia Preston was surprised when he drove past the hotel without stopping.

"I know a better one,| he said.

Soon, the city was behind them, and they continued up into the Hollywood Hills, where Thor Nis Christiansen stopped. Within moments, he produced a .22 caliber pistol and shot Lydia Preston in the head. Bones shattered, and blood gushed out, but the young woman did not die. On the contrary, she managed to get out of the car and flee towards the nearest house. The shocked residents helped her alert the police, who arrived shortly after, but by then her customer was long gone, and although his victim could describe him, she did not know his name.

The Los Angeles police did not think to connect the attempted murder to the student murders in Isla Vista because Lydia Preston was not a student. Thus, they made a mistake similar to the one their colleagues in the Isla Vista area had made shortly after the first bodies were found. One evening, a patrol car had driven out to a natural area overlooking the Pacific Ocean, where young people often hung out, either to kiss and have sex in their cars or to drink beer and smoke hash. The officers noticed a car whose brake lights glowed red in the dark, and they went over to knock on the window. They could clearly smell that the two young men, Thor Nis Christiansen and one of his friends, were both drinking and smoking. For good measure, the patrol asked to see what Thor Nis Christiansen had in the trunk, but at first, he categorically refused to open it. His friend stared at him. The two could probably get away with a warning or a fine for possessing alcohol and pot, but if Thor Nis Christiansen behaved provocatively, they could risk ending up at the police station. Finally, he gave in and let the officers look. In the trunk was a bag that they guessed might contain more hash than the two youngsters could smoke themselves, but when they lifted it, it was much heavier than they had expected. Inside was a .22 caliber pistol. This was not necessarily unusual. Lots of young people passed the time shooting targets in the woods, and the two officers ended up issuing a warning.

"What do you need that pistol for?" the friend asked in surprise.

"Just to shoot rabbits in the woods," was the answer.

The friend couldn't help but think back to when they were younger, and the guy in the driver's seat had started tying fireworks to birds and frogs and then watching them explode.

Thor Nis Christiansen is a good example that it is not impossible for a Dane to develop into a serial killer, for he was born in Denmark in 1957 and lived here until his parents emigrated to the USA when he was five years old. Nor is it the case that Danish genes provide any protection, for Robert Hansen, the baker who hunted his victims in the Alaskan wilderness, had parents who had emigrated from Denmark about 10 years before his birth. Some Danish children grow up under the same terrible conditions as many of the serial killers we have dealt with in the book so far. And although it is fortunately extremely rare that the many factors whip up the perfect storm needed before we are faced with a serial killer, there are certainly some who have the same profile, and thus also a few who have the potential.

This also means that the reason why serial killers are largely unknown in Denmark can be found in the way our society is structured. Firstly, Denmark is a small country and USA is a much bigger country made up of 50 states, a federal district (Washington, D.C.), and several territories where some is much bigger than Denmark. And also the Danish police are very good at solving murders. While the clearance rate in Denmark is over 90 percent, the figure in the USA is just over 60 percent. This means that four out of 10 American homicides are never solved. This is largely because Denmark is a small, homogeneous country with high trust, where almost everything is registered. In other words, it is difficult to disappear into the crowd here. The opposite is true in the USA, where there is not the same type of a CPR register (national civil registration system) and therefore no one ever knows exactly how many people live in the country, though the have a registration system, which is the social security number. In addition, the American police are divided into many levels, and the different states and police districts rarely communicate, special if you go back in time, which means that it can take a long time before murders in one area are linked to murders in another. Serial killers in the USA, therefore, have a lower risk of being discovered than is the case in Denmark. I do this, after working in the system for over 20 years, that we are better here, although not perfect, of course, when it comes to social efforts for children who are struggling in various ways. While there is far less trust in public authorities in the USA, the opposite is true here, and this contributes to us being better at identifying children at risk of developing in a way that makes them a danger to others.

But even if serial killings are an extremely rare phenomenon in Denmark, another serious serial crime is not. It doesn't take many online searches to find a long list of examples of serial rapes here, and the frightening thing is that serial rapists resemble serial killers very much. It is also not an unknown phenomenon for a serial rapist to eventually evolve into a murderer. They often have an upbringing marked by violence, abuse, isolation, and humiliation, as we know from many of the killers we have encountered so far in the book, and their crimes are not about sex. They are about power and control and about living out something psychological, and they often draw threads back to the past.

The beginning of the end of one of the most infamous cases in Denmark began on September 25, 2010, when a 17-year-old girl, on her way home from a night out with her friends, was assaulted, threatened with a knife, and raped in an allotment garden area on Amager. When police and technicians subsequently examined the area, a skilled police dog found a condom containing semen that someone had dropped or thrown into a hedge very close to the crime scene. An analysis showed that the DNA was the same as that found on a milk carton left by the perpetrator behind a rape in a room at the Amager- college. Here, a 24-year-old woman had been raped several times for two hours with a blindfold. He had even forced her to choose which abuses she would be subjected to, a clear sign of power mixed with the urge to humiliate the woman. Between the assaults, the man had drunk milk from the refrigerator. Subsequently, technicians had managed to take a sample of a little saliva on the carton and develop a DNA profile. The same DNA had also been found on the 40-year-old teacher Lene Buchardt Rasmussen, whose body was found on Amager in 1990 after she had cycled there to watch birds. She had been raped and strangled, and the killer had taken a silver ring and a watch, perhaps as souvenirs.

The police were agonizingly close to having solved the murder on the common. One of the many witnesses who called the police in the following days said that he had cycled there the day Lene Buchardt Rasmussen was killed. He had seen two people on the bike ride. The first had turned away from him, and he had therefore been unable to determine if it was a man or a woman. The officer on the phone laughed at the witness and said he probably needed glasses, which made the witness hang up in anger. Thus, the person did not get to say that he had also spotted an old schoolmate named Marcel Lychau Hansen, a man who in 1987 had been one of the police's main suspects in a case of robbery-murder of an elderly woman he had been a mover for.

When investigators of the rape in the allotment garden announced at a press conference that the suspect was behind a murder and at least one other rape, hundreds of citizens called the police. One of them was the mother of the cyclist who had hung up 20 years earlier. She repeated her son's story and gave the officers the name of Marcel Lychau Hansen. A DNA test subsequently showed that investigators had finally apprehended the culprit. And more crimes were added to his record, including a quadruple rape in a villa on Amager in 1995. In that case, the man broke into the residence where a 23-year-old woman and two girls, aged 14 and 15, were sleeping. He first encountered the 23-year-old, whom he threatened into telling him about the girls in the basement. Here he gathered all four, put pillowcases over their heads, and bound them, after which he raped them in shifts for more than two hours in the house's bathroom. Each time, he threatened to kill a victim if any of the others escaped, thus clearly demonstrating that the crime was primarily about exercising complete control over the woman and the three girls. Subsequently, he forced the victims to wash their mouths and bodies to remove biological traces. He left the villa with the 23-year-old's debit card and some gold and silver jewelry. A preliminary conclusion was reached in the case of the "Amager Man" in 2012, when he was sentenced to life imprisonment for two murders and six rapes.

It is difficult to confirm the stories told about Marcel Lychau Hansen, so I make the following analysis with caution. The Amager Man had affairs with many different women, so he had no problem getting sex, but rape is not about sex, but power and control. He showed not the slightest compassion for his victims or the slightest remorse. He felt like a person, that had the right to take what he wanted. The fact that he evaded the police for so many years must also have given him a feeling of invincibility that reinforced his high opinion of himself. In the Amager Man's case, too, my hypothesis would be that something in his upbringing may have affected him. But as far as I know, there are no concrete stories of violence or abuse, and they would be difficult to validate, as the Amager Man has been very closed about his life.

*

The bar on Hollywood Boulevard was home to many of the nightlife's regulars, including Lydia Preston, who, three months after the attempted murder, was back on the streets despite the injuries from the gunshot to her head. She was sitting on a barstool with a drink when the bar door opened. She looked up and recognized him immediately. Standing just inside the door was the man who had tried to kill her. She recoiled and moved as far into the dim light as possible, considering the situation. Then she walked over to a payphone at the back of the room, and with trembling hands, she called the police. The officer she spoke to initially didn't believe her, but she insisted and sounded so terrified that a couple of patrol cars were sent to the bar anyway.

Thor Nis Christiansen was arrested and taken to the police station, where he was confronted with the evidence investigators possessed in an interrogation room. Most importantly, there were the bloody napkins that had been discarded near Patricia Laney's body. One thing was that they came from a restaurant, and that the suspect's parents owned a restaurant in Solvang that served typical Danish food; quite another was the fact that technicians had managed to find a usable fingerprint on them.

On the surface, Thor Nis Christiansen looked like an ordinary young man who had managed to turn his life around after his stay in Oregon, but it wasn't hard to scratch beneath the surface. He grew up in Solvang in USA, which was founded by Danish emigrants and is nicknamed "The Danish Capital of America." The town is somewhat of a curiosity with copies of

Dybbøl Mill, the Round Tower, and The Little Mermaid, and visitors can experience half-timbered houses and folk dancing, just as they can eat *stegt flæsk* (fried pork belly) and *æbleskiver* (apple fritters) at the town's restaurants. His parents opened one of these, and they quickly became known as unusually hardworking people who spent almost all their waking hours in their business. This meant that their son spent most of his time alone, and that his parents primarily showed their love by spoiling him and giving him money.

He was an intelligent boy, and in the first few years, he did well in school, but things later went awry, partly because Thor Nis Christiansen's father was an alcoholic behind closed doors who took out his anger on the family. Friends would later recount how Thor could suddenly become so enraged that he would lash out at other children, especially in sports, where he more than once assaulted classmates. It's not unusual to see that children from homes characterized by alcohol abuse and violence have difficulty with emotion regulation. While the rest of us in a stressful situation manage to count to 10, walk away, or talk our way out of the situation, people who struggle to regulate their emotions risk exploding. Children like Thor Nis Christiansen, in a home that should be a safe haven, constantly have to suppress their feelings because they fear being beaten. The uncertainty is also difficult because they never know what to expect from their parents. They often come into great conflict with themselves because parents can quickly switch from being the sweetest mother or father in the world to being utterly cruel. It is very difficult for a child to grow up in such an environment, and it often leads to strong inner turmoil and insecurity that can be difficult to manage. For Thor Nis Christiansen, it became very difficult to control himself and find an appropriate way to vent.

Already in elementary school, Thor Nis Christiansen began to drink, often before classes started, and he started with animal cruelty, which should absolutely be an alarm bell when it takes the form it did in this case, with birds and frogs being blown up with fireworks. Animal cruelty is a widespread phenomenon in many serial killers' childhoods because, unlike most other children, they don't stop themselves; on the contrary, they discover that they like it because it gives them a sense of control in an otherwise chaotic childhood.

By the age of 16, Thor Nis Christiansen was drinking daily and also abusing hashish. He gained a lot of weight and became more and more introverted and ashamed of himself. His relationships with girls, in particular, became problematic, and he chose instead to drive around aimlessly with friends who, like him, had dropped out of school, in the car his parents had given him as a birthday present. Conversations in the car often revolved around girls and sex and their failures in that regard, and friends would later recount that he had told them about fantasies that included the desire to shoot a woman and have sexual intercourse with the corpse. Of course, there can be a long way from fantasies to action, and there are actually more people than one might immediately think who have quite violent fantasies about violence, rape, and murder without ever acting on them. The problem arises when such fantasies occur in a mind that, as was the case with Thor Nis Christiansen, is characterized by an inability to control emotions and impulses.

When he felt the heat on his heels after having had to show a couple of officers the car's trunk, he settled, as mentioned, for a time in Oregon, where on the surface he got his life in order. He also, so to speak, got his victim types in order by going from female students to sex workers, which some serial killers do because it is more important for them to have low-risk victims than to go after a very specific type. Prostitutes would be easier to get into the car and would also cause less commotion among the public and the police. We don't know if he also killed in Oregon, but there are a number of unsolved murders in the state that bring Thor Nis Christiansen to mind. Whether he was behind one or more of them, we will probably never know.

He confessed to the murders of the three students, one murder of a prostitute from Los Angeles, and the attempted murder that ultimately led to his arrest. He was sentenced to life imprisonment, but his stay behind bars was short, for already the following year, he was stabbed to death by an unknown assailant.

EPILOGUE: WHAT IF...?

"What if...?" This question has surfaced repeatedly during the writing of this book, which you're now nearing the end of. What if Robert Joe Long had killed Lisa McVey, preventing her from alerting the police and describing the killer in such detail? Or what if the police hadn't been so quick to investigate the deaths of the Otero family as a gang dispute, thereby giving Dennis Rader a stronger hand? And I especially think of Danny Rolling; what would have happened if he had received intensive help when teachers and school psychologists recommended it in third grade?

This is, of course, a hypothetical question. What's done is done, and the past cannot be changed, but that doesn't stop us from learning from it.

I have no doubt that early intervention would have been crucial for these different outcomes. It's not certain that Danny Rolling would have become a model citizen, but would he have become The Gainesville Ripper? If he had been connected with psychiatry as a child, he might have had the opportunity and the courage to reach out for help, instead of sitting alone in a tent in a forest, trying to fix his problems with alcohol and a guitar. He was actually encouraged by his girlfriends to seek treatment, and he briefly went to a psychiatric emergency room, but records from that time show that he was so afraid his father would find out that he stopped going after only a few times, despite being an adult man at that point and no longer being abused. That says something about the terror he was subjected to.

In my studies of criminal profiling, I've been particularly struck by the clear connection, in many cases, between childhood/upbringing and the later behavior of serial killers and rapists. When I call the book "Psychology of Evil," it's about trying to understand the psychology behind evil. Because no one is born evil; it's something that can develop. This ties back to my thesis in psychology, where I showed that the profiling method can also be used to predict which behaviors and events in childhood can help determine whether a child might later be at risk of developing in a violent direction. When I finished my psychology degree, it was acceptable to say that children's and young people's problems could, at least partially, be traced back to the family, but this later became a bit of a taboo. The statement still provokes many, but that's simply how it is, and hopefully, that's also clear after reading the stories in this book. There's no point in people taking offense at pointing to parents, because they play a very large role in shaping who we become. Of course, other factors are at play, but it's important not to overlook the people who mean the most to a child. I often meet people who say they grew up in chaos but have a good life today. I'm glad to hear that, and some do manage to overcome a terrible start in life, but that doesn't change the crucial fact that it's possible to damage children from the very beginning, and that it can have catastrophic consequences. This is precisely what we see in profiling: Upbringing can manifests itself in crimes.

Criminal profiling, as mentioned, is not a miracle cure that can lead investigators directly to a killer. That said, I've consistently been impressed by how scientific the method actually is. Behavioral analysis, victimology, personality psychology, and all the other tools we've looked at are based on many years of research by many people and emphasize the importance of including all details and not basing a profile solely on hunches, statistics, or experiences from previous cases. Every single case is unique, and that must be the starting point. If you compare offender profiles today with earlier profiles, you will therefore also see that they are now often less detailed and that they are far more dynamic, because they change as more knowledge becomes available. Criminal profiling should therefore be seen as a tool that investigators can use in conjunction with all the other methods they employ to solve a crime, when they need to exclude suspects, or when they need to interrogate an arrested person.

For me, as a psychologist, prevention is more important than anything else. If we have the opportunity to prevent someone from developing into a serial killer or serial rapist, or from turning anger and fear inward against themselves, that would be optimal. Criminal profiling gives us knowledge about very specific things that are crucial for a child to be damaged.

The key is to identify these children, and the method can help us with that, because we know what to look for. Of course, there's no guarantee that a child won't develop in the wrong direction, but if we act, there's at least a chance that we can prevent it. If a child behaves in a boundary-crossing way, we adults must ask ourselves: Why is he or she doing this? What is the reason for the behavior? We must never abandon children who are subjected to violence, abuse, humiliation, isolation, or bullying; we must intervene as early as possible.

Readers can probably sense that it's the psychologist writing here. Although on paper I can call myself a criminal profiler, I am first and foremost a psychologist. I've said several times that I don't intend to use my education to work as an investigator, and I still feel that way. Nevertheless, as I write this, I am on my way to Spain, where I will be looking at some cases together with Dr. Maria Jose Garrido, a PhD in psychology. She is a commander for the Civil Guard and the police and works in the secretariat for security in the Ministry of Interior in Madrid. What the future otherwise holds is a good question. I finish a Master of Sceince in Criminal Profiling in 2023, and I still find crime, personality psychology, and behavioral analysis very fascinating. These are areas I want to try to understand better, and I see an opportunity to combine that knowledge to spread understanding of how important prevention is, not only for the individual but also for society in general. We simply have to get better at taking care of our children and young people, because there is nothing sadder than sitting across from young people who have experienced abuse their entire lives and tried to say or hint at it, without getting help.

Even though I sometimes reach the point where serial killers and serial rapists exhaust me, I have so far, every time, returned to them, intending to try to understand them. I don't think I'm finished with them yet. At least I'm still in contact with Dennis Rader, the BTK killer, who says he's in the process of answering my questionnaire and other serial killers. And if he ever finishes it, I'll hopefully have another piece to the big puzzle that I and many others are trying to put together.

THANK YOU!

Thanks to Karen McLean, Søren Lykke, Søren Flott, Elise H. Nørholm, Bent Isager-Nielsen, Mark Safarik, Frederik Strand, and all the people who listen, watch, and make use of my knowledge.

A thousand thanks to my wonderful mother, who always supports me and has lent an ear to so much. She has never doubted my ideas, even when they seemed impossible.

Søren Lykke, my partner, who always backs me up and makes it easier for me to go full throttle.

My "ghostwriter," Søren Flott, for your patience and perseverance.

Elise, both for being on board with my idea for this book and for showing respect for my projects.

Bent Isager-Nielsen, my good friend and business partner, who is always there and helps in every way he can. You're always ready when I need a sounding board.

A big thank you to former FBI Behavioral Analysis Unit Criminal Profiler Mark Safarik, who, in connection with my Master of Science in criminal profiling, has been a tremendous help in understanding, especially complex cases. You have generously shared your knowledge with me.

Thanks to Frederik Strand from the Police Museum for giving me the opportunity to read documents and view artifacts related to the Claus Kai Berggren case.

Thanks to TV media, professionals, and private individuals who, since the last book, have read, listened, watched, attended lectures, followed me on Instagram and LinkedIn, and used my knowledge. I greatly appreciate it.

My heartfelt thoughts go out to all the victims of serial killers. For their sake, we must learn from the things that have happened. Since we must also never forget them, I list here the known victims from the cases included in this book:

Joseph Otero (38) – Julie Maria Otero (33) – Joseph Otero jr. (9) – Josephine Otero (11) – Kathryn Doreen Bright (21) – Kevin Bright (19) – Shirley Ruth Vian Relford (25) – Nancy Jo Fox (25) – Marine Wallace Hedge (53) – Vicki Lynn Wegerle (28) – Dolores Earline Johnson Davis (62) – Artiss "Ann" Wick (20) – Ngeun Thi Long (19) – Michelle Denise Simms (22) – Elizabeth Loudenback (22) – Vicky Marie Elliott (21) – Chanel Devoun Williams (18) – Karen Beth Dinsfriend (28) – Kimberly Kyle Hopps (22) – Virginia Lee Johnson (18) – Kim Marie Swann (21) – Marnette Comer (17) – Cynthia Chandler (16) – Gina Marano (15) – Karen Jones (24) – Exxie Wilson (20) – William Grissom (55) – Julie Grissom (24) – Sean Grissom (8) – Sonja Larson (17) – Christina Powell (17) – Tracy Inez Paules (23) – Manuel Taboada (23) – Christa Hoyt (18) – Tammy Homolka (15) – Kvinde (15) – Leslie Mahaffy (14) – Kristen French (15) – James Gibson (19) – Deborah Everist (19) – Simone Schmidl (21) – Anja Habschied (20) – Gabor Neugebauer (21) – Caroline Clarke (21) – Joanne Walters (22) – Guillermina León Oropeza (84) – María Guadalupe Aguilar Cortina (86) – María Guadalupe de la Vega Morales (87) – María del Carmen Muñoz Cote de Galván (78) – Lucrecia Elsa Calvo Marroquín (85) – Natalia Torres Castro (85) – Alicia Cota Ducoin (76) – Alicia González Castillo (75) – Andrea Tecante Carreto (74) – Carmen Cardona Rodea (76) – Socorro Enedina Martínez Pajares (82) – Guadalupe González Sánchez (74) – Esthela Cantoral Trejo (85) – Delfina González Castillo (92) – María Virginia Xelhuatzi Tizapán (84) – María de los Ángeles Cortés Reynoso (84) – Margarita Martell Vázquez (72) – Simona Bedolla Ayala (79) – María Dolores Martínez

Benavides (70) – Margarita Arredondo Rodríguez (83) – María Imelda Estrada Pérez (76) – Julia Vera Duplan (60) – María Elena Mendoza Vallares (59) – María Elisa Pérez Moreno (76) – Arturo Patiño Barranco (74) – Carolina Robledo (79) – Ana María Velázquez Díaz (62) – Celia Villaliz Morales (78) – María Guadalupe Núñez Almanza (78) – Julia Vargas (64) – Mario Cruz Flores (84) – Emma Armenta Aguayo (80) – Emma Reyes Peña (72) – Carmen Sánchez Serrano (76) – Dolores Concepción Silva Calva (91) – María del Carmen Camila González Miguel (82) – Guadalupe Oliver Contreras (85) – María de los Ángeles Repper Hernández (92) – Ana María de los Reyes Alfaro (84) – Shirley Williams (45) – Mary Lou Pratt (33) – Susan Beth Peterson (27) – Celia "Beth" van Zanten (18) – Megan Siobhan Emerick (17) – Mary Kathleen Thill (22) – Eklutna-Annie (16-25) – Joanna Messina (24) – Roxane Easland (24) – Lisa Futrell (41) – Sherry Morrow (23) – Andre Mona "Fish" Altiery (24) – Sue Luna (23) – Robin Pelkey (19) – DeLynn "Sugar" Frey (22) – Paula Goulding (31) – Malai Larsen (28) – Teresa Watson (22) – Angela Lynn Feddern (24) – Tamera "Tami" Pederson (20) – Kvinde (22) – Kvinde (26) – Jack Owen Blake (10) – Karen Ann Hil (8) – Dorothy "Dotsie" Blackburn (27) – Anna Marie Steffen (28) – Dorothy Keeler (59) – Patricia "Patty" Ives (25) – June Stott (30) – Marie Welch (22) – Frances "Franny" Brown (22) – Kimberly Logan (30) – Elizabeth "Liz" Gibson (29) – Darlene Trippi (32) – June Cicero (33) – Felicia Stephens (20) – Richard Charles Mallory (51) – David Andrew Spears (47) – Charles Edmund Carskaddon (40) – Peter Abraham Siems (65) – Troy Eugene Burress (50) – Charles Richard "Dick" Humphreys (56) – Walter Jeno Antonio (62) – Conny Jacobsen (8) – Connie Lund Koue (15) – Pauline Reade (16) – John Kilbride (12) – Keith Bennett (12) – Lesley Ann Downey (10) – Edward Evans (17) – Jacqueline Ann Rook (21) – Mary Ann Sarris (19) –

Patricia Marie Laney – (21) – Laura Sue Benjamin (22) – Patricia Tamez (29) – Lanett Deyon White (25) – Tina Renee Gibbs (26) – Kvinde (16) – Stephen Dean Holmes (14) – Kenneth Ockendon (26) – Martyn Duffey (16) – William "Billy" Sutherland (27) – Malcolm Barlow (24) – Paul Nobbs (25) – John Howlett (23) – Carl Stotter (21) – Archibald Graham Allan (27) – Steve Sinclair (20)

FROM SAME AUTHOR

- *Serial Killers - Understanding and Prevention* (2004) Aarhus University
- *Prevention: A Case Study of Arthur Shawcross* (2012) research report through Aarhus University
- *Serial Killers - The Man Behind the Monster*, in Danish, German, Swedish, and Italian. (2021)
- *Psychology of Evil - Profiles of Serial Killers*, in Danish (2023)
- *A Disturb Mind - Behind the Serial Killers Mask*, in Danish (2025)

Podcasts:

- The Human behind the Monster (Arthur John Shawcross) - Season 1 - Danish (2024)
- The Human behind the Monster (Douglas Clark) - Season 2 - Danish (2025)

ABOUT THE AUTHOR

Florence McLean has an MSc in Psychology and is a licensed psychologist and she is a specialist in clinical psychology, psychotherapy and child neuropsychology and is an approved supervisor. Florence McLean hold a professional diploma in Criminal Profiling and Crime Scene Analysis from The Forensic Criminology Institute v/ Dr. Brent Turvey USA and she has a diploma in Criminal Profiling from Heritage University/Behavior & Law in Washington. In 2023, she obtained a Master of Science in Criminal Profiling from Evidentia University of Behavioral & Forensic Sciences in USA.

For over two decades, Florence has worked with children, young people and adults in Jutland municipality, both in municipalities and in private practice. Since September 2021, she has worked independently as a psychologist and a criminal psychologist.

Florence McLean has dealt with serial killers since 1997, culminating in a thesis in 2004: *Serial Killers – Understanding and Prevention* and in 2012 a research report: *Prevention: A Case Study of Arthur Shawcross.*

In addition, she has investigated well over 100 serial killers, she has communicated with beside that she has reviewed their cases, read court transcripts, watched interrogation recordings, watched and read interviews with them and reviewed court transcripts and more, to gain a deeper understanding of them. But in general, she has been examining cases outside the persons she has communicated with and is closely follow current and active cases.

Florence McLean is an experienced speaker and author of 3 books about serial killers. She has appeared in several TV-series, including as a host in the TV documentary, *Are they too dangerous for freedom?* She acts as an expert in many programs, amoung several: *When Men Kill Women*, *Women Who Kill*, *Criminal*, and *When Crime Shakes Us*. In addition, she has appeared in several radio programs, newspapers, magazines, podcasts, and much more.

Made in the USA
Coppell, TX
14 February 2026

72043531R00156